PENGUIN BOOKS
Native Strangers

Susanne Williams Milcairns was born in England,
raised and educated in New Zealand, and lived for
several years in Europe. She has a PhD in English
literature from Victoria University, Wellington.
While teaching American and English literature at
Victoria, she developed an interest in the American
writer Herman Melville and his travels in the
Pacific during the 1840s. Her subsequent doctoral
thesis on the Pacific beachcombers forms the basis
of this book. In recent years she has travelled widely
throughout the Pacific region and now lives, with
her family, by the sea in Wellington.

NATIVE STRANGERS

Beachcombers, Renegades and Castaways in the South Seas

Susanne Williams Milcairns

PENGUIN BOOKS

PENGUIN BOOKS

Published by the Penguin Group

Penguin Group (NZ), cnr Airborne and Rosedale Roads, Albany,
Auckland 1310, New Zealand (a division of Pearson New Zealand Ltd)
Penguin Group (USA) Inc., 375 Hudson Street, New York, New York 10014, USA
Penguin Group (Canada), 90 Eglinton Avenue East, Suite 700, Toronto,
Ontario, M4P 2Y3, Canada (a division of Pearson Penguin Canada Inc.)
Penguin Books Ltd, 80 Strand, London, WC2R 0RL, England
Penguin Ireland, 25 St Stephen's Green, Dublin 2, Ireland
(a division of Penguin Books Ltd)
Penguin Group (Australia), 250 Camberwell Road, Camberwell, Victoria
3124, Australia (a division of Pearson Australia Group Pty Ltd)
Penguin Books India Pvt Ltd, 11, Community Centre, Panchsheel Park,
New Delhi – 110 017, India
Penguin Books (South Africa) (Pty) Ltd, 24 Sturdee Avenue, Rosebank,
Johannesburg 2196, South Africa

Penguin Books Ltd, Registered Offices: 80 Strand, London, WC2R 0RL, England

First published by Penguin Group (NZ), 2006
1 3 5 7 9 10 8 6 4 2

Designed by Shaun Jury
Typeset by Egan-Reid Ltd
Printed in Australia by McPherson's Printing Group

ISBN 0 14 302015 3
A catalogue record for this book is available
from the National Library of New Zealand.

www.penguin.co.nz

This book is dedicated to
the memory of my father
Alan Richard Williams
(1933–78)

I only wish he could have read it.

Contents

List of Illustrations

Acknowledgements

I have been very fortunate to receive support and encouragement from a number of friends and colleagues during the writing of this book and the doctoral thesis that preceded it. First, my thanks must go to Vincent O'Sullivan whose wisdom, experience, encouragement and good humour gave me the courage to tackle both projects. I feel privileged to have worked with him and to have known him as a teacher, mentor, colleague and, most importantly, as a friend. My blessings continue in the friendship and support of Anne Holleron: reader, critic, part-time editor and movie buddy. Her unconditional and unwavering loyalty means more than she could know. Fellow writer, one-time fellow student and full-time friend, Marie Duncan also gave freely of her time and her literary talents, while Sue Wilkins' expert technical knowledge was generously offered and gratefully received. The staff of the Alexander Turnbull Library and the Beaglehole Rare Books Room at Victoria University provided invaluable assistance over the past few years. The burden of research was greatly lessened by their combined professionalism and expertise. Finally, my family has never wavered in their support, belief and encouragement. As always, it is the love and loyalty of Vicki, James and especially Joseph – my first and most important reader – that makes everything worthwhile.

Preface

In the late eighteenth and early nineteenth centuries, an unlikely group of men made a unique and remarkable voyage of discovery. They were ordinary sailors, men of humble origin and lowly status – common mariners who traditionally travelled 'before the mast'. They left their homelands searching for adventure and excitement, on a quest for knowledge and experience. Like other men of their time and place, they believed they could find what they were looking for in strange and unfamiliar places. But voyages of any sort are always transformative. They are much more than a movement from one place to another. The sailors' voyage to the South Seas would take them somewhere else entirely. It would set them on a perilous journey from civilisation to savagery. It would lead them away from the safety and familiarity of Europe towards their own 'heart of darkness' in the Pacific.

Arrival on Pacific shores was merely the beginning, not the end, of their voyage. It was the start of an arduous, complex and perilous cross-cultural odyssey, unparalleled by any group of individuals before or since. The sailors from Europe, men of limited education and experience, 'crossed the beach', that physical and psychological boundary that separated their world from the unknown world of the islands. They went native on the shores of the Pacific and travelled deep into the heart of an alien culture. Along the way, they left behind the world they knew and forfeited their status as Europeans. They had no way of knowing what lay ahead; they were totally unprepared for the physical and psychological traumas that awaited them. Although they were informed by the age-old tradition of exploration and discovery, their new terrain was uncharted and unknown. These remarkable cultural explorers became known as 'beachcombers', taking their name from the beaches they crossed in their unique and dangerous journeys from European to native.

By living as natives, the sailors would intermarry, become tattooed, adopt native dress and learn new languages. They would enter a foreign culture, adhere to unfamiliar laws and participate in foreign ceremonies, rituals and rites. For a brief time they would lose themselves in that other life. That was their glory and their terror, their salvation and their damnation. Going native demanded a high cost from those who attempted it. It took them far from the world that told them who they were and how they should behave. It destabilised their sense of self, and played havoc with their belief in the innate superiority of the European. It left them bewildered and confused, marooned in the complexities of an unknown and 'savage' culture.

The beachcombers were pragmatic, untutored and hard-working sailors who underwent a transformation on the shores of the Pacific. In order to survive, they became astute and resourceful performers in a theatre of life and death. They learned to be mimics and actors – to hide their true selves and play the part demanded by their new society. They became successful role players in a culture antithetical to the one they knew. They learned to accept and honour other social and political realities as their own. In the process, they discovered something about themselves and about their capacity to become other than what they were. They discovered that identity was flexible and circumstantial, that social acceptance was a matter of role playing, and that cultural voyaging could be liberating as well as dangerous.

In many ways, they were the living exemplars of Robinson Crusoe – that fictional castaway immortalised by Daniel Defoe in 1719 – embodying an archetypal desire to reject the constraints of a civilised life. Like the earlier castaway, they were wrecked on islands, cast up on foreign shores and forced to adapt to native life in order to survive. For a while at least they were free from the demands of their own time and place. They became a symbol of romantic escapism, defiant repudiators of the drudgery and repression associated with an industrial homeland. But they soon found that island life was not always what they expected; it proved to be something completely different, something entirely new. Their first steps across the beaches of foreign shores required a monumental leap of faith. The men from Europe could not anticipate what lay ahead; they could never imagine what they would leave behind. Knowledge would come with experience, if only they managed to survive it. The sailors took a gamble on themselves, on their beliefs and on their expectations, correct or otherwise, about the true nature of primitive people. It was a gamble they could not afford to lose.

The stories of these castaway sailors and their perilous journeys into Pacific societies are taken from twenty-four accounts of shipwreck and survival known informally as 'beachcomber narratives'. Full details can be found in the bibliography. Although similar to other accounts of shipwreck and disaster, these texts have a dimension that is absent from more traditional voyage narratives. They are all concerned with enforced (or, in some cases, voluntary) European interactions with native island hosts. The sailors go native primarily to ensure their continued survival on islands not always hospitable to European strangers. The extreme level of cultural assimilation required, and the negotiations it gave rise to, are the fundamental characteristics of the beachcomber account.

The experience described in this book is a distinctively male one. Throughout the period under discussion, women were shipwrecked and cast away in similar circumstances, but as women their experience of captivity and integration was different to that of the sailor. They require a separate investigation and a story of their own. A similar explanation must also be given for the exclusion of beachcomber experience in Australia and New Zealand. Australia's historical pre-eminence as a trading and economic centre in the early nineteenth century, together with the increased volume of shipping that it gave rise to, necessitates its own full-length study, while the infamous Pakeha Maori of New Zealand have already received considerable attention.[1] Nevertheless, the experiences described here form an integral part of the wider narrative of exploration in the South Seas in the late eighteenth and early nineteenth centuries.

For ease of expression all sailors are described as European, regardless of whether they are American or British by birth. The description identifies both peoples as similarly informed by Western philosophy, history, religion and, at the same time, differentiates them from those who can be regarded as non-European in cultural and ideological terms.

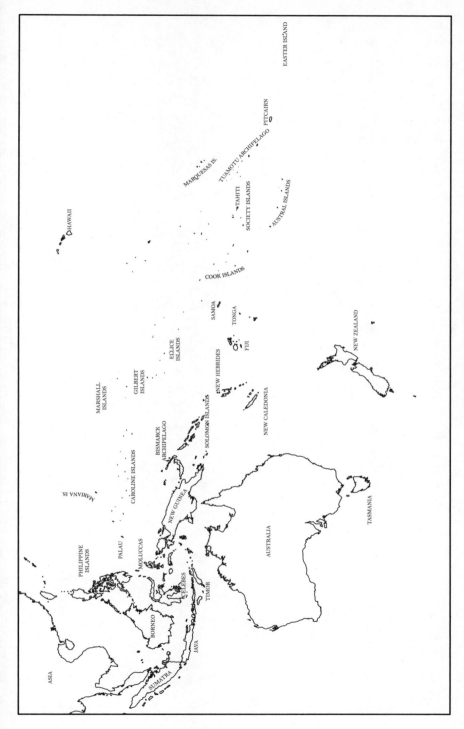

Islands of the Pacific

CHAPTER ONE

The White Heathen of the South Seas

So true is it, that man, left to himself without the restraints of law and civilized life, will, unless the grace of God prevent, soon degenerate into a savage, through the corrupt tendency of his nature to yield to the influence of bad example.

GEORGE VASON, *An Authentic Narrative of Four Years' Residence at Tongataboo*

One day in July 1831, a young man named Horace Holden made a decision that would change the course of his life. He decided to go on a journey. He would leave his home in New England, turning his back on all that was known, familiar and secure. His first step took him to the port of New Bedford, where he signed on a whaling voyage to the Indian Ocean. He knew that in order to become an explorer of a new world, he first had to become a stranger to his own. It was an important act for the son of a New England farmer who had spent his entire life in the village of Hillsborough, New Hampshire, and it was undertaken with a heavy heart. Holden had lived happily with his family until the unexpected death of his father, described by the boy as 'a loss which nothing on earth can supply'. It was a loss that his small, close-knit family experienced on a practical level. It brought about the end of their livelihood and it forced them to make their own way in the world. Holden tried a number of different occupations before deciding on the time-honoured route of all young men with no money and no prospects. He would go to sea. By doing so, he would contribute to the financial well-being of his family. He would gain new skills, learn a little about life, and see something of the world. Along the way, he would have an adventure or two of his own.

He prepared for his journey. He exchanged the clothes of a farmer for those of a sailor. He wore the loose duck trousers, checked shirt and tarpaulin hat common to the nineteenth-century seaman. The trousers were tight around the hip and hung loose and long around his feet. The shirt was thick and warm to protect him on the long, cold night-watches. His black hat with its trailing length of black ribbon was pushed to the back of his head, while a casually knotted neckerchief was tied at his throat. His new apparel did more than signal his metamorphosis from landsman to whaler. It prepared him for a new role in life – one that would soon be reflected in the wide step and rolling gait, in the rough hands and reddened skin of the archetypal Jack tar.

A whaling life was a hard one. Pitting oneself against the leviathans of the deep was a hazardous enterprise, not for the faint-hearted. Whalers were a class of people proverbial for the intrepid voyages that took them away from land for years at a time. It was an arduous, uncertain and physically demanding occupation, not to be undertaken lightly. Holden, though, had little time to contemplate the change in his fortunes, as the *Mentor* sailed the day he enlisted. With the hoisting of the sails, he was effectively cut off from family and friends, from home and nation, 'at the mercy of an element to which I had been but little accustomed'. Holden travelled, without accident or alarm, to the Azores, Java and Timor before his ship was blown off course near the Spice Islands (present-day Moluccas). It was during a storm that lasted three terrifying days and nights that the *Mentor* was forced onto a submerged coral reef running north and east of the Palau Islands. The impact threw the young sailor from his berth and flung him against the opposite wall. He rushed on deck in a state of confusion and dismay. It was only ten months since Holden had become a sailor and suddenly his journey was over. As his ship dashed itself to pieces against the rocks he called out to his family and prayed for salvation.

Half of the crew clambered into one of the ship's longboats, cut themselves free of the sinking ship and headed for open water. Neither the boat nor its occupants were ever seen again. The rest of the men took their chances and waited for daylight. Survival was uncertain but preparations needed to be made. A complete set of nautical instruments, a logbook, a bag of clothes and a small quantity of bread and water were loaded into the remaining longboat, along with a canister of gunpowder, a brace of pistols, three cutlasses and a tinderbox. With their basic necessities safely stowed, the men cast off from the sinking ship 'with little to rely upon but the mercy of Providence'. Daylight brought with it a ray of hope after the horrors of the night. The reef encircled a large land mass which was visible about thirty to fifty kilometres away. A decision was made to head for the island, although many weary hours passed before the sailors finally approached the shore. 'We were on a barren rock, in the midst of a waste of waters,' Holden recalled, 'far from kindred and friends, and the abodes of civilized man.' They did what they could to raise their spirits. Some men collected shellfish and others made a small fire. They shared a simple meal and contemplated their future. Rocks, shingle and dried lumps of coral lay about the shore. A few metres inland they saw nothing but low green shrubs and tangled undergrowth, while wind-beaten trees sloped away from the shore providing little shelter against the hot sun. The sailors had begun to believe the island was deserted when they noticed signs of activity at the other end of the beach. Visions of cannibals and expectations of a bloody death set them trembling in fear and dismay. They watched in silent trepidation as a 'singular looking being' separated himself from the crowd and walked towards them. It was a sight that Holden would never forget:

His appearance was that of a man of sixty. His hair was long and gray unlike that of the natives. His legs, arms, and breast were tattooed. His step was quick and firm; his motions indicating that he felt himself a person of not a little importance. His teeth were entirely gone, and his mouth was black with the use of 'kabooa'. Judge our emotions on hearing this strange being address us in broken English! His first exclamation was – 'My God, you are Englishmen!'[1]

This was the men's first sight of that strange phenomenon known as a Pacific Island beachcomber. The man that stood before them had once been a British sailor. Twenty-nine years earlier, Charles Washington had set forth on his own voyage of adventure and discovery. He had shipped on a man-of-war travelling to the South Seas and, towards the end of a long spell of sentry duty, he had fallen asleep. Rather than face the flogging he was sure to receive, he decided to take his chances on shore. Washington had 'gone native'. He had transformed himself from a European sailor to a Pacific Islander, conforming in all visible respects to the appearance and behaviour of the 'savages' around him. By doing so, he had crossed the invisible but potent line that divided Western man from his primitive other. Dishevelled, darkened by the sun, long-haired, tattooed and dressed in native clothing, Washington had irrevocably severed his ties with Europe. Originally a hatter by trade, he had long since turned his back on those roles that had once given shape to his life. He told the shipwrecked sailors that he had no desire to leave the island where he was one of six local chiefs. In his small world he was an important man; he had prestige, authority and status. The man he had been thirty years earlier had been forgotten. He was now something else entirely. He stood before the stunned sailors as a cultural hybrid, a bizarre embodiment of the encounter between European and Islander, between civilisation and savagery.

Like many sailors before and after him, Washington could not have known that his sea voyage would be only the first step in a unique and remarkable journey. Not only would he travel across oceans, hemispheres and island shores, he would also traverse cultural, behavioural and psychological boundaries that would prove a great deal more perilous. His decision to turn his back on Europe separated him from his customary place in life, requiring him to make a new life on foreign shores. In order to survive, he dressed native-fashion, became fluent in the local language and observed local cultural and religious practices. The level of Washington's assimilation was soon to be paralleled by the young sailor from America, whose pivotal decision to go to sea had dictated the course of his future. Holden's journey took him far from the life he knew. The shipwreck that misplaced him geographically also displaced him culturally. It was the beginning of an adventure that would forever shape the man he would become. On his lonely island, he would be confused and misunderstood. He would suffer unimaginable brutality and hardship and he would experience great acts of kindness and forbearance. He would live intimately with strangers and he would become just like them in order to survive. His island sojourn was to last for two years before he was rescued by a passing ship and taken back to America. On his return to Boston four years later, Holden immediately recorded for posterity his unforgettable journey from civilisation into 'savagery'. His intriguing story will be referred to later.

The Beachcomber Phenomenon

Beachcombers take their name from the beaches on which they lived.[2] It is a term that acknowledges the combination of nature, fate and providence that initially brought them to island shores. Once there, they made the best of what they found, adapting and conforming to an unfamiliar world and awaiting a change in their fortunes. As a nineteenth-century American sailor-turned-beachcomber explained:

> [The term is] much in vogue among sailors in the Pacific. It is applied to certain roving characters who, without attaching themselves permanently to any vessel, ship now and then for a short cruise in a whaler; but upon the condition only of being honorably discharged the very next time the anchor takes hold of the bottom; no matter where. They are, mostly, a reckless, rollicking set, wedded to the Pacific, and never dreaming of ever doubling Cape Horn again on a homeward-bound passage.[3]

However, a less poetic definition also held sway through much of the nineteenth century. It described the beachcomber as 'a seaman who, not prepared to work, preferred to exist by hanging around the ports and harbours and existing on the charity of others'. It became a way to describe those 'loafers around the waterfront, particularly in the Pacific islands, who prefer a life of *dolce far niente* to work of any description'.[4] Certainly by the mid- to late 1800s, as European presence in the islands increased, such men could be found living on the fringes of all the established port towns, scraping together a frugal existence as pearl-fishers, traders and general odd-jobbers.

But the term 'beachcomber' has yet another dimension. Men such as Charles Washington and Horace Holden can more properly be described as 'transculturists' – Westerners who attempt to survive in a culture other than their own. They were men who 'crossed the beach', who traversed those literal and metaphorical boundaries that divided the European world from the native. By choosing to live as islanders within island communities these men were embarking on a perilous adventure. Their ongoing safety in their new society was directly related to their degree of assimilation. The more integrated they became, the more they could rely on the grace and favour of the natives. If they were lucky, they would obtain the support of a chief or a member of a ruling family. This patronage would guarantee their personal safety and would provide them with an extended network of friends and family to call on in times of need. If they were not so lucky, their long-term survival was uncertain. Without the acceptance of the native community their island experience would be brief and brutal.

Beachcombers were cultural explorers. They travelled to places that were unvisited, and often unknown, by the wider European community. They were witnesses to island cultures in ways denied to all other strangers from the sea. However, their decision to cross the beach was often a direct consequence of their own life histories. Three-quarters of the beachcombing population comprised British seamen with increasing numbers of American sailors. They were usually of low social status, traditionally under-educated, often illiterate, and subject to the harsh discipline and rigid hierarchy associated with life on board ship. Convicts with working-class origins comprised the remaining quarter. These men had served their time in the Australian penal colony at Port Jackson or had escaped by signing on as crew members on American ships.[5]

Neither sailors nor convicts needed any incentive to turn their backs on cramped conditions, tyrannical captains, overwork and low pay. Their personal history gave them little reason to be loyal to the land of their birth. They literally had nothing to lose. They often had few prospects for advancement in their own society, while their disreputable social status kept them on the fringes of European society. Island life appeared to offer them greater wealth and security. Tattooed and dressed as natives, they were often provided with accommodation, given wives and offered land. Their technological superiority and their knowledge of the wider world ensured their value to many Pacific communities.

Beachcombing sailors were a fairly common sight during the late eighteenth and early nineteenth centuries. Commercial shipping, the establishment of a British settlement at Port Jackson and the burgeoning north-west fur trade between America and China meant that many more ships crossed the seas.[6] The bêche-de-mer (sea cucumber), sandalwood and fur seal trades brought a constant stream of sailors, craftsmen, convicts, deserters and castaways into the islands. There they joined growing numbers of whalers, traders, missionaries, scientists, naturalists and adventurers looking for a life of excitement and opportunity in the Pacific. It was easy to find. Their voyages had brought them to islands whose very names were imbued with wonder and romance – places such as Tahiti, Hawaii, Samoa, Tonga and Fiji for instance were filled with myth and mystery. They were perfect for adventure. The blue skies, warm lagoons, coral beaches and golden palms of those islands symbolised the freedom, beauty, peace and pleasure sought by all those who voyage far from home. They were also rich with mythical possibilities. New worlds could be made on islands, and old worlds could be re-ordered. They were places of magic, of transformation and rebirth. The area known to our sailors as 'Oceania' or 'Polynesia' or the 'South Seas' was less a place than an ideal. Actual physical positioning was irrelevant. The sailors travelled towards an ideological vision, a collective myth that had cast an enchantment over generations of voyagers.

Pacific Paradise

The Pacific did not disappoint. It became legendary as a seaman's paradise. As early as 1595, when the Spaniard Alvaro de Mendana claimed Las Marquesas (the Marquesas Islands) for Spain, he dwelt on the beauty and sexual charms of the islanders. They were 'almost white and of very graceful shape, well-formed, robust' and 'naked, without any part covered'. The women were 'prettier than the ladies of Lima, who are famed for their beauty' and were 'ready to come near in friendly intercourse'.[7] A ship full of American sailors received a similar welcome many years later. After making anchorage in Nukuhiva Bay, their vessel was boarded by scores of naked Marquesan women who made themselves at home on the decks, head-rails and bowsprits. They were 'dripping with brine and glowing from the bath', recalled one sailor, 'their jet black tresses streaming over their shoulders, and half enveloping their otherwise naked forms'. He added that the 'ship was now wholly given up to every species of riot and debauchery. Not the feeblest barrier was interposed between the unholy passions of the crew and their unlimited gratification. The grossest licentiousness and the most shameful inebriety prevailed.'[8]

Other travellers wrote about the sexual freedoms to be found on the islands. Samuel Wallis and his men described the welcome they received in Tahiti in 1768 — an island paradise defined by sexual exchange and barter. The sailors wanted fresh food and female company and the islanders wanted iron. In order to facilitate trade, the Tahitians brought forward 'a good many fine young Girls . . . this new sight Attract our mens fance a good dale, and the natives observed it, and made the Young Girls play a great many droll wanting [wanton] tricks', recalls the master of the *Dolphin*.[9] It was a profitable transaction on both sides of the beach and before long the 'old trade' became a flourishing pastime: 'The Women were far from being Coy. For when A Man Found a Girl to his Mind, which he Might Easly Do Amongst so many, their was Not much Cermony on Either Side.'[10] Iron was the preferred currency and the ship was so depleted that it threatened to fall apart. By the time the *Dolphin* left the island, most of the men were sleeping on the deck, having no nails on which to string their hammocks.

Despite the documented appeal of the South Seas, not all beach-combers voluntarily chose island life. Some men were kidnapped for prestige value or held for ransom while others were forcibly put ashore by their captains for being troublesome, seditious, or simply too ill to travel. While Charles Washington is representative of those who deserted, shipwreck was the predominant mode of arrival. The beachcomber narratives confirm that disaster at sea, and the loss of ships, accounted for two-thirds of arrivals on island shores. Shipwreck was an unenviable fact of life in the seagoing world of the nineteenth century and it was one that occurred with alarming frequency in the still uncharted waters of the Pacific. Throughout the history of European sea voyaging, it was not unusual for men from every walk of life, from all countries and nationalities, to find themselves cast adrift on foreign shores.

The Romantic Castaway

The popularity of South Sea stories of travel and adventure at this time ensured that the image of the castaway-turned-beachcomber was widespread and pervasive. Tales of white men living as natives, fighting in local wars and taking native wives, generated a great deal of interest and speculation. The castaways from Europe were imbued with their own particular aura of romance. Their distance from Europe had liberated them from tradition and history, from the twin trials of duty and responsibility. They were freed from the constraints of a civilised life, from the limitations of their class and creed. In the history of European exploration and discovery they were unimportant men. They did not travel with an imperial mandate in the tradition of Cook, Wallis and Bougainville. Their pedigree was less impressive, their status a great deal more humble. Ultimately, their experience was a personal one. The beachcombing sailor was an adventurer and opportunist who faced the trials of the world on his own. He was a de-institutionalised traveller, an intrepid individual who repudiated the demands of the civilised world in order to follow his own desires. He was a rover, a wanderer, a seeker of adventure, someone who was cut adrift from his country of origin, his family, his ship. On the shores of the Pacific he found his own sort of freedom.

Those footloose, culturally curious, beach-crossing sailors scattered throughout the Pacific at the turn of the nineteenth century were archetypal voyagers who, voluntarily or otherwise, found themselves severed from their pasts. On island shores they took advantage of the opportunities they were offered. They explored new worlds, and new ways of being, by learning new behaviours, gestures, rituals, habits and customs in accordance with their unique circumstances. They attempted to make themselves at home in an alien place. As lone Europeans on foreign shores, they were imbued with the exotic glamour of Robinson Crusoe. It was a glamour recognised by one contemporary commentator who remarked, 'There is a poetry about these men (a rough class of poetry, it is true) which one finds it very difficult to convey in words.'[11]

But the romantic escapism associated with the beachcombing lifestyle was balanced by a growing emphasis on their cultural disloyalty. This negative image was set in place as early as 1789 by the 'mass act of beachcombing' known as the mutiny on the *Bounty*.[12] The HMS *Bounty* left England on 23 December 1787, charged with transporting breadfruit trees from the Pacific to British slave plantations in the Caribbean. She was not a happy ship. She was small and overcrowded, packed with men, supplies, and breadfruit seedlings, together with scientific and botanical paraphernalia. It was a cramped, restricted and fiercely regulated world made worse by the personal insecurities of its captain. William Bligh interfered remorselessly in all aspects of his men's existence. He rationed provisions, regulated the distribution of food and withheld their legitimate serving of grog if the sailors threatened to disobey his increasingly erratic commands. The lure of the islands proved a dangerous contrast against such autocratic interference. On Tahiti, the men could reclaim their personal sovereignty. They could surround themselves with the bounty of food, peace and freedom denied them by their captain.

The mutiny occurred on 28 April 1789. Under the leadership of Fletcher Christian, a number of sailors seized Bligh and eighteen others, placed them in an open boat, and cast them adrift. The remaining crew sailed to Tahiti, where sixteen sailors chose to leave the ship and live ashore. The rest of the crew, together with a number of Tahitians, male and female, went on to settle on Pitcairn Island. There they founded a colony of which Alexander Smith (by then calling himself John Adams) became the leader. Although unrelated to the French Revolution which occurred in the same year, the *Bounty*

The mutineers evicting Lieutenant Bligh and some of the
officers and crew from HMS *Bounty*, 1790.

mutiny challenged the entrenched status quo.[13] It occurred on a
much smaller stage certainly, but the actions of the mutinous sailors
who violently chose the freedom of the beach over the constraints
of maritime law were equally anarchic. Their rebellious actions in
the Pacific could not be separated from similar events in Europe and
were seen as an unacceptable threat to European political and social
stability.

Captain Edwards of the HMS *Pandora* was sent to Tahiti with orders
to capture the mutineers and bring them back to England for justice.
Some were reluctant to return but others believed themselves to be
innocent of any intentional wrongdoing. They welcomed the chance to
defend their names. All those who appeared for trial were irrevocably
marked by their experiences in Tahiti. While their psychological scars

could only be guessed at, their physical changes were unmistakable. Their skin was darkened by prolonged exposure to the sun, their hair was long and their speech was littered with Tahitian words and phrases. Worst of all to European eyes were the tattoos they carried on their bodies – indissoluble proof of the sailors' journey into the 'heart of darkness' and evidence of their mutinous tendencies writ large. The English society reacted with horror and disgust at the political, social and cultural ramifications of white men gone native. Any lingering admiration for the sailors' bid for democracy on Pacific shores was soon replaced by widespread condemnation of their treasonous acts. Public abhorrence of the absconding, recidivist, culturally treacherous mariner was easily transferred to *all* men who willingly chose island life over shipboard duty.

Cultural Treason

The romantic conception of the beachcombing sailor was under threat. Contemporary commentators were deeply offended at white men who deserted their ships only to lead lives of idleness and dissipation on Pacific beaches. Such men were a 'slur upon the reputation of the English in the Pacific'. White men abroad were to be ambassadors for Europe. They were not expected to degrade their nation by 'getting drunk before savages' – a common charge levelled against the beachcombers. An ex-sailor in Fiji known only as 'Harry the Jew' was a case in point. He had deserted from a man-of-war and was adopted by a chief of the Navua district. With his gun the white man helped his chief wipe out other contenders for power. He later took to the hills where he had fourteen native wives and spent most of his time drinking kava, living a life of 'bloodshed, drunkenness and debauchery'. 'Yankee Ned', a deserter living on York Island in the Torres Straits, was also notorious. 'Clad only in a shirt and pants, and with dirty bare feet', the sailor was interested in nothing but the ship that brought his supply of grog.[14] The men, their names and personal histories are simply indicative of a certain type of person becoming infamous through the Pacific at this period in history. The white-man-gone-native was a growing phenomenon and was fast becoming an anathema to other Europeans. His lifestyle, appearance and behaviour

were seen to reinforce barbarism at the expense of civilisation and he
was regarded with contempt rather than admiration. As one Pacific
traveller remarked:

> They climb trees like apes, and can dive almost as well as the natives with
> whom they live. They wear no shoes, but go at all times barefooted on
> beaches of sharp gravel and reefs of prickly coral. Some of these men have
> as many as twenty children with huge frames and gipsy countenances.
> Their intellect is of a low order, and their morals are very lax . . . The
> civilization they introduce is usually of the square-gin and musket order,
> and they tend to destroy fine races of savages instead of assisting them
> to approach our level.[15]

Sailors who crossed the beach to the world of the native became
synonymous with depravity and dissipation. By living as natives
they had effectively placed themselves beyond the borders of civilised
society by depriving themselves of the progress and enlightenment
traditionally associated with Europe. The root cause of such disdain
was a fairly basic one – a belief that the sailors' ease with native life
had been purchased at the cost of their European civility. It was seen
as a betrayal of the highest order. White savages were markedly more
reprehensible than black or brown ones because they *chose* to throw
off the restraints of civilisation[16] – a condemnation that conveniently
overlooks the involuntary nature of much beachcomber experience.
Going native was seen as socially and morally reprehensible, appealing
only to men already predisposed to venality and licentiousness:

> [T]here are men – one finds them on almost every beach in the wide
> South Sea – who in other days and other climes have held their heads high
> with the highest, but who now because of some queer kink in their mental
> make-up . . . have shed their white men's ways and drifted by easy stages
> into the dingy inertia that places them level with the beasts. They live
> native fashion, in many cases they have native wives. They are not black
> men but neither are they white.[17]

The Rev. Robert Thomson believed that seamen in the Marquesas, for example, differed only in colour from 'their fellow savages; they are tattooed as much as the natives – run as naked – live as loose, and are more openly insultingly vile in our presence than even the natives'.[18] 'They are men of the most desperate wickedness', wrote another observer, 'regarded as monsters even by the ferocious cannibals with whom they associated'.[19] There is no doubt that in some cases the bad publicity was entirely justified. John Bow, an infamous white-man-gone-native, boasted of having killed 300 Samoans. 'Entirely naked', he was 'besmeared from head to foot with the blood of his victims, whose heads were placed in frightful array around him', according to one commentator. Similarly, a beachcomber known as Jack Jones was supposed to have eaten all of his companions on a boat voyage from Rotuma to Nauru. Not content with that, he then murdered all the sailors who had arrived there before him, poisoning seven and shooting four in a single night.[20]

Men who crossed the border that divided the European from the native had, in the eyes of their contemporaries, permanently descended into a life of savagery. Their willingness to assimilate was regarded as a repudiation of civilisation in all its forms and guises. It was an act of cultural treachery especially when the adoptive culture was associated with the worst excesses in human behaviour. The Rev. James Orange, for instance, was quite explicit about the true level of native depravity. Polynesians, he believed, were wicked, covetous and malicious. They were full of envy, murder, deceit and malignity, were haters of God and inventors of evil. They possessed no natural affections, no understanding and no mercy.[21] In fairness to other South Sea missionaries, Orange's views are extreme and cannot be regarded as representative. However, they do reflect the deep European prejudice against white men who turn their backs on their own culture. By becoming like the Polynesians, the beachcombers were subject to the same racist assumptions levelled against all savage people. They were irrevocably tainted with the same vices.

The Lure of the Native

The missionaries had a special interest in the degenerative figure of the white native because of the spectacular fall from grace of one of their own – the missionary-turned-beachcomber George Vason. Vason, a poor village boy from Nottingham in England, was influenced by pious friends to become a missionary. Responding wholeheartedly to the evangelical impulse, he journeyed to the South Seas in 1797 to civilise and redeem the natives. The element of chance and misfortune so common in the majority of beachcomber experiences is absent here. Vason began his journey with a strong sense of duty and an avowed commitment to live among native people. He sailed for Tahiti on a voyage validated by God. After leaving a number of men on Tahiti, the *Duff* headed for Tonga. The verdant hills and calm lagoons encircling the island proved a welcome sight to the remaining missionaries on board, and they began their island life in the security of their faith and the company of their brethren. They were also fortunate to obtain the protection of the local chief, who was keen to gain the advantages of civilisation (trade goods, weapons, iron, technical skills and so on), even if he was not so enamoured of the Christianity that accompanied it. The first months were idyllic. Suffused with a sense of importance and worthiness, Vason wrote: 'there were ten of us in company, all social and friendly, all attached to each other . . . all at this time, united in love and zeal for our divine Master'.

The men decided to split up in order to increase their progress and improve their language skills. Vason was lucky to win the friendship of Mulikiha'amea, a high-ranking chief, and went to live under his protection. However, he still had occasional meetings with the others, which he found of 'considerable use to revive and strengthen my religious principles'. Separation from his fellow missionaries soon proved to be a problem. Without their permanent presence, Vason succumbed to the delights of island living: 'The temptation of my situation, uniting with my natural depravity now no longer restrained by the presence of others, but fostered by all around, gradually corrupted my soul, and overcame me.' With those prophetic words he began his spectacular 'decline' from God-fearing missionary to white native. The man who set off from Europe with such high hopes lost himself in the islands. He was unable to resist the lure of native life. He neglected prayer, stopped reading the Bible and chose not to contact his brethren for spiritual sustenance. At just twenty-five years of age, Vason found himself bereft of the spiritual fortitude needed to 'stem the strong torrent of surrounding corruption'. There is an air of inevitability about the changes in him. He was seduced on all fronts: 'After a time, I was induced to yield to their manners, and to join them in their sins.' His isolation among the natives left him open to 'those temptations with which I was daily surrounded and enticed'.

Ironically, his moral degradation and mental anguish went hand in hand with increased wealth, status and personal happiness. Vason learned the local language, adopted native dress, and was persuaded to take a native wife. He agreed to be tattooed and was marked with the full hip and thigh markings universal among Tongan men. Despite his stated misgivings about cohabiting 'with a woman without the sanction of marriage', he was very happy. He lived in harmony with his wife, growing in wealth and influence. His new life offered him a level of comfort and personal power that he had never experienced. He surrendered to the 'seduction of appetite' and the 'alluring attraction of sensual objects', but is very coy about the details of his depravity: 'I now entered, with the utmost eagerness, into every pleasure and entertainment of the natives, and endeavoured to forget that I was once called a Christian, and had left a Christian land to evangelise the heathen.' His fellow missionaries begged him to renounce his 'wife' and return to the fold. Vason refused. He turned his back on his one-time companions, and went back to the fifteen-acre plantation gifted to him by his chief. When the missionaries left Tonga, they travelled without their wayward compatriot. Vason chose to remain, and sought his own peculiar form of redemption in the hills and valleys of Tonga.

He lived as a native for four years until Mulikiha'amea died in a particularly vicious civil war. Finding himself caught between two opposing factions and in fear of his life, he fled to an English ship moored in the harbour. He pleaded with the sailors to take him on board. His stress and anxiety caused him to forget his mother tongue and he was ignored by the sailors who assumed he was a native. Eventually the captain, recognising his broken English, brought him safely on board. The *Royal Admiral* had been sent by the Missionary Society to bring supplies to the remaining missionary station in Tahiti. Because Vason's own colleagues had already left Tonga two years earlier, the ship's presence in that place and at that time was entirely coincidental. The fallen sailor recognised the hand of providence. He returned to England, recovered his faith and found his way back to God. Eager to promote Vason's story as a redemptive narrative, the Missionary Society published it as an example and a warning to others.

Vason's story warned of the dangerous allure of the islands. Native life, it was believed, had the capacity to seduce unwary Europeans, lulling them into moral turpitude through too much ease and indulgence in forbidden pleasures. They would then be powerless against their own 'natural depravity'. Vason's experience demonstrated how the 'seduction of appetite' could make beachcombers of them all. One such individual was the French beachcomber, Jean (Josef) Cabri, who lived for nine years with the natives of the Marquesas. Cabri was a French sailor who went to sea in 1794 at the age of fourteen. He was taken prisoner by the English, but was eventually allowed to ship on a whaler travelling to the South Seas. It is unclear whether he deserted or was shipwrecked, but somehow he arrived on the Marquesas Islands about the middle of 1796. A Russian expedition, led by Captain von Krusenstern, investigating economic and territorial opportunities arrived at the islands eight years later and met the young sailor in 1804. He was a bizarre and wondrous sight. Tall and well-built, he was fully tattooed in the Marquesan fashion with ornate designs and bands of colour over his legs, body and face. He had forgotten his native tongue – at that point in time he had forgotten his own name – and was Marquesan in all but birth. He had two native wives, had integrated fully into island life and had two children of his own. He fought for his family against other tribes and established himself as cunning, agile, courageous and loyal. He participated fully in all aspects of Marquesan life, seeing his world primarily in terms of the power and domination he could find in theirs.

Cabri travelled freely throughout the islands during his nine years there. He was a familiar sight to the ships that called into port, but he was never fully trusted as an intermediary. The Russian visitors believed the Frenchman had been 'morally and physically transformed into a savage' and that he was not constrained by loyalty to Europe.[22] His allegiance lay elsewhere and he was implicated in a number of

Jean (Josef) Cabri, a Marquesan beachcomber. The level of his assimilation can be gauged by the extent of his tattoos.

anti-European skirmishes. Cabri exerted a fascination over all visitors to the Marquesas. They gazed on him in wonder, at once attracted and repelled by the extremes of his cultural integration. Then, as now, there was a great deal of interest in those men who chose to repudiate

their European identity in such a spectacular manner. What sort of
men were they? What would cause them to compromise themselves
so irrevocably? Men such as Washington and Vason could not have
known how scandalous they appeared to other Europeans. Their
tattooed skins and foreign speech, their familiarity with a savage way
of life, mounted a subtle threat to the stability of European cultural
identity. Their very existence challenged the traditional division
between the civilised man and the savage, between 'us' and 'them'.
Their in-between-ness, the fact that they were clearly neither one
thing nor another, was deeply disturbing. It signalled the fragility of
Western cultural superiority and blurred the edges of civilisation by
threatening to make savages of all Europeans. The exotic strangeness
of these cultural hybrids evoked equal measures of curiosity and
condemnation in all who met them.

It was a response that revealed a deeper psychological impetus.
Europe was fascinated by the sexual freedom of the islands, by the
reports of promiscuity and licence on Pacific beaches. Primitive man
was seen as a living symbol of preconscious European man, free to
live out his regressive fantasies and fulfil his repressed desires.[23] His
imagined sexual freedoms were linked to the uninhibited hedonism
of childhood and to those forbidden urges traditionally repressed
on the journey to adulthood. Anything so rigorously denied is also
violently longed for. Eighteenth-century society was caught between
the need to redeem the primitive and/or to grasp his freedom for itself.
The beachcomber, as semi-savage, was believed to indulge in such
pleasures, particularly those that were explicitly denied in his home
society. Western ambivalence towards the white-man-gone-native, its
combination of fascination and repulsion, arose from that dichotomy
between civilised behaviour and forbidden delight. It was a response
that said more about the state of the European psyche than the actual
experiences of the beachcombers who inevitably became victims of
their own mythology.

CHAPTER TWO

Accidental Authors

Here, with a board for a table, and a shell for an inkstand, I wrote an account of what I had passed through until my arrival in Oahu.

JAMES OLIVER, *Wreck of the* Glide

Those British and American sailors, cast away on the beaches of the Polynesian islands, were much more than the cultural reprobates and irredeemable sinners others thought them to be. In the first instance, their accidental and unplanned arrivals set them apart from other travellers and tourists. They soon realised that survival was a matter of chance and that they would be saved or otherwise solely at the discretion of the natives. Also, for the length of their stay they were completely cut off from outside influence. They suffered the total dependency and powerlessness common to the island castaway, wholly at the mercy of complete strangers and totally unprepared for an alien way of life. They could not speak the language, had no means of communication and no understanding of relevant social and cultural protocols. At no point were they independently able to pick up and move on to somewhere else. The men were soon forced to realise that their safety and continued survival depended on a successful degree of cultural assimilation. They were careful to avoid trouble with their hosts, to treat their adoptive families with respect, and to adhere as closely as possible to local beliefs and practices. Their social flexibility, cultural relativism and dramatic flair for self-invention were valuable skills in their journey from European to native. These talents, together with a sheer determination to survive, were justly claimed as unique by those who lived to write about them.

Although marginal to the larger national and economic forces at work in these historical encounters, the beachcombers had their own unique brand of usefulness. They were the forerunners of Western civilisation, bringing to the islands their knowledge of firearms, and their expertise in a range of technological skills, such as bricklaying, weaving, printmaking, distilling, blacksmithing and so on. They were usually happy to offer what practical help they could. For instance, Archibald Campbell, a Scottish sailor who spent six eventful years travelling around the world, was prized in the Sandwich Islands (Hawaii) because of his facility with a loom – he wove cloth to make sails for King Kamemeha's ships. Other beachcombers repaired muskets, advised on farming techniques or used their superior fire power to the advantage of their host families. It was that skill in particular that ensured them the support of the chiefs. Beachcombers were also invaluable as mediators or go-betweens, facilitating trade and cross-cultural communication between visiting whalers, travellers, traders and missionaries and the island communities. They worked as agents, supercargoes, pilots and interpreters. They warned of native attacks, and saved ships by convincing chiefs not to attack and encouraging them to show mercy. They also provided valuable knowledge of baffling island protocols to visiting Europeans. In 1797, for instance, the missionaries on the *Duff* set sail for Tahiti armed with a vocabulary and grammar, as well as ethnographic notes, prepared for them by *Bounty* mutineers James Morrison and Peter Heywood.

More importantly, the beachcombers redeemed themselves by becoming authors. Publication of their stories implied a return to Europe and set them in opposition to those men who chose to remain on the islands. It also demonstrated their renewed contact with Western civilisation and their preference for Western values over island life. They were at pains to legitimise themselves in European terms and to convince their readers of their authority as credible eyewitnesses. The act of writing involved the sailors in a process of reflection and consideration. Consciously or not, they entered into the larger philosophical debate concerning the nature of the savage, the ideology of primitivism, the ethics of imperialism, the benefits of civilisation and the meaning of humanity. They realised that their experiences, when presented in the appropriate textual format and validated by their appearance in print, had the capacity to reinstate them in European terms. The popular interest in new stories from the Pacific guaranteed them access to an audience that was traditionally denied them. Those sailors-turned-authors literally wrote themselves back into respectability.

Because the majority of beachcombers were anonymous, unimportant men, examination of their lives is, by necessity, restricted to those who were better known. Some entered history through the writings of others or by means of anecdotes, tall tales and stories told about the early days of European exploration. Others have written accounts of their own. It is impossible to know what the absconding seamen thought or felt during their island experiences, without access, after this length of time, to a text of some sort. It is the written accounts – those diaries, notes, logbooks, journals, memoirs and letters – that have survived which vividly bring to life the sailors and their Pacific experiences.

Beachcomber-authors vary in age and experience. William Mariner was a very young man, only fifteen years of age at the start of his four-year stay in Tonga, while the suggestively named 'Cannibal Jack' (also known as John Jackson and William Diaper) was still wandering the Pacific well into his eighties. James Morrison, a boatswain's mate on the infamous *Bounty*, spent two years on Tubuai and Tahiti, while a British sailor, John Twyning, spent over twenty years as a travelling beachcomber. Some of the men remained lifelong sailors, returning to the Pacific in later years. Others were one-time voyagers only and settled back into land-based lifestyles upon their return home. Their adventures took place on a wide range of islands: the crew of the *Antelope* was shipwrecked on the Palaus in 1783; William Lockerby found himself cast ashore in Fiji in 1808; James O'Connell stayed on Ponape for six years from 1826; while William Torrey wrote about life on the Marquesas in the 1840s. Most castaways were isolated from their fellow sailors, but a fortunate few were able to retain the

Herman Melville in 1861, almost twenty years after his life as a Pacific beachcomber and ten years after the publication of *Moby Dick*.

company of other Europeans. Close contact with other white men usually permitted them a greater level of control over their own destiny and those sailors were among the most likely to leave the islands on their own terms. Men who were more dependent on their island hosts, or those who were kept captive, had to escape by other, more violent means. Their stories tell us how difficult it was.

The most famous beachcomber-author was Herman Melville, whose popular narratives of life in the Pacific, *Typee* and *Omoo*, made him infamous as 'the man who lived among the cannibals'.[1] Melville was a young American who took to the sea looking for adventure at the age of twenty-one. The three years he spent in the Pacific were to provide him with material for a number of novels written on his return home. They tell of his experiences on merchant ships, in the American navy and on board a whaler. They were the beginning of a lifelong career as a writer that culminated in his artistic triumph, *Moby Dick*, the legendary tale of a hunt for a great white whale, first published in 1851. His literary career was in its infancy, however, when *Typee* was first published in 1846. It described his desertion, captivity and escape from cannibalistic natives in the Marquesas. Although it was extremely popular, many readers and critics refused to believe that the account was the work of an ordinary seaman. Writing of such sophistication and insight was not expected from a common man who sailed 'before the mast'. At least half of the British reviewers in 1846 refused to believe that the author and the seaman were the same person, supposing instead that it was a fiction created by a practised writer. There was less scepticism in America, where Richard Henry Dana's *Two Years before the Mast* stood as surety that young men of good families and good education did, in fact, go to sea as common sailors. Despite the controversy, or maybe because of it, the book was a runaway success.

Typee is the most interesting of all beachcomber accounts. It is certainly the most literary. Melville's artistry, his powers of observation and expression and his capacity for ideological exploration and reflection set him apart from other sailor-authors. *Typee*, and the later *Omoo*, stand as paradigms for beachcomber experience and its representation in print. Their evocation of the dangers as well as the delights of a beachcombing life keeps Melville at the forefront of our discussions. He offers a breadth of understanding and reflection that universalises his personal experience. His is the literary achievement that other sailors are inevitably measured by. Although we are here describing Melville as a beachcomber, it is not a definition he would have approved of, preferring to regard himself as a sailor-adventurer. His first sight of a beachcomber in the Marquesas Islands in 1843 filled him with disgust. The beachcomber was an ex-sailor called Lem Hardy, whom Melville described as 'a renegado from Christendom and humanity – a white man, in the South Sea girdle, and tattooed in the face'.[2] He was repelled by Hardy's adoption of native clothing, his implied lack of Christian belief and most of all by the prominence of his tattoo. Melville regarded the tattoo as the ultimate marker of cultural assimilation and was horrified to think that any European would voluntarily submit to such disfiguration. His response to Hardy was ironic, given his own later history, as Melville came close to that same 'disfigurement' in his beachcombing experience among the Taipi and found himself on the receiving end of Western prejudice when destitute in Tahiti many months later. All sailors with no visible means of support were regarded as prospective troublemakers by other Europeans and Melville was no exception: 'Prejudiced against us by the malevolent representations of the consul and others, many worthy foreigners ashore regarded us as a set of lawless vagabonds', he remembered.

George Vason, the missionary-turned-native in Tonga, is another man who had little time for beachcombers when he first encountered them. When he arrived in Tonga in 1797, his missionary party was forced to rely on the interpreting skills of two ex-sailors, Benjamin Ambler from London and John Conelly from Cork. Both men had deserted from an American vessel some years earlier and were living with the Tongans. Vason was scandalised by their semi-native status and, despite benefitting from their mediation skills, referred to them as 'base and wicked characters'. James Wilson, a fellow missionary on the *Duff*, was equally unimpressed: 'in their countenance, one of them especially, there was so much of the villain marked, that in England, a well-disposed person would shun them as he would a swindler or a pickpocket'.[3] Their opinions were soon to be vindicated.

Ambler and another beachcomber Morgan Bryan, an ex-convict from New South Wales, proved particularly troublesome. The resident beachcombers feared the growing influence of the newly arrived missionaries and attempted to sabotage their activities. Ambler and Bryan stole the newcomers' possessions and tried to prejudice the Tongans against them. Acting as interpreters, they informed the islanders that the missionaries planned to take over the island. The missionaries – totally reliant on the linguistic superiority of the beachcombers – could neither refute nor deny the accusations. However, the actions of the beachcombers caused their own downfall. Their constant drunkenness, their violence and their lack of goods or resources soon brought them into disfavour with the Tongans. Vason wrote, 'their bad conduct had rendered them too unpopular, to have much sway with the natives; and at length it provoked them to inflict upon them that death, in which they wished to have involved us'. Both beachcombers were in fact subsequently killed by the islanders for disrespectful behaviour to a chief and for the brutal violation of a chief's daughter. Vason was quite insistent on the violence and mayhem associated with men such as Ambler and Bryan. His latent European class consciousness and his own moral standards set him apart in his own mind from men such as these. Despite Vason's success at living as an integrated native, he never identified with other beachcombers.

The majority of beach-crossing sailors tended to view themselves as adventurers and explorers. Their voluntary or enforced adoption of a Pacific Island lifestyle is the factor that identifies them, historically, as beachcombers. It was not a category they chose for themselves. They were men of the sea and their narratives dealt with the age-old maritime realities of shipwreck, captivity, survival and rescue. They described the trials and rituals of seagoing life and focused on the thrill of discovery. Their literary model was the canonical accounts of Pacific exploration – those earlier journals which popularised the idea of travel and adventure. They were also influenced by the success and popularity of such works as *Robinson Crusoe*, Defoe's legendary tale based on the exploits of real-life castaway Alexander Selkirk. The story of a man cut off from all that is known and familiar proved perennially fascinating. Two hundred years later Joseph Conrad wrote of a similar journey into the dangers of the unknown in *Heart of Darkness*. Public interest in all aspects of newly 'discovered' worlds, their dangers and delights, encouraged the publication of other travellers' tales. The beachcombers believed it was an area to which they could contribute. Because of their beach-crossings, they were ideally placed to provide important information about little-known islands and about foreign or unknown cultures. Their native experiences had given them an unparalleled insight into the diversity and complexity of life lived on the native side of the beach, an insight they wished to share. As one sailor explained: 'One object in this publication ... is to give the civilized world an insight into the manners and customs of the children of the island of the sea with whom the author was so long associated'.[4] All beachcomber accounts contain local vocabularies, grammars, glossaries and maps, often in exhaustive detail. They include masses of ethnographic information, what they called 'customs and manners' of the native people. The sailors had found themselves marooned in the complexities of a foreign culture. With no knowledge of native language, form or ritual, they had no familiar frame of reference. The sheer quantity of empirical material outlined in their narratives reflects their naïve, but understandable, belief that an exhaustive focus on the details of island life might help solve the riddle of unknown cultures.

James Morrison, boatswain's mate on the *Bounty*, wrote one of the most interesting beachcomber accounts. His *Journal of James Morrison* is divided into two distinct parts; the first half deals with the *Bounty* mutiny, and the second is described as 'an account of the Island of Taheite . . . and of the Manners and Customs of the Society Isles in General with an account of their Language'. When the journal was discovered in the Mitchell Library in Sydney in the mid-1930s, it was obvious that the first section had been worked on by at least two different people with a view to publication. The second part of the manuscript had not been touched. Public interest has historically centred on the story of the *Bounty* – Morrison was well aware of that. He wrote his narrative after his return to England while awaiting a court martial for mutiny, and he wrote with a political and personal agenda. His account was intended to explain his actions, provoke sympathy and keep him from the gallows.[5] But it had another purpose. Morrison wanted to explore the complexities of Tahitian life and culture. The mass of ethnographic detail (over a hundred pages long and almost equal in length to the first section) balances the sailor's personal story. His painstaking inclusion of all aspects of Tahitian life for his readers demonstrates the value he placed on his role as ethnographer and author. Like many other beachcomber-authors, Morrison saw himself as an anthropologist, if only by default.

The beachcombers may have been common seamen but they believed that their unsolicited and unofficial contribution to Pacific literature was a valuable one. It was meant to serve a number of purposes. William Lockerby, marooned on Fiji in 1808, wanted to 'inform my friends of the particulars relating to myself during this unfortunate voyage'. But there were also economic imperatives – the burgeoning sandalwood trade and its possible benefits to Europe were an important consideration. His narrative included charts of the islands made from his own personal observation and surveys. He achieved his aim: 'having advertised the same on sale to the Public several copies were sold; and ships were sent out in search of Sandlewood [sic]'.[6] Another sailor had advice of a more practical nature to offer travellers to the Marquesas:

I hope, if ever this Narrative should fall into the hands of any one frequenting the pacific ocean, [they learn] to be cautious and not to leave things in the way of these Kind of people, as they are apt to pilfer. Never fire a ball till you are obligated, nor be allured from your boat on any account, as at several Islands in these seas they will entice you from your boat with their young women, who will lead you from the beach into the bush. There you get murderd, and the boat becomes their prize.[7]

Sailors also told their stories to earn money. Samuel Patterson was an American sailor born in Rhode Island in 1785 who spent his early years living with a number of different families – his own being too poor to support all six children. He eventually left his homeland for good when he ran off to sea at ten years of age. Patterson was nineteen years old, a common sailor with very little education, at the time of his first voyage to the South Seas. During the four years that followed, he travelled to a number of different islands, using Hawaii as his base. He claims to have purchased land in Oahu, Hawaii, paying $40 for twenty-four hectares stocked with fruit trees, fish ponds and blessed with very fertile soil. On a short trading voyage to Fiji, the ship he was sailing in was wrecked and he found himself stranded for nearly a year among the Fijians. The islanders perceived Patterson's lowly status among his own people and were unimpressed by his lack of influence – they treated him accordingly. He was unable to obtain the patronage and support of influential Fijians, and never rose beyond the level of a commoner during his time on the island. He was often hungry, frequently ill and on one occasion was kicked and beaten by a native for taking plantains that did not belong to him. He was finally able to leave Fiji on the *Favorite* a year later and continued his travels until he returned to America in 1810 after an absence of ten years.

His trials at sea and in Fiji had ruined his health. He was partially paralysed, crippled and prone to bouts of fever. In his own words, he was 'totally incapable of exertion' – his life was one of 'want and wretchedness'. He decided to publish a narrative of his sufferings and adventures in the hope that his 'misfortunes would be an inducement to a generous publick, to buy my work'. The resulting account, described as a 'mendicant text' by its publisher, was produced in 1817. Before the advent of royalty payments, it was common for aspiring nineteenth-century authors to pay a printer to produce copies of their individual life stories. The books were cheap pamphlets with paper covers – poorly printed, badly assembled and shoddily made. They focused on the suffering, hardships and eventual religious redemption of their authors, who were typically disabled, crippled or reduced in physical and personal circumstances. Their religious agenda is quite specific, as Patterson illustrated:

> Ye sons of the main that
> Sail over the flood,
> Whose sins are high mountains
> That reach up to God,

> Remember the short voy'ge
> Of life soon will end;
> O come brother sailor
> Make Jesus your friend.[8]

Peddling mendicant books was often regarded as a flimsy excuse for begging. However, the promise of religious conversion added an air of respectability to the sinner in the eyes of his prospective audience, who may consequently have been more generous in their support. Patterson bought a horse and cart and took 'to the highways and byways and attempted to persuade a somewhat disinterested public to buy copies one by one'. It was an arduous and time-consuming way to earn a living. He travelled throughout the American countryside between 1817 and 1823, selling his life story for 10–15 cents.

Unfortunately, he was not very successful financially, although he did generate enough interest in his story to consider a second edition. He wanted to raise funds to return to Hawaii, to his native wife ('a very handsome and interesting woman'), his two children and his plantation. His time on Hawaii is remembered as a period of 'domestick happiness' where he enjoyed 'every comfort in life'. The proceeds from his book, Patterson hoped, would 'restore me to the bosom of my family'. He journeyed on foot through 'all the towns in Rhode Island and many in Massachusetts', searching for subscribers in sufficient numbers to defray the expenses of publication. The book was reprinted in 1825 but there is no record of whether its sales generated enough funds for the sailor to return to his Hawaiian family.

Beachcomber accounts vary in quality and interest. Obviously not all sailors are competent authors and for the most part their lack of formal education and social status renders them unlikely writers. But among the stories that have survived are a wide range of personal histories. William Mariner, Herman Melville, and the Californian businessman E. H. Lamont, of whom we shall hear more, can be termed 'gentlemen beachcombers' because of their social and educational background. William Mariner was the son of a one-time ship owner and had already spent several years studying at Mitchel's Academy in Hertfordshire before embarking on his voyage when he was captured

Robert Coffin, an American sailor and Fijian beachcomber,
who spent several months in Fiji in 1855.

by natives on Tonga. Melville, a member of a socially secure American
family, was a well-educated country schoolteacher before signing on
for his first sea voyage in 1839. Lamont was a trader hoping to enrich
himself through economic opportunities in the Pacific before he was
cast away on Tongareva, part of the Penrhyn group of islands in the

present-day Cook Islands. George Vason had a basic education which developed when he trained as one of the Missionary Society's 'godly mechanics'. And Robert Coffin, an American sailor, went to sea solely to earn enough money to go to college. He eventually achieved his aim but it took many years before he received his long-awaited education. He was fifty-three years old when he graduated with an Advanced Diploma from his local state teacher's college.

The Road to Publication

Sailor-authors came from all levels of the ship. They were navigators, first mates, third mates, petty officers and even a captain or two. A number of them had their own specific skills and areas of expertise which they were able to bring to their island lives and later to their written accounts. Less qualified sailors often received editorial help of one sort or another. Archibald Campbell, for instance, told his tale of Pacific adventure in the years 1806–12 to James Smith upon his return to Scotland. His story is particularly poignant. He was nineteen years old when he signed on a voyage to the South Seas. En route he was shipwrecked on the Aleutian Islands (near the Alaskan Peninsula), where he suffered severe frostbite. His boots had filled with water and froze on his feet – both of which had to be amputated below the ankle joints, leaving him with weeping stumps that never properly healed. Shortly afterwards he gained passage to the Sandwich Islands, where he became a favourite of the queen, who took pity on the disabled sailor. Campbell made himself useful. He repaired sails, demonstrated the use of a loom and described the intricacies of European culture to the native court. He was rewarded with land and servants to work it, but he missed his homeland. Succumbing to a desire to see his 'native country and friends once more', he signed on a Europe-bound ship. By the time he met his editor, Campbell was a patient in an Edinburgh infirmary. His legs had refused to heal and were still covered with suppurating sores, but the hospital could do nothing to help him. He was dismissed as incurable. His life as a sailor and as a working man was over. He earned his living 'crawling about the streets of Edinburgh and Leith, grinding music, and selling a metrical history of his adventures'. Smith was interested in Campbell's story, and in view of the sailor's reduced circumstances, and his limited education, he edited his tale for publication in 1816.

Dr John Martin did the same for William Mariner, who was still a very young man of nineteen after his four years on Tonga. Although most of the crew was massacred, the Tongans believed that Mariner was the son of the captain and his life was spared. He was in fact adopted by the family of the chief with whom he lived throughout his stay. His amazing story would never have been told without the help of his editor. The boy's youth and disinclination to publish threatened to keep his adventures out of the public domain until Martin became involved. An educated and informed man, Martin was convinced that Mariner's story would be of great public interest. He asked the boy to write down a 'memoranda' of his experiences, together with a small vocabulary and description of native ceremonies. On the basis of this, Martin agreed to undertake 'the composition and arrangement of the intended work'. It was an extremely popular work, which soon became a classic. Published originally in 1817, it was reprinted often in the following years and was even translated into French.

John Jackson, the beachcomber also known as William Diaper or 'Cannibal Jack', needed no assistance in the writing of his life story. In 1889, on a beach in Mare in the Loyalty Islands, he gave three hand-written notebooks to the missionary James Hadfield. They were meant to be a sample of a much larger autobiography contained in another nineteen copybooks. However, Jackson's remaining papers were subsequently destroyed in a fire and the three extracts were all that survived. Hadfield was fascinated by the sailor's story but hesitated to publish it: 'My regret on closing the book was that the writer had used such coarse language and described events in so realistic a manner as to preclude any thought of publication.' [9] The manuscript was filed away only to be rediscovered many years later by Hadfield's son who clamoured for its publication. Jackson's beachcombing narrative was finally published in 1928 under the name of William Diaper.

Whatever their genesis, the stories of the beachcombers have one thing in common – they describe the life of common seamen, men of limited prospects and low social status. The stories of Vason, Cabri, Melville and others were not authorised by their home nations; they

were not endowed with a scientific purpose or supported by any national or cultural institution. Free from any political agenda, their stories examine the joys and terrors of their lives as natives. They demonstrate how the sailors understood and negotiated unfamiliar parameters of cross-cultural encounters. As testaments of adaptability and survival in unknown worlds they are unparalleled, and it is on that level of courage and personal fortitude that the men, their lives and their stories speak so powerfully to their readers, even today.

To Spin a Yarn

Their accounts are an intriguing mix of personal adventure, geographical information and anthropological data. It was a combination that required its own form of composition and expression. Because the authors were sailors first and foremost, they turned to a genre they knew and understood. Yarning was the means by which sailors traditionally talked about the sights they had seen, the experiences they shared and the stories they had heard. It was a form of storytelling based on exaggeration and hyperbole. Like a yarn of thread it could be spun, teased and drawn out. It could form fabulous shapes and take on its own unique texture and weight. Yarning demanded the active participation of the listener, while indulging the dramatic propensities of the speaker. In the crowded, noisy and public life of the ship, yarning was the way the men interacted with each other – a ritual of sociability whereby they 'exchanged the politics of experience'.[10] It was the chosen form of entertainment for seagoing men, providing them with moments of pleasure during the stress and hard work of shipboard life. Yarns were the tall tales, fabrications and exaggerations from the lower deck that helped hard-worked sailors endure long journeys away from home.

As an oral form of storytelling, yarning forms an inevitable contrast to the prestigious written accounts of the early voyages – those authored by officially sanctioned officers, captains, scientists and philosophers. Traditional voyage narratives were scientifically informed texts that did not always allow for subjective and personal accounts of adventure and survival. Yarning circumvented the objectivity of those earlier texts. It was the sailors' preferred method of imparting first-hand, personal and directly lived experience. It enabled them to incorporate their own personal adventures into the greater project of their accounts – the mass of ethnographic and geographical information deemed to be of national interest. It was a genre they were familiar with and one they felt empowered to use in their reconstitution as authors. Whether he is spinning a yarn or telling a story in print, the yarnster employs a number of dramatic techniques. He acts out events and re-enacts storylines for his avid listeners, while employing a number of different voices and developing different personae. He is also very much alive to audience expectation and aware of the ritual and ceremony of traditional storytelling. Whether spoken or written, a good story rests on its ability to fashion lived experience into dramatic narrative.

Herman Melville's *Omoo* is a perfect example of the force and vitality to be found in the beachcomber narrative. In typical sailor fashion, Melville dealt imaginatively with the facts of his island visit by exaggerating details of time and place. He extended his time on Tahiti from three months to four, while his two weeks on Moorea became a two-month sojourn. His desire to tell a good story also prompted him to develop his original cast of characters by freely characterising a number of people who were with him on board ship and later on the island. As a spinner of yarns, however, he attempted to stay faithful in outline, if not always in detail, to actual events, and *Omoo* is thus regarded as factually correct and culturally astute in its commentary on native life.

It was also extremely popular among all sections of the population when it was published in 1847 and was widely praised for its vivacity, liveliness and for the warmth of the author's writing style. A number of critics commented specifically on Melville's gusto, his sense of humour and his humanity. Reviewers also enjoyed his 'curiously accurate ear' for the sounds of native and sailor speech and celebrated his power as a 'natural' storyteller. One reader went so far as to imagine that, on the basis of his storytelling, the author must be 'exceedingly good company'.[11] The ease, humour and immediacy of Melville's writing style, however, were simply his textual version of a well-told yarn.

Similar skills are seen in the narrative of the young New Hampshire sailor, Horace Holden, whose voyage into the unknown left him shipwrecked. It was not long after his return to America in 1835 that he wrote an account of his adventures with the natives on the Palau Islands. His story received financial and editorial assistance from John Pickering Esq. of Boston, one of two people to whom the book is dedicated. It was a successful venture for Holden. His book, *A Narrative of the Shipwreck, Captivity and Suffering of Horace Holden and Benj. H. Nute*, was reprinted three times in the ten years after its first publication in 1836. It capitalised on the growing demand for information on newly discovered places. His narrative combined ethnographic information with a lurid tale of captivity and cruelty, further cementing its success. Holden's Pacific adventures captured the public imagination and refused to die. Sixty-five years after first publication, he was interviewed by the Oregon Historical Society which republished another account of his island life in the March–December 1902 edition of their historical journal. Although Holden was ninety-one years old at the time of that interview, his verbal account was almost identical in detail to the story he had written so many years earlier. His life as a beachcomber on an almost unknown Pacific island was one that would never be forgotten. It is worth another telling.

Holden spent his first six months on the Palaus after the loss of the *Mentor* in May 1832. The islanders happily accepted the stranded American crew into their small community, and even helped the sailors build a boat in which they hoped to reach the Dutch settlements in Timor. Eleven men set forth on that second fateful journey. Tossed by storms and suffering a lack of provisions, they eventually made it to Tobi Island – a minute and barren coral island, halfway between the Palaus and Papua New Guinea. Tobi was extremely isolated and very primitive. There had been no prior contact with Europeans, and the men received a violent welcome: 'They attacked us with brutal ferocity, knocking us overboard with their clubs, in the meantime making the most frightful grimaces . . . like so many incarnate devils', wrote Holden. Their boat was destroyed and the men were stripped and divided up, like chattels, among the natives. Holden and Benjamin

Nute, a fellow sailor, found themselves allocated to the same family.

Life for the castaways on this remote and isolated island was extremely hard. A storm had destroyed most of the food supplies, and four men from the *Mentor* died from hunger and disease. Holden and his remaining compatriots were treated as slaves. Burned and blistered by the sun, they were forced to carry coral rocks on their lacerated shoulders. They were also forcibly tattooed. Holden begged and pleaded to be spared what he regarded as the ultimate sacrilege, but was ignored. Until the day of his death, his body bore the marks of his captivity, recording in indelible swirls and bands of colour his trials on the island. Throughout the following months, several of the men died of malnutrition and overwork. Holden, extremely weak and desperately ill, was reduced to crawling on his hands and knees. Any man who refused or was not able to work was beaten with clubs. Dead and dying men were placed in canoes and sent out to sea. Holden suffered the agonies of near starvation: 'Our flesh had so fallen away', he wrote, 'that on lying down, our bones would actually pierce through the skin, giving us the most severe pain.'

By 1834 the nine men that had arrived with Holden were dead, except for Benjamin Nute. The two sailors were unable to work. The islanders agreed to leave them be, but would not feed them. They ate leaves, insects and occasionally begged pieces of coconut from their more soft-hearted captors. At the point of certain death, a ship was sighted and Holden managed to convince the natives to ransom him and Nute for iron. They were placed in canoes and rowed out to the ship, crying out desperately to the men on board. They were eventually taken on board by the captain, who heard the American voices among the calls of the natives. Emaciated, sick, shrunken and feverish, Holden finally ended his island adventure. His overwhelming relief speaks for itself: 'Never shall we find words to express our joy at once more finding ourselves in the company of civilized men.' He returned to America on 5 May 1835.

Holden was an adventurer, a sailor, a hostage, a slave and a survivor, but even more significantly, he was an author. His story recalls an island experience less egalitarian and more brutal than most, but like all other beachcomber accounts, it was a valuable addition to European knowledge of the Pacific. Sailors like Holden were not writers – they were hard-working, untutored and pragmatic men who spent their lives in the depersonalised and regimented seafaring world of the late eighteenth and early nineteenth centuries. They had little time for leisure and little inclination for poetics. Their stories are told in the straightforward, matter-of-fact prose common to nineteenth-century seamen. They contain contradictions and errors. They mix fact and fiction. They come from a world of tall tales, yarns and outright fabrications – a world of casual violence and careless brutality. Their voices are not always educated, but they are compelling. They are also timeless. They tell of fear and uncertainty, about losing one's place in life and having to find another. They describe the difficulties of constructing a sense of self in a strange new world. They question the nature of personal identity, the randomness of fate and the relativity of human nature. Although they were written 150–200 years ago, the stories of the beachcombers resonate with power and conviction. They paint a vivid picture of a perilous existence on the fringes of savage societies far from the safety of Europe. Above all, they record the fortunes and misfortunes of ordinary individuals who found themselves in extraordinary circumstances. They have much to tell us.

CHAPTER THREE

The Myth of the Castaway

The solitary life of Robinson Crusoe, or, more correctly speaking, Alexander Selkirk, appears to be anything but singular in the annals of the Pacific.

Chambers Edinburgh Journal

There is no doubt that the beachcomber was one of the most exotic and intriguing figures of early Pacific life. His appearance and his lifestyle identified him as a particular type – a restless, wandering, beach-crossing and culturally transgressive adventurer. But this was a type primarily defined by others. Those beachcombers who left written accounts identified with a more literary hero. Their predominant role model was Robinson Crusoe – that archetypal castaway. It is not surprising that Crusoe, the ultimate survivor, was a highly resonant figure for men who lived with the constant threat of shipwreck on unfamiliar islands. Although the castaway is traditionally an isolated individual, and beachcomber experience involves integration and assimilation, beachcomber experience became romanticised when it was refigured in castaway mode. Their choice of the Robinson Crusoe model was an important one. It endowed their individual experiences with a universal significance. It dignified the common sailor through an implicit identification with the romance inherent in the literary figure. Their familiarity with the first novel of the English literary canon also legitimated them as little-known authors. They were connected by means of their experiences, and their accounts of them, to the greatest fictional castaway in history. Their repudiation of civilisation could now be seen as revolutionary in its disavowal of social constraints and established order. Beachcombers were a symbol of romantic escapism. They had turned their backs on the impotence and impersonality of mass industrial society and opted for lives of noble simplicity. They embodied a universal desire to go native, to take to the bush, to return to nature. The castaway experience functioned allegorically as a meditation on the courage of the human spirit, the vicissitudes of fate and the workings of providence – stranded on a desert island, man is forced to find within himself the resolve, determination, adaptability, strength of character and depths of faith that will ensure his survival.

The adventures of the literary Crusoe were based on the exploits of real-life castaway Alexander Selkirk, a Scottish mariner who was marooned on the island of Juan Fernandez (now renamed Robinson Crusoe Island), 640 kilometres off the coast of Chile. He arrived on the island in 1704 and was not rescued until four years and four months later.[1] Selkirk (variously spelled Selcraig, Selchriage, Sillcrigge, Silkirk) was born in 1680 in Fife, Eastern Scotland. He was a troublesome youth whose violent behaviour and antisocial acts resulted in his enforced departure from his native village. At just fifteen years of age and seeking the only sort of freedom available to young men without education or private means, Selkirk ran away to sea. Eight years later he returned home, a hardened man and an experienced mariner. In need of work and money, he quickly signed on as master of the *Cinque Ports Galley* – one of two ships conscripted for a privateering expedition led by the buccaneer William Dampier. Dampier's 1697 edition of *A New Voyage Round the World* had established his reputation as a first-class navigator, experienced pilot and a world-renowned pirate, privateer and adventurer. When Selkirk met him in 1703, he was planning to sail to the South Seas in search of Spanish gold. This act of piracy was legitimated by the English crown and regarded as a patriotic gesture in service of Queen Anne. England was at war with Spain and France, and an assault on Spanish ships was seen as an assault on the enemy. The promise of gold and other booty was an even greater enticement. The *Cinque Ports Galley*, under the captaincy of Thomas Stradling, was travelling in consort with Dampier's ship, the *St George*. Both men hoped to enrich their investors, owners, crew and themselves by capturing Spanish galleons laden with riches on their journeys from Manila to Acapulco.

The expedition that set off from London with such high expectations did not fare well. A number of factors – scarcity of Spanish ships, the lack of plunder, the illness of the men, the shortage of supplies and disintegrating relations between officers and crew – resulted in attempts at mutiny and in damage to the ships. Under threat from inhospitable seas and with a crew of sick and disgruntled men, the *Cinque Ports Galley* was forced to sail for Juan Fernandez, arriving there some time in September 1704. The ship was leaking badly and most of its crew were suffering from the effects of scurvy and dysentery, caused by a lack of fresh food. Stradling was unhappy with the detour and was keen to return to sea as soon as minor repairs had been carried out. Selkirk, as master or navigator, remonstrated with his captain. He was convinced the ship was unsafe and refused to board. Worms had infested the bottom of the vessel and had devoured its oak timbers. The hull was so fragile and disfigured it resembled a honeycomb and before the ship returned to sea the worms needed to be killed, the hull treated and the timbers replaced. In a hurry to get back to the business of gold, Stradling accused Selkirk of mutiny and marooned him on shore. Faced with the reality of abandonment, Selkirk pleaded with his captain to be allowed on board. Stradling refused to be moved and offloaded Selkirk's sea chest and personal belongings and then cast off from the island. The abandoned sailor abused his captain. He railed against the cruelty in consigning him to such an uncertain and lonely future. As the sails disappeared into the horizon, Selkirk's four solitary years as a castaway were about to begin.

Juan Fernandez was uninhabited. It was a small piece of land, nineteen kilometres long by six across, located almost 10,000 kilometres from London. It was a place of hills and craggy precipices, interspersed with lush valleys and deep bays offering anchorage to passing ships. A mountainous ridge formed its spine and at the highest point it rose

Cumberland Harbour, Juan Fernandez Island, *c.* 1800. Its mountainous ranges and precipitous bays testify to the island's rugged beauty.

900 metres above the ocean. The ridges were thick with forests and its escarpments sheered down to the sea where the land came into contact with the seething ocean that surrounded it for 16,000 kilometres. The island was a place of natural springs and waterfalls that began in the rocky heights and plunged through valleys towards the sea. It was a place of squalling winds and heavy rains. Its slopes supported stretches of sandalwood, mountain palms and other greenery that could withstand the salt-laden winds. Wild plums and herbs grew among the hills. It was fertile, but it was remote.

The island was known to booty seekers, pirates and privateers of the late 1600s and early 1700s. There was a small natural harbour, ringed by green pastures, where a small boat could land, but larger vessels had to sail around to the deep-water anchorage located on the other side of the island. Within the high mountain walls the anchorage offered sanctuary from the perils of the sea. Goats that had previously arrived on Spanish ships populated the hillsides, offering a welcome source of fresh meat to those ships that stopped for rest and repairs, while colonies of fur seals and sea lions – some as long as six metres – could be found around the coastline. Rats, mice and cats were also plentiful, having arrived on visiting ships and made their home on shore. Juan Fernandez offered sailors a place to rest, recuperate, and prepare themselves for further travels ahead. It was the original desert island for men travelling inhospitable seas.

A Myth of Islands

There is something primordial, fresh and untouched about islands. In the Western imagination they are traditionally seen as places of abundance and simplicity, like the Garden of Eden before the Fall. Deserted and delightful, primitive and alive with uncorrupted nature, they are expressions of innocence and joy. Life on islands promises happiness and personal fulfilment. Their wild and solitary nature imbues them with connotations of magic, wonder and romance. Prospero's Mediterranean island in *The Tempest* is described by Caliban as

> full of noises,
> Sounds, and sweet airs, that give delight and hurt not.
> Sometimes a thousand twangling instruments
> Will hum about mine ears; and sometimes voices
> That, if I then had waked after long sleep,
> Will make me sleep again; and then, in dreaming,
> The clouds methought would open, and show riches
> Ready to drop upon me, that when I waked
> I cried to dream again.
>
> (*Act III, Scene ii*)

However, the islands of the South Seas were places of paradox. They were beautiful and bountiful as well as dangerous and unforgiving. The castaway was subjected to both extremes. He was freed from the obligations of civilised society, but was also overwhelmed by the terror of the unknown, living in fear of cannibals and savages. Isolation concentrated and focused the emotions. All castaways vacillated between poles of jubilation and despair. They were ecstatically free, jubilant and celebratory, or they were plunged into the depths of melancholy and despair. Selkirk's island experience began in just such a mood, but by means of hard work and solitude he was renewed physically and spiritually. He was later to claim that he 'was a better Christian while in this solitude than ever . . . before'.[2]

Like all castaways, Selkirk had to make a new life for himself in an alien place. He constructed rudimentary accommodation from boulders, branches and trees. He hunted goats for food and fished for lobsters and crabs. He ate wild greens, birds' eggs, found root vegetables growing wild in the hills, and ate plums, berries and all manner of edible plants. He domesticated some of the feral cats he found wandering around the island to help keep the rats at bay – rats that swarmed through his hut and 'gnawd his Feet and Clothes while asleep'.[3] He was bereft of all comforts, but he was not completely helpless. He had common sense, his training as a sailor, and an adaptability and resourcefulness that is the inheritance of any seagoing adventurer. The captain had left him with his clothes and bedding, a pistol, gunpowder and bullets. He had a knife and a pot in which to boil food – a Bible and a book of prayers. Food, shelter, solace and courage he had to find for himself. In true castaway fashion, he made use of what the island had to offer and he learned to make do.

He scavenged, beachcombed and salvaged all manner of objects left on or around the island. He found nails, iron hoops and pieces of rope left by previous ships, lying by the shore. He modelled tools and equipment from wood, fired clay to make pots, and heated iron to make axes, fish-hooks and knives. He domesticated the goats in order to gain a supply of fresh meat without having to chase them all over the island. When his original clothes disintegrated with the passing of time, he fashioned a skirt and a cloak out of goatskins that he scraped and tanned himself. His beard and hair grew long and unkempt, his skin darkened with the constant exposure to sun and air and his long nails functioned as claws. He killed fur seals and their cubs for food and used their fat as tallow and cooking oil, and their skins as bedding.

Selkirk's intense preoccupation with structuring and ordering his environment was not just a physical endeavour. It was also, and more importantly, about establishing a relationship to disorder and to strangeness. There is a mythic appeal in the business of island making, as Greg Dening, the eminent Pacific historian and scholar, explains:

> A narrative that tells how someone constructed and furnished a house, not a makeshift dwelling, but a permanent home, using, with ingenuity, new materials and new designs to catch nonetheless old metaphors of security and comfort and status, or a story that tells of reinventing technologies to

manufacture dyes, clothes and medicines out of foreign plants and minerals creates a liberating wonderment at how much else is a building block in life. Island making sublimates a sense of alienation.[4]

Reinventing the Self

For four long years, Selkirk, the original castaway, learned to live without society. He functioned in a world deprived of human contact and devoid of social obligations. But his solitary state provided him with compensations. He was free from the claims and expectations of others. An important element of the castaway myth is the idea of self-sufficiency on a spiritual as well as a physical level. Clothed in skins and living off the land, the castaway was free of the social and political restraints imposed by society. He was answerable to no one but himself. There was much pleasure and excitement to be had from the dissolution of social ties. The castaway was freed from the tyranny of time, from dates, work, stresses, anxiety, from past and present. The castaway myth promotes freedom from hardship and overwork and posits a life of ease – unselfconscious and uncomplicated. There was a Utopian element to island dwelling, as celebrated by Gonzalez, shipwrecked on Prospero's magical island in Shakespeare's *The Tempest*. He outlined his ideal community:

> I'th'commonwealth I would by contraries
> Execute all things. For no kind of traffic
> Would I admit, no name of magistrate.
> Letters should not be known. Riches, poverty,
> And use of service, none. Contract succession,
> Bourn, bound of land, tilth, vineyard, none.
> No use of metal, corn, or wine, or oil.
> No occupation: all men idle, all,
> And women too, but innocent and pure.
>
> (*Act II, Scene i*)

Islands could be places of rejuvenation and self-invention. The castaway who arrived, displaced and suffering, could be remade or reformed on islands. He could refashion himself into something new –

something better or something different. This remodelling was based on a distinction between nature and art, between social responsibilities and personal freedom. The castaway, through his own actions and determination, could turn disaster or misfortune into providence. He could emerge victorious from a calamitous situation. He could remake the space in which he found himself into something wondrous and romantic, and experience a delight at his own inventiveness, adaptability and resourcefulness. He could become what Selkirk's rescuers believed the Scottish castaway to be: the 'governour of the island' and the 'monarch of all he surveyed'.[5]

Selkirk was rescued in 1709 by Captain Woodes Rogers, who stopped at Juan Fernandez for repairs and supplies. Like Dampier before him, Rogers was also on a privateering expedition against the French and Spanish in the South Seas. When his men went ashore they were unable to believe their eyes. Selkirk appeared before them as some strange cultural hybrid, a mythical wild man of the forests.

Alexander Selkirk and his companions on the island of Juan Fernandez. Images such as these depict the romantic aspect of the castaway myth.

Selkirk himself was literally lost for words. Four years without human company had left him unsure of his powers of expression. When questioned by the curious sailors, he became agitated and confused. 'He had so much forgot his Language for want of Use', wrote Rogers, 'that we could scarce understand him, for he seem'd to speak his words by halves.'[6]

Rogers' own account of his journey, *A Cruising Voyage Round the World*, was published upon his return home in 1712 and brought Selkirk's story to public attention. An additional version of his story appeared shortly afterwards in *The Englishman*, a journal published by Richard Steele. Steele, a journalist, essayist, pamphleteer and literary man about town, became fascinated by Selkirk's story, which he heard directly from the sailor in 1712. He presented the story as 'as Adventure so uncommon, that it's doubtful whether the like has happen'd to any of human Race' and it was not long before the castaway became the talk of the town. Influenced by the mythic possibilities of the castaway state, Steele reworked Selkirk's story as a meditation on Christian piety, the vanity of riches and the indominability of man. The solitude experienced by Selkirk, according to Steele, was sheer romance. The island was 'the most delicious Bower, fann'd with continual Breezes and gentle Aspirations of Wind'. Selkirk's days were joyous and his nights were untroubled, according to the journalist. He was enriched by his loneliness and his solitary state, and 'He never had a Moment heavy upon his Hands.' A return to the world, after such an experience, could only be understood as a loss of simplicity, and a return to anxiety. In his own way, Steele was propagating the myth of island primitivism. He also advocated the Christian ideal of the virtue of poverty: 'This plain Man's Story is a memorable Example, that he is happiest who confines his Wants to natural Necessities; and he that goes further in his Desires, increases his Wants in Proportion to his Acquisitions; or to use his own Expression, *I am now worth 800 Pounds, but shall never be so happy, as when I was not worth a Farthing*.'[7]

Any island seen from the sea is a place of sanctuary. It offers a solid and tangible refuge against the terrors and hardships of seagoing life. Selkirk's island, however, was a place of incarceration. It imprisoned him, condemning him to a solitude and loneliness that would only be reprieved by the fortuitous arrival of another ship. He experienced the reality, not the romance, of island life. Frightened, alone, forsaken and cast out by his fellow company of mariners, Selkirk faced a life adrift from the rest of the world. In his despair at his abandonment and his overwhelming desire to sight a rescue ship, he perfectly typified the paradox of the castaway. His island offered him freedom from responsibility, from the hateful tyranny of an incompetent captain, but it denied him the longed-for companionship of others, the comforts of friends and the familiar security of shipboard life. In reality, his experience was probably closer to the sentiment immortalised by William Cowper in 1782:

> I am monarch of all I survey,
> My right there is none to dispute,
> From the centre all round to the sea,
> I am lord of the fowl and the brute.
> O solitude! Where are the charms,
> That sages have seen in thy face?
> Better dwell in the midst of alarms,
> Than reign in this horrible place.[8]

Fact or Fiction

Daniel Defoe heard Selkirk's amazing story apparently from the man himself at the Red Lion Tavern in Bristol. Intrigued by the inherent literary possibilities of the castaway's story, Defoe published the first part of *The Life and Strange Adventures of Robinson Crusoe, Mariner of York* in 1719. He took pains to disguise his indebtedness to Selkirk, however. The mariner's four years on Juan Fernandez was extended to twenty-eight years and he was relocated to an island near the mouth of the 'Oronoque' river off the coast of South America. *Robinson Crusoe* was presented to the public as a true story: 'the editor believes the thing to be a just history of fact, neither is there any appearance of fiction in it'.[9] Defoe also insisted that his hero was a real individual. 'I Robinson Crusoe', he wrote in his preface, 'do affirm that the story though allegorical is also historical . . . Further, that there is a man alive, and well known too, the actions of whose life are the just

subject of these three volumes . . . and to this I set my name.' It is not
Selkirk's name he signs but that of Robinson Crusoe. Despite these
discrepancies, it is obvious that the novel is based on the exploits of
the Scottish sailor. The novel was published anonymously on 25 April
1719 and was reprinted a further three times before August. It was
translated into French in 1720 and into Dutch, German and Russian
in the 1760s and has since been copied, performed, serialised, abridged
and pirated. It has become a world classic.

Robinson Crusoe is the story of a man shipwrecked on an uninhabited
island. Forsaken, alone and forgotten, Crusoe creates his own world.
He tames and breeds goats, plants corn, grows food, builds a house, a
boat, tables, chairs and shelves. He is the archetypal pioneering settler
as he transforms his island home, rendering it bountiful and productive. He becomes a farmer, tanner, builder, potter, miller, fisherman,
salvage expert, cook and tailor. In a life that veers between introspec-
tion and industry, Crusoe brings order out of chaos with God as his
right-hand man. He replicates a family – he has a dog, two cats and
a parrot called Poll that speaks his name. Like Selkirk before him, he
creates a new but not so different life for himself on foreign shores.

Robinson Crusoe is also the quintessential survival story. To a large
extent Defoe reworks the story of his adventurer hero into a scriptural
pattern of disobedience, punishment, repentance and deliverance.
Man, in the image of God, and by means of his own ingenuity, is
able to transcend his improvident circumstances. The story tells of
the fight to overcome fate, misfortune and to wrench victory from
vicissitude. It is a testament of adaptability and survival – it rejoices
in spiritual and physical strength, personal character and fortitude.
It is the story of a man who, reduced to nothing, attempts to rebuild
himself and his environment. It celebrates a resourcefulness borne of
necessity. The story demonstrates how life on an island, far removed
from society, can provide all the necessities of life. Nearly all sailors
had read the novel – the majority of their autobiographies begin with
the phrase 'After reading *Robinson Crusoe* I decided to run away to
sea'.[10] It is certainly the most imaginatively powerful of all voyage
narratives and its influence is pervasive. A young sailor, passing the
island of Juan Fernandez in 1830, wrote: 'Its rough aspect gave it but

little claim to beauty, yet being connected with Robinson Crusoe and his man Friday, it delighted my fancy. I longed to wander over it, and recall the adventures of the solitary Selkirk.'[11] Another traveller to the Pacific reflected: 'I often used to think on Robinson Crusoe and the dangers and privations he endured: and the reflection, that he was preserved under greater circumstances of difficulty much greater than those I was placed in, enabled me to submit to my hard fare with greater cheerfulness.'[12]

Crusoe became part of the mythic imagination. He was the epitome of flexibility and ingenuity. He made his own clothes from animal skins:

> I had a great high shapeless cap, made of a goat's skin . . . I had a short jacket of goat-skin, the skirts coming down to about the middle of my thighs; and a pair of open-kneed breeches . . . made of the skin of an old he-goat, whose hair hung down such a length of either side . . . stockings and shoes I had none, but had made me a pair of somethings . . . to flap over my legs, and lace on either side . . . I had on a broad belt of goat's skin dried . . . At my back I carried my basket, on my shoulder my gun, and over my head a great clumsy ugly goat-skin umbrella.[13]

Barefoot, in his goatskins, accompanied by his dog, his parrot and his cat, Crusoe entered the collective unconscious. A sandy beach and a leaning palm tree likewise became an icon of all desert islands everywhere. A group of English sailors shipwrecked on Vatoa Island in Fiji in 1829 describe themselves as 'so many Robinson Crusoes with the skins of the trip-birds (turned inside out) for morgasins or shoes'. In a direct and somewhat jaunty descent from their mythic forefather, they too carried 'a stick in the hand, and a knife made of the iron hoops of our boat keg slung about our necks'. Others decorated their caps with 'the red plumes of the tropic birds'.[14]

The novel established a model of an ideal castaway – a Crusoe-like figure distinguished by his steely determination and personal resourcefulness. '[B]y making the most rational judgment of things', claimed Crusoe, 'every man may be in time master of every mechanic art. I never handled a tool in my life; and yet in time, by labour, application, and contrivance, I found at least that I wanted nothing but I can have made it.' The inventive capabilities of the castaway were thus mythologised and relate to all aspects of his island existence – an ingenious creativity that faced its greatest challenge in the act of boatbuilding. Building a boat on an island became a way of establishing a link to the castaway's country of origin. In utilising tools and building a vessel, he identified himself as a craftsman, as someone with the appropriate skills to facilitate a return to European society. Crusoe made the attempt after four years on his island. He selected a very large tree which he planned to hollow out in the style of a native *periagua* (canoe). The cedar tree measured five feet near the stump and 'four feet eleven inches at the end of twenty-two feet'. The effort required was prodigious. It took him twenty days to fell the tree and another two weeks to trim all the branches and limbs, working all the time with the most rudimentary tools. A month was spent shaping the log to resemble a canoe, and another twelve arduous weeks hollowing out the bottom of it. Working only with a mallet and chisel, Crusoe's labour was backbreaking and soul-destroying.

His earlier experience was replicated in one form or another by the later castaways. In Tahiti, James Morrison and his fellow *Bounty* crew members decided to build a boat to return to England. For nearly a year they felled wood, carved planks, curved a hull, produced pitch, and improvised sails and masts:

> Nor was the making of Plank less troublesome, having no Saws (except handsaws) the largest tree would afford no more then [sic] two thicknesses of Plank, Some of the trees Cut for that purpose measuring six feet round which took a deal of Labour to reduce into plank of inch & a quarter with axes & adzes; and as we had but two Adzes we were forced to make the Small trade hatchets . . . answer that purpose, by lashing them to handles after the manner of the Natives which answered our purpose very well.[15]

Morrison and others like him can be identified primarily as 'bricoleurs' – the name given to a jack of all trades, a master of resourcefulness

An attempt at boatbuilding by shipwrecked castaways. Nearly all sailors spent
a great deal of time and effort constructing a means of escape.

and adaptability. Bricolage is the art of scavenging, of creating
something new from derelict material. Improvisatory and imaginative,
it is the art of sailors. In the absence of European tools, they had to
make their own. When they needed bellows, 'Canvas supplyd the place
of Leather, and the Iron handle of a Sauspan made the Nozzel, a Frame

of Plank filld with Clay was made for the Forge, and Coleman Cut a hole through a stone to point the Nozzel of the Bellows through, the Pig of Ballast made a good anvil & the Carpenters maul answerd the purpose of a Sledge.' Their resourcefulness was evident throughout the entire process:

> We formed an anvil of the spindle of a windlass, and a pair of bellows we contrived to manufacture out of an old canvas clothes bag, and the half of a gun barrel; we used wooden pegs instead of tacks, and the canvas was made air tight, with the mixture of the gum of the bread fruit-tree, and a little cocoa nut oil. We had neither of us seen the inside of a pair of bellows; we had therefore, to puzzle our brains to put our materials together, but we succeeded tolerably well.[16]

Monarchs of All They Survey

These latter-day Robinson Crusoes were influenced by a myth of experience and survival, adaptability and determination that was integral to their image of themselves as 'true' castaways. It was a potent myth that affected all who went to sea. It was also a myth that found a perfect terrestrial location in the islands of the Pacific. The Pacific has always had more than its share of island dwellers fleeing from the stresses of modern life. The size of the ocean, its thousands of islands, its temperate climate, its atolls, reefs, harbours and hills were seen as conducive to the castaway lifestyle. The islands provided breadfruit, bananas, cocoa palms, pandanus, fruit trees and other luxuriant vegetation. Their warm waters were full of fish, shellfish, lobsters, oysters, clams and other bounty. A man needed only build a small hut, cultivate a few plants, help himself to the bounty of the sea and live in peace and plenty. On an island one was able

> to spend one's days in a rock-bound haven where the waters are eternally at rest . . . to run about bare-foot upon silvery sands, where the cool sea breeze all the year round conquers the sultriness of the tropic sunshine; to paddle about on the still waters of a calm lagoon . . . to sleep softly and to dream sweetly . . . to know nothing of what is going on in the outer world, and to care as little; to have no ideas beyond those included

within the horizon of vision; to climb to the summit of some lofty tree and to see at one glance all which constitutes for ourselves the material universe – is indeed to revel in nature, and nature as she only exists in Coral Lands.[17]

In a four-year voyage around the Pacific, Dr John Coulter, a British surgeon, encountered many remote Crusoes with identical expectations of island life. His book, *Adventures in the Pacific,* which was first published in 1845, tells of men completely cut off from the bustle of trade, travel and exploration taking place around them. An English sailor called Thomas Holt, for instance, created a 'little kingdom' on Robert's Island, the most northern of the Marquesas archipelago. He was marooned by his captain after causing a continual disturbance on board ship. The captain, exasperated but not cruel, provided Holt with a frying pan, iron pot, axe, spade, saw, cutlass and a bagful of ship's biscuit. Somehow the sailor survived. When a British whaler arrived at the island seven years later, the crew found a well-tended plantation of breadfruit, coconut and bananas. At the end of a well-cleared track leading towards the hills, they saw a timber building, six metres long by three and a half metres wide close to a small pool of water which was supplied by a spring gushing out from the cliff above. There was a small cookhouse adjacent to the main dwelling and inside it the sailors found Holt, enjoying a meal with a Swedish sailor and a native of the Marquesas – who had both escaped from their own ships and decided to join the castaway on his island. While expressing great joy at meeting the new arrivals, Holt was adamant about remaining in his own domain. He had everything he desired. He was 'monarch of two subjects and all he surveyed'. He stayed – and died – a Crusoe.

Coulter's own experiences in the Pacific forced him to conclude: 'There is an isolated pecularity of mind which induces men voluntarily to take up their abode on uninhabited islands . . . There is scarcely an uninhabited island in those seas, in the thorough-fare of shipping, on which there is a fertile spot of earth with a supply of fresh water, that has not its Robinson Crusoe on it.' He was soon to become one himself. When his ship moored at Chatam Island, one of the Galapagos, he was quick to leave his companions and explore the interior. He set off alone after noting that the other seamen were reluctant to put too much distance between themselves and the ship. Coulter felt no such concern:

> The question may be asked, did I not feel lonely? I say no; I had the fowls of the air; the lovely landscapes in all directions, the rich forest, the park like lands, with abundance of everything on them, to gaze upon. No, there was nothing of loneliness here for me; all creation appeared in its primitive state; and I delighted in contemplating such a scene – one that had been, perhaps ever undisturbed by man.[18]

He found fresh water and plenty of wild fruits on the island. He killed and ate birds and terrapins. He tramped through hills and valleys and climbed the highest peak in order to survey the land around him. He caught fish, wrapped them in large leaves and cooked them on the hot ashes of his fire. As the days passed, and his shoes started to fall apart on the harsh landscape, he tied the soles to his feet with lengths of goat skin. He also shot a large seal stranded on the beach and by cutting through the thick hide he obtained enough skin for three or four pairs of moccasins. In true castaway fashion, he improvised and made use of available materials. All he had to do 'was to spread out the skin, place my foot upon it, and cut it of an oval shape about four inches all round from the foot . . . make a range of holes all round near the edge, then a thong off the hide to reeve through the holes would serve as a drawing string and it was complete'. His delight at his own ingenuity and his enjoyment of his temporary castaway status was short-lived, however. When he returned to the shore expecting to be welcomed by the crew and captain, he found the beach deserted. His dismay and despair threatened to overwhelm him. At that moment he noticed a bottle on a stick with a note inside. The note explained that the ship had been forced away from the shore because of bad weather and would return for him as soon as it could.

Safe with the knowledge of eventual rescue, Coulter continued to perpetuate the castaway myth. He promised 'ease of mind, and independence' to those who choose the freedom of island life over shipboard regulation and control. A castaway had 'no one to control a man, no one to demand anything of him'. He emphasised the romance by ignoring the reality – a reality highlighted by many castaways themselves. While the myth celebrates Crusoe and Selkirk as fearless, enterprising and indefatigable – the 'Absolute Monarch of the Island' – the beachcombers are more honest. Their island histories reflect the dismay and fear acknowledged only briefly by Coulter. They focus instead on the confusion, uncertainty and danger of island life.

Sanctuary or Prison

Sailors were quite explicit about the reality of island abandonment. William Cary, an American sailor, was forlorn and forsaken in Fiji in 1825. It was approximately 3 a.m. when his ship, the *Oeno*, struck an unmarked reef off Vatoa Island. The order was given to abandon the vessel and by daylight the crew had cast off and made it safely to shore. Initially, Cary and his comrades were welcomed by the islanders. The Fijians helped themselves to the sailors' belongings, but provided food, water and aid in return. 'The natives were friendly and endeavored, by every kindness in their power, to make our situation as pleasant and comfortable as possible', Cary recalled. In order to ensure the relations stayed amicable, the captain gave his watch to the chief who 'appeared to be mighty pleased with it'.

Unfortunately, circumstances changed after the arrival of twenty war canoes from another island. The visiting natives were hostile and over a period of days became increasingly threatening and aggressive. Cary described them as 'a frightful looking set, being hideously painted with red and black, and all armed with clubs and spears'. The captain and crew believed they would be safer in the village. Cary, however, feared the worst and stayed behind, hiding himself in a cave. Days passed and he remained out of sight. Eventually, driven by hunger and thirst, he was forced out of hiding. His worst fears were realised. As he crossed the beach he saw signs of a scuffle, displaced sand and strange shapes littering the shore. 'I searched around until I found a place which had evidently been dug over', he wrote. 'I scooped away a few inches of sand with my hand and came to the face of a man. I uncovered one other, but could go no further.' Evidence of a massacre was everywhere – the entire party of white men had been killed.

Cary threw himself on the mercy of an old man he had met before and was taken to the village to have his fate decided. Unable to understand the discussions taking place, he was unnerved by a large party of men who were swinging their clubs and looking 'as though they would like to have a crack at me'. Luckily, he was accepted into the community and was eventually adopted by the old man, who claimed ownership of him. Although given a reprieve from death, he knew his long-term safety and survival remained precarious.

There was danger on Crusoe's island as well. The fear of the unknown savage and the threat of cannibalism was a universal one, shared by all castaways and it permeated fictional accounts of island abandonment. Crusoe's relationship with Friday, the Caribbean native whom he meets on the island, brought that fear to life. Friday was the intended victim of a cannibal feast and was rescued from certain death by Crusoe who attacked the perpetrators and saved the victim. His presence coincidentally provided the lonely Englishman with a native companion whom he begins to educate and civilise. 'I beckoned him again to come to me', said Crusoe, 'and gave him all the signs of encouragement that I could think of.' In return, Friday lay down on the sand, lowered his head on the ground and placed Crusoe's foot on his head: 'This, it seems, was in token of swearing to be my slave for ever', interpreted Crusoe.

His relationship with Friday establishes a myth of race relations informed by colonial ideology. In this iconic encounter the native becomes a willing subject to a European father figure, propagating a myth of 'permanent colonial tutelage'.[19] Crusoe is authority figure, spiritual tutor and cultural ambassador to his native companion. He taught him English, showed him how to use and repair tools and then instructed him in the true Christian faith. The unredeemed savage soon becomes an ideal Christian servant. Although Friday is the South American native, he is nevertheless represented as the newly arrived stranger who crosses the shore into Crusoe's world on the island. The dichotomy of civilised versus savage, which structures so many encounters on the shores of the new worlds, is reversed. It is the primitive who comes ashore to the waiting European. It is the newly arrived savage who had to adapt to the civilised model of displaced colonialism that had been established on the island. That colonial framework was put in place at the beginning of the encounter: 'I made him know his name should be Friday', Crusoe said, 'which was the day I saved his life . . . I likewise taught him to say master, and then let him know that was to be my name.'

Danger and Despair

There are of course many differences between real and fictional castaways. The similarities arise from the romantic treatment of the castaway myth – a legacy based on the myth-making potential of literary history. Defoe did not set out to create a myth when he wrote his story of an English castaway. Its mythic dimensions manifest themselves in the novel's archetypal themes. Myths deal with situations of conflict, and in *Robinson Crusoe* the individual's conflict with the social order is at the heart of his story. Crusoe himself is an archetypal Western man involved in a twofold pursuit. Firstly, he steps outside his assigned role in life seeking an alternative route to follow, and secondly he is forced to come to terms with the cultural diversity that arises from any confrontation of cultures.[20]

His colonial model of race relations was not one employed by the real castaways. They were not able to impose their own particular reality onto people who had their own culture, politics and history. Instead, they were forced to become part of those existing indigenous structures. If they were lucky, they were accepted into existing native families via name exchange. This important process granted the beachcomber a measure of safety and independence by enlarging his network of friends, contacts and family members. It allowed him to call on his extended family for support, food and shelter. It enabled him to exist and to move with some degree of freedom in an environment that would otherwise be hostile, dangerous and unsustainable. Name exchange also enmeshed the beachcomber in a wide range of family politics which left him at the mercy of larger family or tribal dynamics. The sailors were outnumbered and unable to impose their personal desires on those around them. On the beaches of the Pacific, beachcombers were renamed, re-educated, culturally challenged and changed. They soon came to doubt themselves as white men at all.

When William Mariner finally boarded a ship in 1810 after living with the natives in Tonga he received a harsh welcome. He was knocked overboard by a sailor who 'took him for a native, for his skin was grown very brown, his hair very long, and tied up in a knot, with a turban round the head, and an apron of the leaves of the chi tree round his waist'. Other nativised sailors told of similar transformations: 'My body was sometimes painted black, sometimes white, according to their different rites and ceremonies. My hair was at times painted black, at other times red; in this way I was apparently metamorphosed sometimes to an African Negro, and then to a native of Bengal', wrote an American sailor in Fiji in 1808.[21] The sailors' ambiguous cultural status on the islands jeopardised their sense of personal identity. They were no longer able to recognise themselves, or be recognised by others, as Europeans. When one captive sailor finally escaped from the loving clutches of his native hosts, he was a changed man. He was unable to recognise himself when he reached the ship that was to restore him to civilisation:

> I walked up and down, and passing the captain's cabin, stared wonderingly on a looking-glass, in which I caught a glimpse of a figure as savage as that of any of the natives. My hair and beard almost covered my face; my head was protected from the sun by the remnant of a Panama hat, held together by fish bones; my bronzed skin appeared through my thread-bare shirt, which exposed my neck, chest, and arms; and a remnant of blue dungaree trousers, whose ragged ends scarce reached my knees, left my feet and legs bare. Well might I start at the strange figure I presented to myself.[22]

In Defoe's fictional account, Crusoe suffered no such confusion. Unlike his true-like counterpart, Alexander Selkirk, Crusoe was the archetypal Englishman abroad. He recreated the world that he knew, he marked out the days and years of his ordeal, kept his hair and whiskers groomed and remained in control of his own small community. He also insisted on wearing clothes: 'I could not go quite naked, no, though I had been inclined to it, which I was not, nor could abide the thoughts of it, though I was all alone.' Crusoe's

William Mariner dressed in Tongan costume.

story suggests that a civilised man on a desert island will recreate the structures of his own world. In the blank space offered to him by an unknown land, he will inevitably surround himself with things he knows and understands. He lessens his alienation by imposing the familiar on the foreign. Crusoe's island society was based on property rights, agricultural production and control, individual ownership and personal autonomy. His cultivation and fortification of the island, and his later organisation of peoples (Carib, Spanish and British) into a structured hierarchy, was a complex representation of colonial expansion.[23] Crusoe civilised his natives and brought religion to his little kingdom. As 'monarch of all he surveys' he is honest about the pleasure of possession:

> I descended a little on the side of that delicious vale, surveying it with a secret kind of pleasure . . . to think that this was all my own; that I was king and lord of all this country indefeasibly, and had a right of possession; and, if I could convey it, I might have it in inheritance as completely as any lord of a manor in England.[24]

That proud possessiveness was replicated by a later beachcomber. George Vason's properties and holdings on Tonga, it might be remembered, were gifted to him by his grateful chief. The ex-missionary spent a large proportion of his time, and his text, extolling the productivity of his little plantation: 'Already fancy painted to my view rows of sweet canes, embowering new walks of refreshment, and pleasure.' Vason's island vision is closely linked to an English ideal of cultivated order incorporating bowers, enclosures and harvests. He celebrated the beauty and the productive capacity of the land under his control: 'The idea of having an island of my own much delighted me; and I set off for my little dominion with the greatest joy, already anticipating the happiness I should find in being freed from the many inconveniences of dependence, as a resident with a chief.'

A Home Away from Home

He was not the only beachcomber to subscribe to the colonially informed myth of European appropriation and control. Fletcher Christian and the *Bounty* mutineers, those archetypal revolutionary castaways, were also keen to establish a secure base for themselves in the Pacific. Their mutinous actions against their captain, William

Bligh, had marked them for life and they wanted to ensure their future safety. The penalty for mutiny was death, and the British Navy would never let them escape. So they loaded up the *Bounty* in Tahiti and set sail for another island, further off the established shipping routes. Pitcairn lay in the future. The island they decided on in the first instance was the small reef-ringed island of Tubuai, which seemed to promise them a haven from their disturbing political history. Mutineer James Morrison wrote that the island produced breadfruit, coconuts, yams, taro and plantains, while there were plenty of fish and turtles in the reef. There were also plenty of Tubuaians, all with their various allegiances to the three chiefs who ruled the different parts of the island.

In order to be as self-sufficient as possible, and thus avoid becoming embroiled in local island politics, the mutineers brought meat, supplies and native men and women with them from Tahiti.[25] On 10 July 1789, Fletcher Christian went ashore determined to built a fort. He wasted no time: '[T]he Ground being Measured out for the Fort posession was taken by turning a Turf and hoisting the Union Jack on a Staff in the Place. On this occasion an extra Allowance of Grog was drank and the Place Calld Fort George'. Fort George was 100 yards square, with walls twenty feet high and eighteen feet thick at the bottom. It was to have a drawbridge and be surrounded by a moat or ditch eighteen feet wide. Most importantly of all, the *Bounty*'s forty pounders were placed in the corners with swivel guns on the walls. The sailors were living the Robinson Crusoe dream of island dominion.

Again, their experience made a mockery of the myth. The sailors fought among themselves. There were quarrels over the availability of women and the allowance of grog. Those men without wives of their own refused to work unless they were provided with one. They were permitted to form relationships with Tubuaian women but were not allowed to take them away from their villages. Drunken fights broke out and different factions began to challenge Christian's authority. His answer was to ration the liquor and put all men to work. It took six weeks of hard labour before the walls began to rise, the ditches to widen and the posts to be placed for the gates and drawbridge. But the raising of a fort on native land does not guarantee possession of an island.[26] The islanders were not impressed by the activities of the strangers. They withheld supplies of food, forbade any interaction with the women, and raided the sailors' supplies and strongholds.

Eventually 700 Tubuaians, armed with clubs, spears and stones, ambushed the white men. Morrison described the fury and confusion: '[T]hey started up in a Swarm all round us, rushing on us with great fury & horrid yells . . . they kept pouring in from all quarters, seeming not to regard death or Danger.' The Europeans rallied with their superior fire power and when the fighting was over they claimed to have shot over 120 native men and women. However, their colonial desires remained unfulfilled. The sailors, still divided among themselves, agreed to leave Tubuai and return to Tahiti. There the party would split – sixteen men, including beachcomber James Morrison, would take their chances at Matavai Bay, while Christian and eight others would take the *Bounty* and continue their search for a safe haven.

Those men who decided to stay in Tahiti, however, did not go native. Although they acknowledged the authority of the local chief and were respectful of local practices and behaviour, their native life was lived along English lines, not local ones. They were made welcome in the homes of the Tahitians but they chose to build their own houses in a separate compound. Like Pacific Crusoes they flew the English flag on Sundays and observed the appropriate religious observances. They said their prayers, they worshipped at Easter and they celebrated Christmas with a meal of roast pork.[27] Life in this colonial English enclave was a gift permitted by the forbearance of the natives. Their tolerance and understanding was remarkable. They obviously made allowances for the sailors and permitted them their own customs and practices. They did, however, ask for a return for their generosity. The English mutineers were required to fight on behalf of the local chief, lending their bodies and their fire power to support the local cause. Their life as ex-patriot Crusoes was made possible by the largesse of their hosts. It was a gift that always had to be repaid.

Although it was a model most predominantly chosen by the beachcombers themselves, the use of *Robinson Crusoe* as a model of beachcomber experience was problematic. The novel, and its literary reworking of the castaway myth, established a set of expectations and beliefs about islands and castaways that ignored the realities. Actual reality was beside the point – the poignancy and power lay in its mythic representation. A deserted island, blue seas and waving palm trees form the basis of all island mythology. The castaway is the archetypal Man Alone, cast adrift from his own place and time. Forsaken and alone, he creates a new world for himself far away from the obligations and responsibilities of modern life. There is romance and heroism in the individual who proves able to sustain physical and mental well-being in the face of such adversity. There is also pathos.

John Coulter wrote of another 'Robinson Crusoe' that he found on a small uninhabited island in the Galapagos group. Travelling through the interior of the un-named island, he unexpectedly came across a space that had been cleared in the undergrowth. Pumpkins, melons, corn, sweet potatoes and tobacco had all been planted at one time and were now growing wild. Leaning on a small stone-walled well was a rusty spade that disintegrated when Coulter tried to pick it up. Continuing further through the plantation he saw the outlines of a small hut, partially covered by trees and nearly obscured by tangled vines. It was crudely built; the sides and front were posts of wood interlaced by vine branches covered with dried mud. Locating a small opening, he hacked through the vines with his axe and stepped inside.

The inside was dry and warm. On one side of the hut was an old pot, a frying pan, some wood and an axe. On a rough-made table lay a tobacco box and a home-made pipe. On the other side was a long shelf covered in skins that once served as a bed. Lying in the centre of the floor, near a small table, was the skeleton of a man, partially concealed by what had once been a covering of animal skins. Coulter moved towards the body and leaned over to touch it. It disintegrated into powder. Struck by the pathos of the scene before him, he searched for information that would identify the remains but could find nothing. He moved outside, at a loss to know how to honour 'this remnant of humanity'. He decided to cover it with the ruins of the house so he felled the posts, which caused the hut to collapse on itself and bury the unknown sailor. With a heavy heart Coulter made his way back to the shore. Subsequent enquiries proved worthless – he was never able to identify the forgotten castaway who had lived and died alone.

The beachcombers were not castaways in the narrowest sense of the word. While the mythical castaway was traditionally located on isolated, uninhabited islands, beachcomber experience involved integration. The castaway was an isolated individual – the beachcomber a stranger in an alien community. He was forced to assimilate with native people on islands with their own cultural and political histories. Beachcombers were not able to stamp their native culture on the indigenous people they came into contact with. The natives they met were not 'Fridays' and could not be remade into Englishmen. While Crusoe represented and reaffirmed the values of his home society, the beachcombers challenged them.[28] Their experiences taught them that such certainties were insufficient to the power dynamics at work on the beaches of the Pacific. They were not colonialists abroad. They were, after all, predominantly outcasts from their own society. They were unofficial Europeans, unauthorised representatives of their own culture.[29] Despite their efforts, they were not able to replicate European cultural institutions on islands but were themselves remade into new members of 'foreign' cultures.

They were, however, heir to the themes of the castaway myth – long voyages, personal suffering, arduous labour and overwhelming trials that can only be overcome by sheer determination and endurance. Castaway sailors were living exemplars of inventiveness, adaptability, resourcefulness and personal courage. Their cultural voyage from European to native marked them off from other travellers of their age. They were participants on a nineteenth-century quest as mythologised in the age-old tales of chivalry and romance. Like those earlier adventurers, they too left their familiar worlds, journeyed into unknown waters, confronted marvels and wonders and relayed their stories to those that stayed behind. Clad in tapa cloth or dressed in skins, barefoot or wearing fur moccasins, long-haired and bronzed, tattooed and scarred, the beachcombers epitomised the exotic danger associated with European exploration at the turn of the century. Their self-identification with the figure of the castaway state romanticised them. Their stories and their experiences became shrouded in history and myth. Despite their insistence on a contrary reality in their island experiences, they were inevitably imbued with the glamour and romance that lie at the heart of all desert island mythology.

> They have burst each band of habit
> They have wandered far away
> From island unto island
> At the gateways of the day.[30]

CHAPTER FOUR

Going to Sea:
Surviving the Journey

I must go down to the seas again,
To the lonely sea and the sky,
And all I ask is a tall ship
And a star to steer her by

JOHN MASEFIELD, *'Sea Fever'*

In the late eighteenth and early nineteenth centuries, going to sea was an adventure. It offered men of all ages a route to the far-flung places of the world. It set them on a journey to new worlds and an encounter with the unknown. Going to sea was a monumental act. It separated those who travelled from those who stayed behind. It differentiated men of curiosity and adventure from those who remained content with the familiar. It was grounded in the personal compulsions of the travellers, men in whom 'the desire to roam was paramount to all others'.[1]

In *Moby Dick*, Melville's alter-ego Ishmael elaborated. As well as needing money he wanted to escape the despondency and depression he felt on land. 'Whenever I find myself growing grim about the mouth; whenever it is a damp, drizzly November in my soul', he explained, 'I account it high time to get to sea as soon as I can.' Ishmael was contemptuous of a genteel life. He scorned the safety of home: the comforts, the hearthstone, the supper, the warm blankets and

the friends. He was searching for something mysterious and wonderful that can only be found in a life at sea. He was, in his own words,
'tormented with an everlasting itch for things remote'.

The beachcombers, following the mythologised Robinson Crusoe,
also responded to the romance of travel and the thrill of discovery.
They shared the same primeval urge to move beyond the 'middle state'
celebrated so famously by Defoe through Crusoe's father. Going to
sea, he warned his son,

> was for men of desperate fortunes on the one hand, or of aspiring, superior
> fortunes on the other . . . these things were all either too far above me, or
> too far below me; that mine was the middle state . . . which he had found
> by long experience was the best state in the world, the most suited to
> human happiness, not exposed to the miseries and hardships, the labour
> and sufferings of the mechanic part of mankind, and not embarrassed with
> the pride, luxury, ambition and envy on the upper part of mankind.[2]

Crusoe's father instinctively understood the transgressive nature
of travel. He saw it as a means by which one would escape from the
responsibility and commitment owed to one's family. A sea journey
would lead a traveller from the familiar to the foreign. It would
take him away from his accustomed place in life to a new range
of experience. But any voyage is more than just a movement from
one place to another. It is more truthfully about a transcendence of
boundaries and a traversal of limits. All journeys comprise obstacles
to overcome, tests to be passed and dangers to be faced. Crusoe's
father knew that the sailor's urge to exceed geographical borders
would have other consequences. It would lead him to challenge the
traditional boundaries that govern behaviour, personality and belief.
It would expose him to the lure of the forbidden and would test his
moral and ethical certainties. No one could return unchanged from
such a voyage.

Our prospective beachcombers repudiated the safety and security
of that 'middle state'. They placed no value on the 'temperance,
moderation and quietness' advocated by Crusoe's father. Instead,
they shared with Crusoe a compulsion to turn their back on prudence

and caution, choosing to seek new knowledge and experience on a voyage to the unknown. 'I had long seen clearly that a great part of the pleasure of travel . . . is rooted . . . in dissatisfaction with home and family', wrote Freud in his analysis of the impulse to abandon the familiar. 'When one first catches sight of the sea, crosses the ocean and experiences as realities . . . lands which for so long had been distant, unattainable things of desire – one feels oneself like a hero who has performed deeds of improbable greatness.'[3] A sense of restlessness drove our sailors beyond their assigned stations in life towards an encounter with the otherness of foreign people and places. Like Ishmael, they too wished to 'sail forbidden seas and land on barbarous coasts'. Their adventures were consciously sought, motivated by curiosity and informed by a compulsion to challenge boundaries. In the words of a sea-struck sailor, 'The life of a sailor was the most wonderful and noble in the world.'[4]

Their appetites were whetted by the stories of returned seamen – tales of exotic encounters that proved far more engrossing than any fiction of the time. They were captivated by the wonders and marvels that supposedly existed beyond the seas, and hoped to 'live among savages and meet with strange occurrences' of their own.[5] They had seen the young men, sometimes only sixteen years old, who had returned from such journeys – men who hinted at a life of adventure in the swagger of their walk and in their knowing smiles. Others were inspired to follow their lead. 'I frequently fell into long reveries', wrote one such sailor, 'about distant voyages and travels, and thought how fine it would be, to be able to talk about remote and barbarous countries; with what reverence and wonder people would regard me, if I had just returned from the coast of Africa or New Zealand; how dark and romantic my sunburnt cheeks would look; . . . and how grocers' boys would turn back their heads to look at me, as I went by.'[6]

All sea journeys began at the wharves and docks of the sailors' home towns – bustling nineteenth-century ports surrounded by warehouses, inns, taverns, shipping offices and stores. Ships of all shapes and sizes thronged with people and activity. Sailors, carpenters, stevedores, artisans, riggers and livestock all jostled together for space on board. Provisions were loaded, goods stored and weapons and equipment stowed for the long voyage ahead. The individual sailor's needs were few. His clothes, papers and personal effects together with a sheath-knife, a spoon and a tin cup for tea and coffee were all that he would take. His life would then be demarcated by the universe of the ship – a living thing of oak and pine, rope and canvas, copper and iron. It was a disturbingly fragile refuge from the force of the sea, but to those on board it was their entire world. It was their only haven against the hostile and landless world they travelled through. But it was more than that. Any ship after all was a vessel of opportunity. It was a passport to new experience. It enabled the sailors, however briefly, to surmount the limits placed on them by their society, their education and their personal history. Along the way they would make journeys of personal discovery. They would come to understand that it is only by exploring the world that one begins to know oneself.

The Thrill of Discovery

Throughout the ages the sea has been seen as a refuge for the free spirit, an arena for the tortured soul. It offers an escape from the madness and congestion of cities and from the restrictions of the machine age. It is the site of a hero's struggle with the elemental forces of nature. The mariner was the classic solitary outsider – alone against the vastness of the natural world. The young man high in the riggings, hostage to the wind and the sea, was a romantic figure. The sea was his wilderness, the chief testing ground of his young manhood. By the nineteenth century, the Pacific Ocean was the proper place for such adventures. It was the last frontier. As the world became more travelled, it remained one of the few places where voyagers of all kinds could test themselves against a power greater than themselves. '[The] mysterious, divine Pacific,' wrote Melville, 'rolls the midmost waters of the world, the Indian ocean and Atlantic being but its arms.' To the small, fragile, wooden ships that ploughed their way southwards, it must have seemed like the 'tide-beating heart of earth'. Its mystery and its vastness identified it as a place where adventures could be had, where discoveries could still be made.

For many it was a road to the markets of the world and a route to Empire. John Hawkesworth, writing from the heart of a maritime nation, celebrated the territorial and commercial impetus of the great southern voyages: 'Nothing can redound to the honour of this nation, as a maritime power, to the dignity of the Crown of Great Britain, and the advancement of the trade and navigation thereof, than to make discoveries of countries hitherto unknown.'[7] But to the common sailor, following in the footsteps of Cook, Wallis and Bougainville, it was something else entirely. It was a place where he could make his own voyages of exploration and discovery.

> I cannot describe my sensations on finding myself afloat on the mighty Ocean. My soul seemed to have escaped from a prison or a cage. I could now breathe more freely. But large and boundless as the world of waters appeared, I was afraid that it was not large enough for my wholesale desires. So many had traversed it before me that I felt apprehensive that they had gleaned the vast field of research, and left nothing new for me to discover and describe.[8]

The sheer scale of the Pacific is difficult to grasp. It is 17,700 kilometres sailing due west from Panama to the Malay Peninsula – almost four times the distance that Columbus sailed to the New World, and it is 15,450 kilometres from the Bering Strait to Antarctica. It is also deep. Beneath its waves lie spectacular mountain ranges with canyons plunging almost ten kilometres into the watery depths. Although it encompasses thousands of islands, the waters of the Pacific cover a third of the globe. In the midst of that ocean, a ship could sail for 8000 kilometres and never make landfall. Land was hard to find; it had to be searched for in the midst of the sea. Maps, with their huge empty spaces, told of terra incognita – their blankness a testament to the undiscovered and charted regions of the world. It was an emptiness framed by illustrations of mythical beings, marvels and monsters, suggesting that travel was as much a journey into imagination and myth as it was a voyage into vacancy. By travelling into the void and crossing that immense and uncharted body of water, sailors participated in a rite of passage that transgressed the laws of nature. Oceans kept people apart. They fixed worlds and continents in their place and those who ignored those natural boundaries committed a perilous act. Going south was a remarkable adventure for men whose entire world was north.

Reality of Life at Sea

The ocean was not just a place to be traversed; it was also a place to be endured. Sea life was full of dangers and privations. The young greenhorn who signed on in a flurry of adventurous idealism was soon to have his romantic preconceptions sorely tested. He found himself mocked by older sailors, ordered about roughly, given dangerous duties, terrified by high rigging and overcome by debilitating seasickness. 'Although but a few hours before I had been so eager to go [on] this voyage', wrote a fifteen-year-old sailor, 'there [now] seemed a sudden gloom to spread over me. A not very pleasing prospect [was] truly before me, that of a long voyage and a hard overseer.'[9] Herman Melville would have agreed with him. He described conditions on the ship that rescued him from the Marquesas in 1842:

> The general aspect of the forecastle was dungeon-like and dingy in the extreme. In the first place, it was not five feet from deck to deck, and even this space was encroached upon by two outlandish cross-timbers bracing the vessel, and by the sailors' chests, over which you must needs crawl in getting about . . . All over, the ship was in a most dilapidated condition; but in the forecastle it looked like the hollow of an old tree going to decay. In every direction the wood was damp and discoloured, and here and there soft and porous . . . In some vessels, the crews of which after a hard fight have given themselves up, as it were, for lost, the vermin seem to take actual possession, the sailors being mere tenants by sufferance.[10]

The sailors' world was small, overcrowded, unsanitary and infested with disease.[11] Their quarters in the forecastle were traditionally cramped, stifling and congested – a breeding ground for infection and disease. Syphilis, malaria, rickets, smallpox, tuberculosis, yellow fever, dysentery and typhus spread easily throughout the crew. The men, who slept in hammocks only thirty centimetres apart, breathed the same foul, tainted air and easily succumbed to endemic shipboard diseases. Typhus, spread by infected lice in bedding that was frequently shared and rarely cleaned, was so prevalent on board ship that it was known as 'ship's fever' or 'gaol fever'. The holds were crammed with festering and spoiled provisions and in some cases rotting corpses. On English ships, dead Protestant sailors were traditionally sewn into their hammocks and buried at sea, but Catholic ships from France and Spain carried the decaying bodies of their dead in the holds. They would remain there for months at a time, mouldering in the heat and damp until they could be returned home for burial. All ships leaked and their ballasts of gravel or sand quickly became putrid. The bilge gases were so noxious that men occasionally suffocated from inhaling the fumes.

The wooden world of the ship quickly became waterlogged and remained permanently damp. The men lived, worked and slept in a cold, wet environment. James Morrison, on board the *Bounty* in 1789, complained about the intense cold as the ship neared Cape Horn. In rough seas and bitter weather, the men were forced to remain on deck through all watches, unable to dry themselves or their clothes between shifts. Sodden, chilled and overworked, many succumbed to sickness and fatigue. When they were finally able to retreat to their quarters they were no better off. Morrison described the 'uncomfortable situation of the Men between decks which were always filld with smoke while the Hatches were fast' resulting in congestion and illness. 'The straining of the ship tho perfectly sound, kept the hammock[s] always wet, which made them very uncomfortable, Not only for the Sick but for the Well.' Peter Heywood, a young midshipman, remembered the *Bounty*'s run to Cape Horn, its inclement weather and stormy seas. The ship was leaking so badly it required pumping every hour and many people were becoming ill 'by the severity of the weather, and want of rest (there being seldom a night but all hands were called three or four times)'. Heywood, young and inexperienced, was awed by the experience: '[T]here never were seas, in any part of the known world, to compare with those we met off Cape Horn, for height, and length of swell; the oldest seamen on board never saw anything to equal that.'[12]

But inclement weather was not the only danger of life at sea. Discipline was severe, as the ship's boy on board the *Hercules* in 1827 discovered to his peril. When the ship began rolling heavily in deep seas en route to Madras and Calcutta, third mate John Twyning ordered the boy to climb on the yard 'and pass the heal lashing to secure the boom'. The boy's competence was not an issue. He had been at sea for three years and was known to be highly efficient in his seaman's duties, but it was midnight – dark and dangerous. He was understandably reluctant to ascend the mast, given the time of night and the condition of the sea and did so only when the mate threatened to flog him. When Twyning went forward to give the boy his orders he was horrified to see him lose his balance and pitch over the yard. 'He came down head-foremost, and falling on the iron monkey, smashed his skull to pieces.' The doctor was quickly summoned to his assistance, 'but when he arrived he was already dead'.

There were other hazards on board ship. The warm air of the South Seas provided a perfect breeding ground for vermin of all kinds. In 1856 the brig *Thomas W. Rowland* was carrying a freight of fruit that hatched a cargo of insects as the journey progressed. The captain's wife, Mary Rowland, recalled:

> White crawling worms about an inch long come out of the cargo of figs and raisins, and large numbers make their appearance in the Cabin, and more particularly in my room. They keep hid during the day time . . . and make their Debut at night, they crawl up on the ceiling overhead and then fall down in a short time . . . they like to hide in my mattress best of all places and . . . often I am awakened during the night by them as they drop down upon me and then commence to crawl over me occasionaly taking a nip as their appetites suit them.[13]

The crew of the *Bounty* had a different battle on their hands: 'the ship began to swarm with Cockroaches to get rid of which evry Method was tried but to no purpose after repeated washing and Carrying evry Chest & box on shore . . . they appeard as plenty in two or three days as ever, the Cables appeard alive with them and they seemed to Encrease instead of diminish tho great quantitys were destroyd evry day.' While travelling from the Marquesas to Tahiti, the *Lucy Ann* was infested with cockroaches and rats. They were host to a legion of diseases: fleas transmitted plague; flies spread dysentery and diarrhoea; and mosquitoes were the bearers of dengue fever, yellow fever and malaria. Hatchways were sealed and the hull fumigated in order to kill the pests, but enough survived to repopulate the ship. The cockroaches were especially active at night. Emerging from their hiding places among the timbers, the larger ones immediately infested the sailors' chests and bedding, running over the bodies of the sleeping men. Still more flew around the close quarters, battering the sailors who could do little more than slap them away. Not to be outdone, the rats also made their presence felt. 'Often they darted in upon us at mealtimes', recalled one sailor, 'and nibbled our food.'[14]

Food was another problem. The seamen's diet of the late eighteenth and early nineteenth centuries was extremely limited. It consisted primarily of salt beef or pork (known as 'sea horse'), dried beans, dried peas and ship's biscuit along with whatever could be picked up on the way.[15] Flour and water puddings (known as 'duffs') enlivened with a few raisins were also a staple of the seagoing diet. The main qualification for a cook at that time was the loss of a hand or foot, a dismemberment that ruled him out of traditional duties. His primary skill was an ability to boil water. A ration of salt beef or salt pork, taken out of the 'harness' cask and soaked in sea water to remove the crust of dried brine, was boiled in a cauldron and served with a ration of hard bread or ship's biscuit. The following day any leftover meat would be chopped with potatoes and onions and served again. The meat was coarse, fatty and extremely salty, while the dried goods harboured pests in abundance. Weevils infested the biscuit and had to be tapped out onto the table before the men could eat. Maggots were also a feature of many a meal. Pea soup was always an unpopular option with the crew because of the maggots that floated to the top after the peas were cooked, and rice, another staple, was usually filled with bugs of some sort or another. James Patten, a surgeon on Cook's second voyage, remarked that 'our bread was . . . swarming with two different sorts of little brown grubs . . . Their larvas, or maggots, were found in such quantities in the pease-soup, as if they had been strewed over our plates on purpose, so that we could not avoid swallowing some of them in every spoonful we took.'[16]

Any bread that was stored in casks was often wet when opened and had to be dried in the open air before it could be consumed. Cheese, also kept in casks, was frequently rancid, along with the butter which smelled so foul the men refused to eat it. The availability of fresh water was also a major problem on ships that were often out of sight of land for months at a time. Water kept in casks for long periods became musty and briny. Tainted with pitch, and pine from the cask, it was often a breeding ground for insects and bacteria of one sort or another. It is no surprise that ale, port, beer, wine and rum were drunk in such great quantities. In the absence of refrigeration, livestock were kept on board to provide fresh meat, and all ships travelled, like Noah's ark, with a complement of animals crowding their decks. Chickens, cows, sheep, goats, pigs and ducks were all food for the crew. On some ships, special pens were made for larger animals; on others, the ship's longboats were put into requisition, the pigs and sheep living on the bottom and the hens in coops placed across the gunwales.[17] The fresh meat did not last long and was not able to be readily replenished without regular contact with land. One of the most nutritious foods found on board were the rats that infested the ships. Only marginally less revolting than the maggots and weevils, the rats had grown plump on the ship's supplies and were reputedly 'full as good as rabbits, although not so large'. Known as millers because they were white with flour dust, the rats were often the only source of fresh meat available to far-voyaging sailors.[18]

The 'Spoyle of Mariners'

Given the substandard living conditions and the frugal diet, it is not surprising that scurvy had such a devastating effect on the crews of long-distance ships. The disease was the curse of the sailors, responsible for more deaths at sea than storm, shipwreck, combat and all other diseases combined. In 1499 Vasco da Gama lost 116 of his crew of 170, while Magellan lost 208 out of 230 men in 1520. In the eighteenth century especially, scurvy decimated the ships' companies with George Anson in 1742 losing more than 1300 out of his crew of almost 2000.[19] The disease was caused by a lack of vitamin C in the diet at sea, particularly on long voyages, where the best source

of ascorbic acid – fresh fruit and vegetables – was not available.
It was merciless in its effect on the human system, with its most
recognisable symptoms being the appearance of large, discoloured
spots over the entire surface of the body. Scurvy caused the body's
connective tissue to degenerate, resulting in bleeding gums, wobbly
teeth, reeking breath, anaemic lethargy, the opening of old wounds
and the separating of once-healed bones. Sailors' gums would swell
so much that the excess dead tissue had to be cut off with a knife.
The later stage of scurvy was the most gruesome, as the body seemed
to rot while still alive. Blisters, as black as ink, discoloured the skin
as if it were putrifying. Eventually the ulcers festered and the flesh
turned fungous, splitting apart to expose the bones underneath. The
men's faces were also disfigured and their skin broke out in black,
blue and green bruises. Overwhelming lassitude and fatigue left the
sufferer unable to work and facing inevitable death. The effects of
scurvy are immortalised in Samuel Taylor Coleridge's *Rime of the
Ancient Mariner*, his epic poem about forsaken men on a doomed
voyage:

> His bones were black with many a crack,
> All black and bare, I ween;
> Jet-black and bare, save where with rust
> Of mouldy damps and charnel crust
> They're patch'd with purple and green

James Morrison described the arrival of scurvy on the *Bounty*, when
his fellow seamen 'particularly the oldest began to complain of Pains
in their limbs and . . . weakness and debility became to be observed
through the Ships Company, for which Essence of Malt was given to
those who appeard worst'. Morrison also recorded that after obtaining
a supply of fresh coconuts, the men made a speedy recovery. It was
long known that fresh fruit and vegetables, taken on land, would
cure scurvy; however, the task of preventing it at sea, or containing
it once it had broken out, was still the subject of vast debate and
experimentation. It was regarded as a failure on the part of the captain
if the disease appeared and most commanders made determined efforts

to keep their crew healthy. Any captain dedicated to extended travel and conquest in the Pacific had to overcome the disease known as 'the Spoyle of Mariners'. By attacking the bodies and minds of the sailors it risked the effective management and morale of the ships.

Men such as James Cook, William Bligh and George Vancouver were dismayed and disbelieving when, despite their best efforts at prevention, their crews displayed symptoms of scurvy. Bligh tried a number of novel experiments. He provided ground wheat and sugar for hot breakfasts, and rationed out barley in lieu of oatmeal. He even hired a fiddler to provide music for dancing in the dogwatch (4–6 p.m.) in an attempt to keep the men 'chearful' and healthy.[20] Cook, influenced by the views of Scottish surgeon James Lind, believed in the anti-scorbutic powers of lemon juice, sauerkraut and portable broth (made from blocks of meat essence boiled in water).[21] He also provided his men with spruce beer and wild celery in order to build up their resistance. Combined with his policy for regular airings of his ships, good supplies of fresh water and dry clothes, and a plentiful distribution of fresh fruit and vegetables when available, Cook's ships were hailed as a model for the control of scurvy.

Despite his precautions, it is commonly accepted that Cook's men did suffer from the disease on their expeditions to the South Seas, although he was justly lauded for the fact that none of his men died from it.[22] It was to take another thirty years before the greatest medical minds of the age made the implicit connection between scurvy and fruit and vegetables rich in vitamin C, resulting in a mandatory serving of lemon or lime juice to each enlisted sailor in the English navy (causing them to be known thereafter as 'limeys'). While it was not the scourge it had once been, scurvy remained a recurring reality to vast numbers of seamen during the early to mid-nineteenth century – especially on ships with unenlightened captains and small supplies of fresh fruit and vegetables.

Scurvy was a disease that also affected the mind. Physiologically it manifested itself as a morbid susceptibility to sensations of light, smell and sound. As the physical symptoms of the disease increased, it led to an extraordinary alternation of moods termed 'scorbutic nostalgia'.[23]

Suffering sailors would veer erratically between ungovernable yet equivocal emotions, and be subject to powerful feelings of joy and despair, pleasure and disgust. Those emotions were pathologically intensified, and victims of scurvy would find the same phenomenon both intensely beautiful *and* profoundly depressing. Sufferers craved the sights, sounds and smells of land; they fantasised about fresh food and clean water, about the colours of the sunset and the beauty of the land. Nerves became sensitised to a more vivid spectrum of emotions. Melville recalled a mariner so scorbutic that the very smell of flowers wafting from the shore caused him to cry out in agony. Brutalised physically and mentally by long sea voyages, sailors developed deep longings for the comforts of home, and focused themselves on a desire for land. 'Oh! for a refreshing glimpse of one blade of grass – for a snuff at the fragrance of a handful of the loamy earth!' wrote Melville. 'Is there nothing fresh around us? Is there no green thing to be seen?' Unsurprisingly, the long-suffering victim of scorbutic nostalgia tended to 'form exquisite ideas of island paradises'.[24] The sheer physical beauty of the Pacific Islands seemed to promise the sea-worn sailors the comfort, peace and plenty they so ardently desired. The fertility and fecundity of the islands contrasted most painfully with the aridity and bleakness of maritime life.

Longing for Land

By the end of their long journeys, morale was at its lowest point. The heat, the monotony, the complete absence of anything green, except the mould in the interior of the ship, the continual damp and the ever-present mildew all combined to depress the hardiest sailor. Even their ships were weary of the voyage. Paint was puffed and cracked, timbers were covered with barnacles from which lines of seaweed trailed, and copper-bottomed hulls were torn and jagged. Whether they were sick with scurvy or ill with the deprivations of shipboard life, the sailors knew they would be cured on islands. The land, the food, the very air itself was seen as conducive to health and happiness. The islands were oases of perfection, places of solace and sanctuary promising life, vigour and rejuvenation. There was a practical and physiological dimension to their longing for land. It was a common belief at the time that immersing a scorbutic sailor in soil would cure him. Known as a 'sand-bath', it was a popular treatment, particularly among those who sailed the slave routes. Many commanders and ship's surgeons were so convinced of its effectiveness that they kept on board a quantity of sea-washed sand together with a double-bottomed boiler. The boiler would heat the sand into which the sufferer would then be immersed. According to one ship's doctor, such a patient would display an amazing recovery (whether this was due to mere coincidence or whether it had a medical aetiology is unknown):

After two hours rest . . . the condition in which [I] found the patient, seemed to border on a miracle; no more swelling; no more stiffness, even

Marquesan women on board a ship in Nukuhiva, Marquesas. The arrival of native women on board vessels moored in Pacific harbours was an event eagerly anticipated by visiting sailors.

in the tendons; . . . the soles of the feet before very painful, no longer
causing any sensation . . . . A week's sand-bath's the second of one hour,
and the others of two, were sufficient for effecting the most complete cure:
all the symptoms of scurvy disappeared never to return; and the man who
had been threatened with sinking, in a few days, under the attacks of the
disorder, enjoyed, during the last ten months of the expedition, the most
perfect health.[25]

Discipline at Sea

There was yet another facet of life at sea that took its toll on the common
sailor. His wooden world was a highly structured environment, full of
boundaries and divisions that enforced their own particular form of
order and control. Sailors lived and worked by a series of complex and
complicated rules that dominated every aspect of their lives.[26] Strict
guidelines dictated when, where, what and how much they ate. They
demarcated hours of duty, hours of sleep, areas of work and areas of
punishment. They divided the sailors' days into different messes and
watches, division and duties. All men knew their position on board ship
and understood their proper place in their small but highly regimented
seagoing community. Any lapse in obedience was often followed by
the use of physical punishment. Herman Melville elaborates.

In 1834 Melville was a humble seaman on board the *United States*,
an American man-of-war, when he first heard the cry feared by all
serving sailors – 'all hands witness punishment, ahoy!' It was a call that
spread terror and foreboding throughout the ship. It demanded the
presence of the entire crew at the flogging of a shipmate and implicated
them in his punishment. They were forced to collude, silently and
unwillingly, in the humiliation of their comrade, a man of 'their own
type and badge', to quote Melville. Simply by being there, they became
participants in an act of degradation, pity and shame. All seafaring men
lived with the same threat of physical punishment. Any one of them
could suffer the same fate. Given an unlucky combination of misfortune
and circumstance, any man might find himself 'stripped like a slave'
and 'scourged worse than a hound'. No one was exempt from the laws
of the ship and the omnipotent authority of the captain.

The dreaded call to punishment required all men to gather before the main mast. The five hundred men on the *United States* took their places in silence, crowding into the open space at the centre of the ship. The officers and midshipmen stood together in a group on the starboard side with the surgeon, whose presence was always required at a flogging. When everyone was assembled, the captain emerged from his cabin. Walking to the centre of the group he began to read the daily report of offences committed, together with the punishments decreed. He then called for the culprit to be brought forward. A man was led through the crowd. He was escorted by the master-at-arms on one side and an armed marine on the other. He stood silently, head bowed, as the charges were formally read. His justification for fighting while on duty was disregarded. The captain was judge and jury, allowing no excuses and refusing any appeal. 'I would not forgive God Almighty', Melville recorded him as saying.

The unlucky sailor was then led to the gratings – square frames of barred wood standing upright against the main mast. Once his shirt and jacket had been stripped off, he was tied to the gratings by his hands and feet. The boatswain waited on one side with the 'cat' (a whip made of nine separate pieces, or 'tails', of leather) in his hands. At the word from the captain, he took his position behind the bare-backed, spreadeagled man. He then began 'combing out the nine tails of the *cat* with his hand, and sweeping them round his neck' before bringing them 'with the whole force of his body', wrote Melville, upon the skin of the sailor. 'Again, and again, and again; and at every blow, higher and higher rose the long, purple bars on the prisoner's back.' The standard punishment, a dozen lashes, would not usually cut through the surface but would raise severe welts and dark bruises on the skin.

Different men reacted in different ways to a flogging. Their responses depended on their age, experience and their individual temperament. Some bowed their heads and remained silent throughout. Others cursed and shouted and when cut down, swore vengeance on their persecutors. A large majority, careless of their self-respect, broke down and howled in anguish. The young landsmen or impressed sailors, especially, suffered all the terrors of pain, anguish and humiliation, often becoming morose, sullen and uncommunicative for the rest of the journey. Their previous lives had not prepared them for the tortuous

realities of a life in the navy. The victim on the *United States* was a
nineteen-year-old sailor on his first voyage away from home. 'I don't
care what happens to me now!' he wept, going among the crew with
bloodshot eyes as he put on his shirt. 'I have been flogged once, and
they may do it again if they will. Let them look out for me now!'[27]

Plays of Power

In the highly institutionalised world of the naval vessel, particularly,
physical punishment was regarded as an absolutely fundamental
instrument of control.[28] It was part of the theatre of discipline and
order necessary for the effective management of the ship. It was
unambiguous in its intent and implacable in its purpose. The captain who ordered it and the men who carried it out were merely
instruments, symbols of the power invested in the ship and in its
venture. As men of the quarterdeck, they were empowered with the
authority of their commissions, which identified them as proper and
appropriate representatives of king and country. They made the
power of the sovereign visible to the men of the forecastle and they
were to be shown the diligence and loyalty owed to one's nation.

Men could be flogged for a number of reasons: insolence,
contempt, disrespect, quarrelling with shipmates, fighting, disorderly
conduct, laziness, neglect of duty, carelessness, to name but a few.
The interpretation of each offence was highly arbitrary. What was
regarded as a punishable offence on one ship might be overlooked on
another, depending on the temperament and personal response of
individual officers. They had the sole power to impose their particular
interpretation, often by violent means. It was an imperfect system
that relied on the integrity and professionalism of the man in control
– and it was ripe for abuse. Richard Henry Dana was a well-educated
American, like Melville, who spent two years travelling 'before the
mast', this time in the merchant service, where he was witness to the
following encounter between a sailor and his captain:

> 'Can't a man ask a question here without being flogged?'
> 'No,' shouted the captain; 'nobody shall open his mouth aboard this vessel
> but myself;' and began laying the blows upon his back, swinging half round

between each blow to give it full effect. As he went on his passion increased, and he danced about the deck, calling out as he swung the rope, 'If you want to know what I flog you for, I'll tell you. It's because I like to do it! – because I like to do it! – It suits me! That's what I do it for!'[29]

It was no surprise that the sailors longed for land. Like all travellers before and after them, they fantasised about a life of ease, comfort and pleasure on island shores. But the hardships were still not over. Long, exhausting and debilitating sea voyages often ended in violence, even death, at point of landfall. Famous voyagers sometimes met infamous deaths – Cook himself was killed in Hawaii, Marion du Fresne was killed in New Zealand, and La Perouse disappeared forever in Melanesia. There was no doubt that Pacific islands were perilous places. The reports that filtered back to Europe were not imaginative writings, but authentic eyewitness accounts written by experienced and credible travellers.[31] Expectation of a violent welcome prompted many shipwrecked sailors to face the rigours of the open sea rather than take their chances on shore. It was a common belief among such men that landfall was no guarantee of safety: '[T]hough we had escaped the dangers of the ocean,' they wrote, 'others awaited us.' The experiences of an American sailor called Leonard Shaw provide a brutal example. He was one of a group of men captured by islanders in the northern Solomons in 1830. The sailors were attempting to set up storage facilities for the curing of bêche-de-mer when they antagonised the native people.[32] Their ship was forced to sail, leaving thirteen men behind at the mercy of the outraged natives. Those who remained were chased, beaten and slaughtered, except for Shaw who managed to escape. He watched in horror as the islanders roasted and feasted on his murdered comrades. Determined not to suffer the same fate, he stayed out of sight for fifteen days before hunger drove him to the nearest village. There he threw himself on the mercy of the local chief, promising to become his slave in return for his life. From that moment his existence was one of abject misery. He was brutalised, beaten, starved and overworked until he had 'pined away to a mere skeleton'. The only food available to him was the rats that infested the island. 'In the darkness of the night I entrapped many a fat fellow', recalled

The massacre of part of the crew of the vessel *Perouse* at Maouna, 1806.
Native attacks on European crews were a constant hazard of early
European exploration in the Pacific.

Shaw, 'and feasted upon him in the silence of my seclusion with more
true joy and a sweeter relish than the proudest monarch ever knew
. . . when banqueting upon the choicest viands of the world.'

As he became weaker and more emaciated, he found he had outlived
his usefulness. The natives decided that he would be killed and roasted.
The hapless sailor was then forced to make the preparations for his
own death. He fetched the wood, brought the water and harvested the
fruits and vegetables that were to complete the feast. He was made to
sit down, axe at his side, and await the moment of his death: 'As I was
prepared for my fate, I received this annunciation with calmness and
fortitude, and awaited the happy moment of my death with impatience.'
Before it could take place, however, his ship returned, and in the hope
of finding some of its crew alive, began firing on the village. Shaw was
sent to the ship as an intermediary to plead for leniency. The hope
of salvation, long since dormant, flared again in his heart. He was a

pitiful sight to those who watched from the deck – entirely naked, bedaubed with paint, emaciated and 'lacerated with wounds'. They were horrified at his condition, describing him as the very epitome of wretchedness. After the terrors of his island life, his reunion with his compatriots was ecstatic: '[T]he scene, the occasion, and the bliss are so engraven upon my memory, that they can only be effaced when the last spark of life is extinct.'

Those men who set sail from Europe and America responded to the romance of travel and the thrill of adventure. They all travelled towards the promise of a safe harbour and a warm welcome in a Pacific island paradise. However, it was not long before they learned the harsh realities of a seagoing life: the poor food, the rampant disease, the rigid discipline and the dismal conditions. They also realised that their trials did not cease with the end of their journey. Before they could set foot on the long-awaited island shores there was often one more challenge to overcome. Shipwreck was a disturbingly common occurrence in the dangerous, partly charted waters of the Pacific. The loss of their ships turned many sailors into accidental beachcombers – victims of misfortune and misadventure. It was a brutal and sometimes fatal end to a journey that had begun with such high expectations months, or even years, before. Shipwreck violently catapulted the hapless sailors into the harsh realities of native life. It also left them stranded, destitute and powerless, on unfamiliar shores, thousands of miles from the place where their voyages had begun.

CHAPTER FIVE

Stranded in a Strange Land

Having found a good haven and being brought safely in sight of land, they fell upon their knees and blessed the God of Heaven who had brought them over the vast and furious ocean . . . again to set their feet upon the firm and stable earth, their proper element.

WILLIAM BRADFORD, *History of Plymouth Plantation*

In the early hours of the morning of 17 September 1829, the whaleship *Minerva* ran aground on an unmarked reef south-east of the Tonga group. John Twyning, the boat-steerer, was woken by the force of the impact and ran on deck. There he was greeted by scenes of chaos and panic as men grabbed their possessions and loaded boats in a rush to clear the ship and save their lives. Twyning collected the chronometer, the quadrant and a number of charts and took them to one of the longboats. The captain, in a 'state of mind bordering on despair', refused to leave his sinking ship. The men pleaded with him to join them: 'I then told him we must leave him if he would not consent to go with us', recalled Twyning. When the captain finally agreed, high seas forced the boats away from the ship, leaving him, the carpenter and another crew member, stranded on board. All night the three boats stayed close despite being pushed against the reef by huge waves. They refused to abandon their captain and spent a perilous night battling the breakers. It was a long twenty-four hours later before calmer waters enabled them to effect a rescue. The overloaded boats then set a course for Tonga, 640 kilometres distant, and began their trial on the open sea.

Twyning's boat contained one bag of bread, one case of wine, and a keg of what the sailors thought was water. It was in fact mixed with one-third sperm oil, which Twyning wrote 'went down very sweet'. There were eight men on board and one large 'Kangaroo dog'. The three boats tried to remain together, but lost sight of each other at night. By morning, one of them was missing and was never sighted again. The two remaining boats sailed on together for the rest of the day, until the second boat sprang a leak, forcing all the men into one overloaded vessel. It was not a popular move: 'Our boat was the smallest of the three. The addition of so many men would greatly over-load it, and place us in most imminent danger . . . Some argued, that self-preservation was the first law of nature . . . and if we took them in, it would render the destruction of the whole almost a certainty', Twyning recalled. The dictates of humanity prevailed and men from the disabled boat came aboard the third vessel. The sinking boat had been followed by two large sharks throughout the morning and the men were desperate to get to safety. There were now fifteen men in a boat only 6.4 metres long, loaded to within twenty centimetres of the water's edge in the middle of the wide Pacific. If they were to survive, they had to lighten the boat. Every man threw his jacket overboard. Everything else that could be spared was also thrown overboard, including some muskets and the case of wine. The dog was saved 'only that he might be the last resource to satisfy the craving of our appetites should we not make land before such a sacrifice might become necessary'.

For two days the sailors suffered from hunger and thirst. Their allowance of oil and water (half a glass) was served out twice a day but could not sustain them. In desperation they tried to drink salt water, which only increased their thirst. At other times they chewed pieces of lead, which helped to moisten their mouths. Twyning wrote that some men were reduced to drinking their urine, 'so violent was the thirst that consumed us'. By 24 September, just over a week into their ordeal, the men were in a desperate state and agreed to kill the dog at midday. 'Noon arrived, a knife was taken out, and the poor dog was about to be put to death, that we might appease our raging thirst with his blood' when land was sighted. The men were jubilant and headed for the island, despite the captain's warnings that it was inhabited by savages. The weary sailors had no choice but to swim across the reef while dragging their boat behind them to ensure that neither they nor the boat were dashed to pieces on the coral. Finally, in a weakened state, torn and scratched by their passage across the reef and half dead with hunger and thirst, a small group of sailors dragged themselves up onto the shore.

The moment they stepped upon the shores of the Tongan island, John Twyning and his weary band of survivors unwittingly enacted one of the most iconic moments in the history of European exploration. Their first steps into a new world heralded an archetypal confrontation. It was the moment when the Western world came face to face with its geographical, historical and cultural other. Those early encounters between Europeans and islanders were violent in nature and apocalyptic in scope. Baffling rituals, mysterious ceremonies and inexplicable acts signalled the collision of two widely diverse world views. Not surprisingly, many of these initial encounters were bloody and brutal. Several sailors already mentioned could all attest to that: Horace Holden's experience of hardship when stranded on the Palaus; William Cary's narrow escape from massacre in Fiji; and Leonard Shaw's witnessing of his comrades being murdered and eaten in the northern Solomons. The European sailor was a stranger from the margins. To the native on the beach, he was an unimagined wonder – a mysterious visitor who was sometimes assumed to have mythical antecedents. When John Jackson stepped ashore in Samoa he was presented with a number of hogs because 'according to the rules of Samoan hospitality' he was 'one of the most distant strangers that dwelled among them, and came from a country at the back of the sky'.[1] Welsh sailor Edward Robarts, one of the first white men ever seen by the Marquesan Islanders, was believed to be a ghost who came from beyond the horizon. He was studied with great interest to see if he was human. On Tonga, the natives regarded the white missionary George Vason as a sky dweller because 'the sky appeared to touch the ocean, in the distant horizon, and knowing that we came from an immense distance, they concluded that we must have come through the sky'.

Irrespective of origin the newly arrived sailor was an intruder. He belonged to a different land, culture and soil from those he confronted and he embodied all the terror of the unknown. He was an uninvited guest on islands that had their own political, social and cultural histories, none of which could fully account for the unexplained arrival of so many strangers. White men were peered at, prodded, poked and examined. They were threatened, beaten, kicked and speared. They were also mocked, teased and stared at. Herman Melville recalled the fixed and unblinking examination he received from a Taipi native who 'placed himself directly facing me, looking at me with a rigidity of aspect under which I absolutely quailed . . . Never before had I been subjected to so strange and steady a glance; it revealed nothing of the mind of the savage, but it appeared to be reading my own.' John Jackson was an object of great astonishment to the natives of Fiji. Their location, deep in the interior of the island, meant he was one of the first white men they had ever seen. They were not impressed:

> They evinced much curiosity at seeing me, some of them scarcely believing their own senses, putting forth their hands towards me to prove whether I was tangible or not; while others would come and shake their hands before my eyes to ascertain if I was blind, then say I was not blind but had eyes like a cat. Others would say I was a leper, or like one, which others would contradict, by saying I resembled a pig with all the hair scorched off . . . the young girls would not come nigh at all, and if any of the young men laid hold of them to force them close to me, they would scream as though they were going into fits.[2]

In the early days of contact it was believed that strangers were sent by the gods expressly to be eaten. A man who arrived on shore, destitute and distressed, was regarded as a gift for the people of the land and would promptly 'have the salt water knocked from his eyes'.[3] Sacrifice of strangers became less prevalent as the natives realised there were gains to be made from the European newcomers, and in many instances sailors were offered sanctuary and salvation from the perils of the sea. Melville and Vason, for instance, safely crossed their respective beaches in the Marquesas and in Tonga, and were treated as honoured guests and honorary family members.

European crews were still operating under orders when first contact was made, and felt protected by the security and authority granted them by their country of origin and by their roles on board ship. The castaway sailor, however, was different. He usually arrived alone without the cultural security of his European community. By leaving his ship and the society of which the ship was an emblem, he detached himself from his fixed place in a familiar social structure. Although free of his shipboard role, he was not yet involved in the social life of the islands. He had no attachment to the culture that he encountered on the other side of the beach. Like all liminal or marginal

European visitors welcomed ashore by the local inhabitants. The majority of sailors had to undergo extensive and highly ritualised ceremonies before they could be accepted into native communities.

figures, he was neither here nor there, neither one thing nor another, neither European nor native.[4] But all beaches are places of transition; they require a movement from one place to another, from one set of rules to another. The bewildered sailor was powerless on his own. His only hope for survival lay in his movement towards, and acceptance in, the culture of the island. His first steps 'across the beach' were very important ones. They set him on the road to becoming a native. They carried him across a physical boundary, but more importantly they transcended a psychological barrier – one that divided Western-based ideologies and beliefs from indigenous ones.

Friend or Foe

Pacific societies traditionally had well-developed strategies for the assimilation of strangers. Despite their relative isolation, travel and movement were continuing aspects of island life.[5] Most island groups had contact with each other and there were established customs everywhere for the reception and treatment of newcomers. Ritual was an important part of that process and all foreign visitors were expected to undergo some form of ceremonial incorporation into native communities. The Polynesian belief that all travellers were to be offered courtesy was problematic in the case of the European stranger. His novelty destabilised traditional patterns of behaviour. It was unclear whether he should be regarded as a visitor and welcomed, or treated hostilely as an alien. The ambiguous status of the castaway sailor, particularly on previously unvisited islands, identified him as a liminal being. To become a social entity, with a name, role and status within the community, he had to be incorporated into the host society.

Gentleman beachcomber William Mariner was fifteen years old when he arrived in Tonga in 1806. His ship, the *Port-au-Prince*, was badly in need of repair when it approached the islands, and communication with the Tongans was necessary to receive supplies and assistance. A Hawaiian who had served on an American ship acted as interpreter and made arrangements for the provision of water and fuel. But treachery was afoot. The captain and a portion of the crew were decoyed ashore and 350 Tongans infiltrated the ship. At a signal from their chief they attacked the unarmed and unsuspecting crew

STRANDED IN A STRANGE LAND 111

that remained on board. Mariner had hidden himself below decks and along with the cooper decided to blow up the ship and all on her rather than let it fall into the hands of the Tongans. Their plan failed and they decided to give themselves up. They preferred to face what they believed was certain death than suffer protracted cruelties at native hands.

Twenty-two crew members were killed in the attack on the ship. The thirty-four who remained ashore were spared, including Mariner and the cooper, who had both taken the fancy of the Tongan chief. But their relief was short-lived. In particular, Mariner's initial treatment at the hands of the natives confirmed his worst fears. He was stripped of his clothes, treated as a curiosity and was teased and bullied. He was led about barefooted 'without anything to cover him, the heat blistering his skin in a most painful manner'. He was finally sent for by Finau, the Tongan chief, who had taken a liking to the young boy, thinking he was the son of the captain. Before Mariner was presented to the chief, however, he was washed, fed and 'oiled all over with sandalwood oil, which felt very agreeable, alleviating the smart of his wounds and greatly refreshing him'. With that small ceremony Mariner was accepted into Finau's household. Mafi Habe, one of Finau's wives, was appointed as Mariner's foster mother. She instructed him in Tongan language and customs, ensured he behaved with the decorum required by his position as a young chief, and made sure he was properly provided for and treated with respect.[6]

John Jackson's Pacific landfall was equally traumatic. He was an English seaman who arrived in Samoa with a party of sailors in 1840 on a trading expedition. Although the sailors were initially treated as special visitors of possibly supernatural origins, they were allowed no personal freedom. Shortly after setting foot on shore, Jackson was kidnapped by the natives, who were determined to keep the white man as their own unique 'resident'. Although the sailor tried to return to his ship, he was forcibly detained on shore when the rest of the crew departed:

After the boat's crew were well off from the shore, they [the natives] brought me down to the beach, stripped me of my clothing, and gave me a large tapa, which they said was lelei [good], and faa Samoa [Samoan fashion], and then put me in the fresh water and washed me clean; then led me back to the house and told me to go in first.[7]

With the removal of his clothes, Jackson was stripped of his European culture and his identity as a sailor. He was then subjected to a baptismal washing and cleansing that continued when he was led inside a hut. Oil was taken from a large calabash and wrote Jackson, 'I had the rest of the oil emptied on my head and rubbed on my body, and then they combed my hair on end'. The sailor was not impressed at the Samoans' attempt to make him more 'handsome': 'I cursed them,' he confirmed, 'for pouring so much oil on as nearly to blind me'. The small ceremony was meant to cleanse and purify the newcomer, enabling him to be reborn as an accepted member of the native community with its own set of rules and regulations. It is a story repeated again and again in the narratives of other castaway sailors. They were all reduced to a state of uniformity on arrival – stripped of all weapons and belongings. Their nakedness effectively symbolised their lack of status, rank and role, leaving them unidentifiable except for their white skin. The bathing that followed identified them as blank slates on which a native identity could then be inscribed. Participation in these native rituals, whether voluntary or not, helped all sailors transcend the invisible boundaries that divide one culture from another. It is an anthropological reading that would have been completely nonsensical to the beachcombers themselves, but it helps explain many of the specific and baffling rituals experienced by all castaways.

Mysterious Ceremonies

E. H. Lamont was an Irish businessman and prospective South Seas trader, resident in California, who set sail, in 1852, on a trading voyage to the Pacific. In the company of Dr R., an acquaintance from San Francisco, he took possession of the brig *Chatham*, sailing under Captain George Snow of Nantucket. Lamont went to sea with the intention of making money. He sailed with a cargo of wines, spirits, firearms, tobacco and cloth, which he hoped to trade for sandalwood, oranges and pearls. While he soon began to harbour doubts about the sobriety and professionalism of his captain, the companionship of Dr R. ensured that he enjoyed his first journey to the South Seas. The *Chatham* sailed to the Marquesas and the Society Islands, establishing trading contacts in Nukuhiva, Tahiti and Domenica, and then headed for home.

Unfortunately, Lamont's fears about the captain's abilities proved correct. On the night of 6 January 1853, when the ship was just offshore of the Penrhyn Islands, he retired below to his cabin. He was uneasy about the progress of the ship, in particular its proximity to a number of small islands not marked on the captain's charts, and was unable to sleep. He returned to the deck just in time to feel the ship strike something under the water. Stretching out on either side was a long line of low, black breakers. As the danger of the reef was revealed the crew sprang to attention, but it was too late to save the ship – she was caught by waves and dashed against the rugged banks of coral. Preparations were made to abandon her when a shout from the bows warned of natives approaching the ship. 'We saw them advancing with spears and clubs', recalled Lamont, 'which they brandished, uttering at the same time, the most frightful yells, accompanied by horrid grimaces and contortions.' The islanders began to board the ship. Lamont was horrified to see 'a savage face peer above the rail on the quarter, near where I stood'. Brandishing his sword he swiped at the man who immediately dropped into the sea. At every point around the rails, the islanders attempted to climb on board. When attacked, they would fall back into the water and then recommence their climb. The sailors began to throw things from the ship thus distracting the intruders who dived after the goods and took them to shore.

One of the men on board was a native of Aitutaki (one of the Cook Islands) who attempted to communicate with the islanders. After some discussion, he was able to confirm that the sailors would be welcomed on shore, in return for the coconuts stored on the ship. But arrival on land was not the end of their trials. The sailors were taken under guard to a bleak clearing of land filled with weeds (identified by Lamont as a 'mara' or sacred ground). The mara, located deep in the shade of a pandanus grove, was demarcated by huge blocks of coral rock that lay strewn about the area. Because the area was taboo to women and children, the sailors were led forward by the men of the tribe, four of whom rushed into the clearing yelling and brandishing their weapons in what was later discovered to be a cleansing ritual. Once the purification ceremony was completed, two of the men plaited an effigy in the shape of a man from the leaves of the coconut tree. This was presented to the high priest who mounted a rocky altar and thrashed it against a rock until it was destroyed.

Baffled by actions that were totally inexplicable at the time, the frightened sailors were led away to a nearby pool. They were made to strip, bathe and reclothe before being taken back to the beach where the women had congregated. Facing each other in two opposite lines the women began to dance, waving their arms and beating the ground with their feet. A mournful chant, rising to a piercing and unearthly yell, was accompanied by frenzied handclapping which, according to one of the sailors, was 'stimulated by sundry pokes behind from the men's spears'. The frenzy increased in tempo and intensity and as the women became more excited, they began to cut themselves with small clam shells. In the hysteria of the moment, it was not long before their arms, legs and even faces were streaming with blood. Amid all this confusion, the sailors were led back to the mara and were temporarily abandoned. 'I afterwards learned', wrote Lamont, 'that the ceremony through which we had passed was a form of adoption, each of us becoming from that time forth the chosen child of some leading man in the place; standing in the same position to all his relations as his own children.' Until that moment the sailors had no social or cultural status in their new world.

Included in the original edition of Lamont's narrative was an illustration that is reproduced on the following page. Entitled 'A pehu' (ceremonial gathering), the picture shows him seated on a mat between two groups of islanders, in each case the women are sitting cross-legged in front of armed warriors. Lamont is illuminated by a shaft of light that falls between thick rows of palm trees. The light draws attention to his liminal status. He is an isolated individual, symbolically positioned between two groups of people, those behind him and those in front. Although he is the focal point of the picture,

E. H. Lamont at a pehu or ceremonial gathering.

Lamont is nevertheless marginal to the society that surrounds him. He has already been accepted by certain island families and is free to travel to other islands within the Penrhyn group. But as the picture demonstrates, his beach crossings are far from over. His participation in the pehu reinstates him as a traveller from afar and formally re-incorporates him into the community: 'Several of the chiefs made lengthened speeches, accompanied by a short dance, on the conclusion of which they approached the spot where I stood apart and performed the most abject salutations. A mat was then placed in the centre where I was compelled to sit.'

Speaking in Signs

Their first steps on native soil took the beachcombers towards another reality – a place where their traditional roles and historical understandings no longer carried the same weight and meaning. When cultures first come into contact, the dividing lines are sharp and distinct; attention is drawn to all that is strange and different. For any meaningful interaction to occur, those divisions have to be softened. Barriers to understanding and communication have to be lowered. In the absence of a shared language and history, Europeans and islanders were forced to communicate by signs. They relied on what they hoped was a shared human response to a universal gestural language. But signs can be unstable and cross-cultural encounters were a risky business. Sailors might have been familiar with Crusoe's fictional deployment of signs that were easily made and readily understood by Friday – his demonstration of the master–slave dichotomy – but these did not work on Pacific islands. There was some recognisable consistency between various trappings of power, though. Figures of authority and symbols of power could be understood across both cultures. Westerners could readily identify the prestige of the native rulers while the chiefs, in turn, had no difficulty recognising the status and authority of captains or expedition leaders. But other symbols and gestures did not always share the same significance. It soon became apparent that new signs had to be formulated for the unique particularities of Pacific–European encounters.

E. H. Lamont, for instance, was forced to extemporise in an unexpected meeting with an unfamiliar party of islanders in Tongareva (present-day Penrhyn in the Cook Islands). He had slipped away from his adoptive family and was resting under the shade of a coconut tree when he saw a group of strangers approaching. As they drew near, he stepped out in front of them. The women and children screamed in fright at the unexpected sight of a white man and ran for protection into the undergrowth. The men, however, 'threw themselves at once into an attitude of defence, brandishing their spears in a threatening manner'. In the face of native hostility and personal danger, Lamont improvised:

> To run away, or even evince fear under such circumstances, would have been to provoke instant death, for if I had fled their spears would undoubtedly have been sent after me. I therefore put on as pleasant a face as I could, and held out my hand in a frank conciliatory manner. They hesitated about making too ready an acquaintance; but as I approached within reach, they, one after the other, placed their hands in mine, giving the back instead of the palm to my grasp, showing that they were unacquainted with our manner of salutation.[8]

He was lucky. In this instance his 'pleasant face' and 'conciliatory manner' were recognised as signs of friendship and peace and the men accepted him into their group. Other sailors were not so successful.

When William Cary and a small group of shipwrecked sailors approached the Fijian island of Vatoa, they did so with a great deal of trepidation. It might be recalled that Cary was the lucky sailor who survived the brutal massacre of his shipmates, a horrific event that, at this point in time, still lay ahead of them. For the moment, the men were uncertain of their welcome and fearful of the islanders' violent reputation. As they approached the waiting natives, they were subject to a bewildering display of actions, gestures and signs:

> Seeing us hesitate the man beckoned to us in a friendly manner to row along the beach, which we did, until we came opposite a landing. Seeing a number of natives sitting in the grass and apparently making hostile demonstrations, we again paused for consultation . . . Mr Shaw, however, urged that the natives showed no signs of hostility, that what we had taken to be clubs and spears was nothing more than sugar cane that they had brought down to treat us. . . .
>
> Seeing our hesitation, the natives sent one of the oldest of their party out in a small canoe. He paddled off until within a few feet of us but said nothing. We had the New Zealand boy in our boat, and the captain told him to address the native in his language, which he did, but our visitor did not understand him, and soon returned to the shore. Supposing he was sent off to invite us to land, we concluded to do so.[9]

Mr Shaw was right. The islanders did indeed hold sugar canes rather than spears and clubs, but the sailors' hesitation was only to be expected. Without understanding the language, they were unable to communicate. Even the New Zealand (Maori) boy proved ineffectual in this respect. The sailors' lack of local knowledge placed them at a severe disadvantage where misunderstanding or misinterpretation could mean instant death. They tried to 'read' the activities taking place around them but they failed to recognise the danger they were exposed to. Even after the massacre occurred, Cary was still unable to understand what had happened and why: 'I several times endeavored to learn some particulars in regard to the massacre, but they did not wish to talk about it and would only say that they had nothing to do with it. I did not understand their language and could only learn from them what they were disposed to tell me by signs.'

Dispossession and Loss

Other sailors were similarly confused. On the evening of 21 March 1831, a storm blew up off the north end of Tackanova (Vanua Levu). Lying off shore at the time was a 310-tonne ship, the *Glide* of Salem, which was on a trading voyage to the South Seas. Most of her crew was young and a number were green-hands, all under the command of Captain Henry Archer. One of the young men on board was the third mate, William Endicott, a twenty-two-year-old sailor on his second sea voyage. The *Glide* had weathered a number of storms previously and had been lucky to escape without serious damage. This time she was not so fortunate. Ferocious gales forced the ship to drag her anchors for a distance of nearly 13 kilometres before she was finally driven onto one of the many unmarked reefs surrounding the perilous Fijian coastline. Leaving the ship to save their lives, Endicott and his fellow crew members were eventually washed ashore. Their moment of landfall is described as follows:

> We soon met with a party of mountaineers, exceedingly fierce, who robbed us of our clothes, hardly leaving each one with a single garment, it not being in our power to prevent them, and leaving us exposed to the storm, without any shelter and perfectly ignorant of the road to the King's town, nor would any one of them be prevailed upon to show us the way.[10]

As soon as they set foot on shore the sailors were dispossessed and humiliated. They had lost their ship, their cargo and their belongings in the shipwreck. They were stripped of their clothes, their weapons and their dignity when they arrived on land. They found there was little safety in numbers. They were powerless against the islanders who simply took what they wanted and who were able to do so because of the power dynamics at work on the islands. To those who survive a shipwreck, the beach is their sanctuary and salvation. But the sailors soon realised that it was also a testing ground. Forgotten by their own world and displaced from their own culture, the sailors had to familiarise themselves with a completely 'foreign' set of social expectations.

This was not Endicott's first Pacific landfall nor his first contact with Fijian natives. The *Glide* had been collecting and curing bêche-le-mer on other parts of the Fijian coast, but it was his first meeting with a group of natives from the inland mountain regions – a group for whom the sailors were a new and unknown quantity. These natives were fierce and uncompromising. To them the strangers on the beach were marginal beings. They did not belong to any traditional or historical realm of experience. They were strangers from the sea, washed up on island shores. They were stripped and exposed naked to the storm, herded together and led to the nearest village. The sailors' unfamiliarity with the terrain made their journey long and frightening. Upon arrival at the village they learned that the king and his men had gone to plunder the ship and had taken everything except 'the salt provisions and bread'. Two days later, after the wind had abated and the storm had died down, the king returned and the sailors learned their fate. Fortunately, their lives were to be spared and they were given accommodation in the village.

The stealing of goods and personal possessions described by all castaway sailors was a pan-Polynesian trait. It was linked to a system of distribution, the control of which was a chiefly prerogative. Only the chief, as the most powerful member of the community, had the power to bestow goods and favours. His personal prestige rested on his generosity and on his ability to command the resources that supplied that generosity.[11] As one beachcomber commented, 'It forms an important part of the religion of this island to consider every thing that arrives there, whether of great or little value, as the property of their gods.'[12] It was an experience familiar to Peter Bays, the sailing master on *Minerva*, and a fellow shipmate of John Twyning. He took part in the same shipwreck and participated in the same journey on the overcrowded longboat to Vatoa in search of safety. Twyning, a pious and self-righteous man, was unimpressed with the older sailor. He accused Bays and the two mates of calculated self-interest and claimed they were among the first men to reach the boats: 'They cared not who were lost provided they were saved', he remarked.

Bays' account provides an interesting description of the arrival of the *Minerva* crew on Vatoa Island and their reception by a party of islanders who were 'entirely naked' and who 'indicated much agitation'. All articles and items of clothing (especially shirts and loose-fitting apparel) were taken from the sailors and divided up between their captors. Clothes, hats, jewellery, knives, combs, razors, needles, thread, papers and documents were all confiscated. The sailors could do nothing about native appropriation of their worldly goods. They started to 'feel about our clothing', wrote Bays, and by one means or another, 'they completely plundered us of every useful article, though they might not know the use of it themselves'. The sailors could only sit and watch as their possessions were removed and re-employed in unfamiliar ways:

> The natives had already collected everything they could find about the camp, and had brought the spoils down to the boat to divide amongst them. One had a small tooth comb stuck in his beard; another, his arms through the legs of a pair of drawers; a third, a jacket buttoned up behind; a fourth, a shirt the hinder part before, and another had the broken ring of our boat lantern on his arm.[13]

Crossing the Beach

Castaway sailors stood alone on the beaches of the Pacific. Deprived of the national or institutional authority traditionally associated with their ships and their roles as sailors, they felt isolated, uncertain and fearful. But the trauma of shipwreck and the confusion engendered by those first encounters had an unexpected impact. It provided the sailors with the chance of cultural and social mobility. It stimulated personal creativity and allowed them to create something different for themselves in island society. It forced them to rely on their wit and ingenuity in order to survive. In 1826 James O'Connell, an Irish sailor, displayed a uniquely personal and inventive response to the dangers and drama of landfall. He was eleven years old when he signed on as a cabin boy on the *Phoenix*, a ship chartered by the Government to carry female convicts to Botany Bay.[14] He spent six years in Australia from 1820 to 1826 and then shipped on board a whaling ship, the *John Bull*, leaving Australia and sailing to the Bay of Islands in New Zealand. Eight months later, in a heavy storm, his ship struck a reef near the Caroline Islands (Ponape).

O'Connell's experience is similar to that of Twyning and Bays. Together with five others, he escaped the sinking ship and spent four miserable days in an open boat. When land was finally sighted, the castaways found themselves surrounded by hundreds of canoes full of natives who showered them with stones, arrows and spears. While the boat was being plundered, the men were forcibly escorted to shore, stripped, and led across the beach to a canoe house where they faced a gathering of islanders. They were regarded as curiosities. They were examined and prodded by inquisitive natives who 'took hold of our persons very familiarly . . . and gave frequent clucks of admiration at the blue veins which were marked through our skins'. The sailors were so terrified that 'they gave themselves up as lost' but O'Connell refused to despair. Against the advice of his fellow sailors he decided to try and impress his 'savage audience' by dancing:

> I accordingly sprung to my feet and took an attitude; a cluck of pleasure ran through the savages, and one of them, readily understanding my intention, spread a mat for me. I struck into Garry Owen, and figured away in that famous jig to the best of my ability and agility; and my new acquaintances were amazingly delighted thereat.[15]

This incident is featured in the illustration overleaf that appeared in the pamphlets sold by O'Connell on his return to Europe. The drawing shows him dancing on the shore of the beach and not in the canoe house as described in his narrative. Although it was produced long after the event it describes, it reflects O'Connell's instinctive apprehension of the instability of first encounter. As the stranger from the sea, he is located symbolically between the sea (with his five anxious companions waiting in the background), and the forbidding natives, fully armed and ranked in front of him. He obviously recalls the terror, uncertainty and thrill of the moment. He is positioned

James O'Connell saved his life dancing for the Ponapeans.
Unsure of his welcome, the sailor improvised a demonstration
in order to gain the favour of his native hosts.

precariously between two opposed and distinct worlds, literally
dancing for his life.

When a shipwrecked sailor took his first steps across an unknown
beach towards a new cultural reality, he embarked on a monumental
journey. He did not know what to expect and he did not expect what
he found. 'The fact was', wrote John Twyning of his relationship with
the Fijians, 'we were ignorant of each other's language, our wants and
wishes were but imperfectly communicated to each other . . . [and]
actions were often misinterpreted.' The sailors' expectations and
preconceptions may well have been born of traditional myth-making,

but it soon gave way to the reality of island existence. Initially, their journeys were marked by dispossession and loss. They lost their clothes, their weapons, their papers, their books, their names and their contact with home. They lost a world that told them who they were and how to behave. In dramatic fashion they were forced to confront the relativity of their social and cultural identity. They had to find new ways of thinking about the world and their places in it. Their first steps towards a new life may have been hesitant and uncertain. They may have faltered along the way. But for all our castaways those iconic first encounters were only the beginning of their long and hazardous journey towards total integration.

CHAPTER SIX

Strategies for Survival:
The Mechanics of Going Native

He loomed up through the mist, shadowy and gigantic,
a drunken dissipated south sea Rip Van Winkle, an
empty bottle in his hand.

JULIAN THOMAS, *Cannibals and Convicts*

Going native was a fundamental prerequisite for beachcomber survival.
The more the sailors conformed to the customs and manners of their
hosts, the more likely they were to live in safety. But the process
of becoming at home in an alien culture, of subjugating a Western
identity for a native one, has long been regarded with distrust and
suspicion. Joseph Conrad, for instance, explores Western response
to the spectre of white savagery in his novel *Heart of Darkness*.
Published in 1902, his tale of Kurtz, the European chief of station
who discovered his own 'heart of darkness' in the depths of Africa,
is deeply concerned with the perils of going native. Although it tells
the story of a civilised man's descent into barbarism in the African
continent, adventuring sailors of the South Seas would have also been
able to identify with some of the physical and psychological dangers.
The novel explores the fragility of European identity, authority and
control on the borders of the unknown. It portrays the struggle against
moral dissolution at the outposts of empire. Wherever it occurred – in
the African interior, the Indian islands or on an atoll in the South Seas

– a white man's reversion to a state of savagery was something to be feared and despised. It was a universally felt concern, particularly relevant to those Western powers with imperial aspirations. How does a civilised man retain his moral integrity when surrounded by savages? How does he perpetuate the values of the European centre, an ideology of progress and enlightenment, when his life and work take him into primitive worlds? Civilising the savages was seen to be a physically perilous and psychologically hazardous business. Conrad's story explores the vulnerability and corruptibility of men who find themselves in dangerous isolation – men who succumb to the 'fascination of the abomination'.[1]

Kurtz was such a man. His journey into Africa took him somewhere else entirely. 'You lost your way on that river', mused Conrad's narrator, 'till you thought yourself bewitched and cut off for ever from everything you had known once – somewhere – far away – in another existence perhaps.' Kurtz's river led him into the darkness of his own desires, into the deepest blackness of his soul. It took him beyond the imperatives of Western civilisation towards a more ancient understanding of life. Kurtz was a man, reduced by climate, alienation and solitude, to the level of the savages around him. His story is a parable of the 'night journey'; a solitary voyage of mythical proportions that always involves a profound spiritual change. In classical form it is an archetypal descent into the bowels of the earth, or the depths of the sea, followed by a return to the light. Night journeys are spiritual journeys of self-discovery, voyages into the subconscious. They move through darkness before they approach the light. Descent is always followed by restoration and return.

Except in Kurtz's story. Described as an extraordinary individual and a courageous idealist, Kurtz was nevertheless overcome by the 'mysterious life of the wilderness' and by the power of savagery. His long, solitary years were lived without the promptings of a socially informed European conscience. They were spent in 'utter silence, where no warning voice of a kind neighbour could be heard whispering of public opinion'. He suffered a moral relapse through his dislocation from home and his spiritual isolation in the heart of Africa. Inhibitions fell away, lifelong reserves were broken. Like the ex-missionary George Vason in the Pacific, he 'lacked restraint in the gratification of his desires'. Kurtz lost himself as a European. He was known to have taken part in 'certain midnight dances ending with unspeakable rites'. His station house in the interior was surrounded by human heads impaled on fence posts, grisly reminders of the barbaric acts that enforced his supremacy. He was a man assaulted by the powers of darkness and ultimately unable to repel them. He had seen into the heart of life, he had plumbed its depths, and named it a 'horror'.

Kurtz's story reflects a very deep and abiding concern about the fragility of European identity. The key image is one of regression. Any adaptation to an alien, foreign or savage way of life is seen as an irretrievable loss. The European loses his culture and identity, he is deprived of the benefits of civilisation, he is morally and spiritually impoverished. Kurtz's story demonstrates the great abyss that exists between human ideals and human practice. It is a chasm that few wished to confront within themselves. The issues raised by the fictional Kurtz were the same as those faced by the historical beachcomber one hundred years earlier. When the castaway sailor crossed the boundary that divided the tourist from the 'transculturist', he compromised himself in the eyes of his European contemporaries. He was no longer a detached observer (the ideal model for a European traveller), and became, like Kurtz, an active participant in a foreign culture. 'It is an undoubted fact that when a white man becomes an outcast, lives with savages, and adopts their manner of life, he soon sinks into such a state of barbarism that he becomes the greater savage of the two', one contemporary commentator asserted.[2]

Kurtz's nativisation was seen as a weakness of character. Conrad described him as 'hollow at the core', unable to withstand the tide of corruption that surrounded him. The disapprobation of the Pacific white-man-gone-native shares the same psychological roots. Any willing assimilation of the culture and language of another was seen as a withdrawal from the growth and dynamism associated with Western civilisation. It symbolised degeneration and regression. It spoke of an abandonment of control, self-discipline and virtue.[3] But going native was more complicated than that. The high incidence of shipwreck suggests that sailors did not turn their backs on civilisation as much as they were wrenched from it. And once on island shores, they had to conform to survive. Many died because they failed to do so; others learned their lessons after narrow escapes. The reality facing the captain and crew of the *Antelope*, shipwrecked on the Palau Islands in 1783, is relevant to all castaways: 'They [knew] nothing of the inhabitants of that country; . . . [were] ignorant of their manners and dispositions; . . . they found themselves, by this sudden accident, cut off at once from the rest of the world, with little probability of their ever again getting away.'[4]

Going native stripped the sailor of his ethnocentrism. He faced a cultural crisis in order to survive. He had to forfeit those everyday thoughts and actions that enforced the difference between his original culture and island society. He could not rely on personal relations and cultural forms that he had previously taken for granted. He was confused, directionless and overwhelmed. Beachcomber narratives showed that going native is a complicated psychological and physical process encompassing a number of different stages, all of which involved the participants in a constant process of education. They had to familiarise themselves with different concepts and rules of classification, new gestures and language, new rituals and patterns of behaviour, and new ways of understanding the world and their place in it. Success or failure depended on a number of variables: the mode of arrival; the age at which assimilation into that culture began; the beachcomber's previous attitude to the host culture; the length of their residence; their personal motivation and individual temperament; and the nature of the roles they played in that culture.[5] Going native was not the inevitable consequence of a simple decision to conform to the customs and manners of a particular society. Rather, it was a complex procedure played out across a wide variety of literal and metaphorical boundaries – a dangerous journey into unknown waters with no guarantee of safe harbour.

The moment he crossed the beach (whether through choice or by chance), the beachcomber lost something of his former self. His search for a new and stable identity demanded that he conform to the patterns and rhythms of a different way of life. He did so when all hopes of

Fijian men outside a native hut in the late 1800s. Beachcombers in Fiji were expected to fully conform to the customs and manners of their native hosts.

escape were gone. There is a moment in all beachcomber accounts that centres on that loss of hope – the realisation that rescue is unlikely and a return to Europe a lost dream. The sailors embraced island life with a greater level of enthusiasm only when they decided to accept their fate. They resigned themselves to the rhythms and pace of their new life by distancing themselves mentally from the concerns of the rest of the world – a characteristic noted by an observer of the time: 'The want of curiosity about passing events, and indifference to the past and future, seem to be the necessary conditions of the adoption of the half-civilised style of life by Europeans.'[6]

Learning the Language

The first step in any act of assimilation is mastery of the language. Life was easier and more rewarding when a sailor could speak as a local, and linguistic proficiency typically took between seven months and a year.[7] But from the perspective of a seafaring captain, for instance, the acquisition of a new language was a dangerous undertaking. It was an important first step towards integration and a willing act of submission to the exigencies of a foreign way of life.[8] As always, the exploits of James Morrison and the *Bounty* mutineers prove instructive. The sailors had learned some basic Tahitian in the five months that they spent in Matavai Bay collecting their cargo of breadfruit. Lieutenant Bligh, keen to deflect attention away from his own accountability, believed that their growing identification with Tahitian life was one of the causes of the mutiny. After long months at sea with a dictatorial captain, the sailors were enamoured of land. Some had formed emotional attachments on shore, and all revelled in the contrast between island life and naval discipline. Tahiti offered them the bounty of food, comfort and companionship that their lives at sea could not. For a few brief months they forgot who they were. They crossed the beach emotionally as well as physically and allowed themselves to be distracted by the pleasures of island life. Their immersion in that life was reflected in their grasp of the language. They found new ways to express themselves as they learned new words for a new way of life. This was a potentially anarchic act. It was a commonly held fear that a European immersed in a foreign language was automatically accepting of the beliefs and practices expressed in that language. To eighteenth-century minds speaking like a native comes perilously close to thinking like a native. Instead of focusing on all that keeps them apart, the European begins to recognise all that they have in common. The dividing line between self and other becomes dangerously blurred.[9]

This was nowhere more apparent than in the figure of Jean Cabri, that heavily tattooed French beachcomber that so scandalised von Krusenstern's Russian expedition on their arrival in the Marquesas in 1804. It was not his tattooed body that shocked them, although the extent of his savage markings was regarded with a mixture of awe and disgust; it was not his semi-nakedness, the cloth around his waist and the feathers on his head; it was not his adoption of native gestures and body postures that demonstrated his true level of assimilation; rather it was the fact that he had almost forgotten his native tongue. His first words to the Russians were, '*Moi beaucoup françois. Americanish ship. Uh damson la Carmagnolè*'.[10] He had forgotten who he was, where he had come from and the name of his parents. It took him a long time to remember his own name. His absorption of Marquesan society was such that he never wanted to leave. Cabri was given a good quality shirt by the visiting Russians, which he promptly exchanged for an inferior red jacket. Red is the colour worn only by the tapu class, as Cabri well knew. It was a colour he valued as highly as did the islanders. He revelled in his unexpected windfall. Putting the jacket on, he began to dance, 'capering and jumping in a most extraordinary manner', according to the astonished Russians, with feathers in his hair and a lance in his hand.[11] Marquesan life had become his life. His ease with the language was a telling indication of the true extent of his integration. By forgetting the French language, he forgot France and he forgot his Western self. To all intents and purposes he had ceased to be European.

Family Ties

Another important step on the road to assimilation involved marriage. All sailors understood that by choosing to marry, they solidified and expanded the network of family ties already established by their native adoptions. The shipwreck that stranded John Twyning on Vatoa Island in 1829 was the starting point for an island sojourn of nearly twenty years, during which time he moved freely between various island groups. Recognising the economic opportunities offered by the profitable bêche-le-mer trade, Twyning and his companion John Jones decided to build their own schooner and go into business for themselves. The decision was made in 1837, about eight years after Twyning's shipwreck, and with it he committed himself to a future life in the islands. He had given up hope of returning to his homeland. He was no longer fit to work on whalers and he had failed several times to buy a passage to Europe. 'Thus, thinking I was doomed to remain on the islands for life, I conceived it a duty I owed to myself to endeavour to make that life more comfortable.' Comfort, prestige and security on the islands meant marriage. Twyning's native wife Twochillow was the daughter of a priestess and a minor chief. She was brought to him painted with a dye made of curry powder and coconut oil:

> while I can't say this . . . improved her personal appearance . . . I had determined not to oppose any of the customs of the people, so I took her to my home, and thus ended this important transaction, and I never had any reason to repent my engagement.[12]

Native women, as wives or mothers, played an important role in the integration of beachcombers.[13] They were frequently used as property. They were given as rewards for service or to reinforce friendship and loyalty. Nearly all beachcombers married, or at least cohabited with native women. This was more common in those islands whose leaders were eager to foster relationships with Europeans. Chiefs such as Kamehameha in Hawaii and Finau in Tonga were quick to recognise and utilise the skills of the sailors – brickmaking, farming, weaving, distilling – and their knowledge and possession of firearms. They were keen to ensure the loyalty of the Europeans by means of marriage. The matter was easily arranged and the sailors required little encouragement. The beachcomber was promised a greater level of personal comfort and security if he was a member of a family. He was ensured full membership in society and enmeshed in a wide range of family concerns and commitments. Marriage also gave him a claim on the obligations of others. In Polynesia a man without a wife, and without the wide range of relations that came with her, was, in effect, a non-person. He was an oddity within the community and often an object of ridicule. Marriage effectively tied the white man to his native community. He was not free to leave or to change allegiance, as his immediate family became potential hostages for his good behaviour and loyalty.[14]

Marriage was also connected to status. Few beachcombers married high-ranking women unless their own status within the native community was semi-royal or influential in some other way. Some beachcombers were presumed to have higher status than others. The Tongans for example believed William Mariner to be the son of the captain, which elevated him in their eyes, while others such as E. H. Lamont gained their status by their perceived influence over other sailors. However, those sailors who arrived on shore destitute and powerless, without the authority granted them by their ships or captains, were extremely unlikely to be offered aristocratic women. Often their loutish behaviour and lack of resources also prejudiced the chiefs against them. The best they could aspire to were women of lower status who were easy to obtain and easy to leave. As always there are exceptions. George Vason married the niece of his chiefly patron a few weeks after leaving the mission. His novelty status and his popularity with his chief ensured his preferential treatment. James Read, a sailor stranded on Tonga twenty years later, was also fortunate to receive the patronage of a high-ranking chief who 'took a liking to me [and] adopted me as his son'. Read found no obstacle to total assimilation and was content to end his days in the islands:

It is now six years ago [since his shipwreck] and though I have twice left to indulge a whim, I have most gladly returned to a mode of life which has become so natural and so pleasant. I am now living in Tonga [tapu], patronized by a chief named Fatou, who has adopted me as his son, – married me to his daughter, and given me a house to live in and land to cultivate: I have also three children, to whose education my life is devoted . . . [15]

Serial marriage and polygamy were common. If a particular wife did not suit, it was easy to return her and take a new one. John Jackson, a typical peripatetic beachcomber and alleged cannibal who became notorious for his island exploits, had a large number of wives on different islands. During the time he spent on Fiji, he acquired another two. His growing level of commitment encouraged him to 'give up the idea of roving', and to settle down in a small village. He planted taro, cultivated land, collected pigs for breeding and fowls for eating, and built a little bure 'for the purpose of taking an afternoon's nap in, and drinking my angona [alcoholic beverage]'. His idyll did not last. Before long he resumed his restless wanderings, leaving his wives with little compunction or regret, claiming only that he was living in 'trying times'. Years later, in Tonga, he entered the marital stakes once more when he agreed to marry the fifteen-year-old daughter of a local chief. He decided to forgo a Christian wedding as 'there were so many other ways of acquiring wives open to me'. The fact that he already had, in his own words, 'six bona fide wives' does not seem to have inhibited him.

Edward Robarts was less acquisitive than Jackson. Robarts, a Welsh sailor, was twenty-seven years old when he deserted from the whaler *New Euphrates* on the Marquesas Islands in December 1798. Conditions on the ship were unstable and in the face of incipient mutiny Robarts preferred to take his chances on shore. He was lucky to have the help of a Hawaiian beachcomber named Tom, who eased his transition from ship to shore by introducing him to Marquesan society. Robarts was a great novelty. He was one of the few white men the islanders had ever seen, and his introduction by a person known to the islanders ensured he was treated with kindness and respect. The sailor soon integrated into the native way of life. He rejoiced in his improved social status, his freedom from the back-breaking labour of a sailor, and in the warm and hospitable island climate. He believed that his future lay in the islands and he decided to marry.

His wife was the sister of the high chief of the valley and with his marriage he secured a large tract of land and further political and social influence. He built a house, planted crops and wrote, 'I pass away my time with my lovely consort in a state of true happiness.' In his journal, dated 27 May 1804, he recorded the following:

> Just after sun rise, my royal consort was deliverd of a fine daughter. I was at the back of the house. On hearing the child, I started out of my store pitt and ran to the house. No midwife being at hand, I did the office myself . . . My tinder box and dry wood was ready in case of a squall in the night. I cutt the navel string and securd it, sent the child to rest, made some gruel and sent of the news to my Brother in Law. The family wish me much Joy, and they repaird to my Cottage and was much pleasd at their new relation.

Robarts acted as midwife in the births of his other two daughters (he also fathered two sons) and remained with his Marquesan wife till her death in 1813.

The Mark of the Native

Going native required the eradication of all points of difference. The European was more likely to survive if he became as much like the natives as possible. The most dramatic step in this direction was the adoption of a tattoo, the Polynesian mark of manhood. In Pacific societies it was a necessary step to full social membership. A non-tattooed man was a visibly marginal man. In the eyes of his native hosts, he was not fully a man and not fully a member of the island community.[16] Sailors who wished to cement their alliances with powerful families voluntarily submitted to the operation. But even unwilling sailors were forced to endure painful operations that left them bleeding and swollen. George Vason agreed to be tattooed because he 'determined no longer to be singular and the object of ridicule'. He was pleased with the result: 'When it was completed I was very much admired by the natives, as the European skin displays the blue colour, and the ornaments of tattooing to very great advantage: I looked indeed very gay in this new fancy covering.'

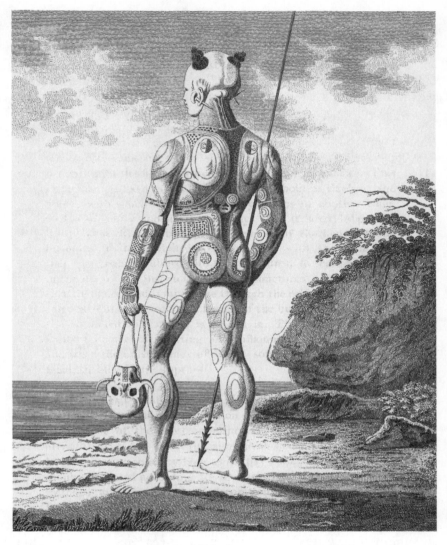

A Marquesan warrior with the full body tattoo worn by all Marquesan men.

During the five years he spent among the Ponapeans (the Caroline Islands), James O'Connell, the Irish sailor who 'danced for his life' when he first encountered the natives, became fully assimilated, complete with a full body tattoo. His companion George Keenan was unable to countenance either the discomfort or the ignominy of being branded so permanently, and was not so obliging. The operation was a gruelling ordeal. Both O'Connell and Keenan were taken by canoe to a mysterious dwelling place hidden away on the banks of a creek, unaware of what was planned for them. The entrance way was completely arched over with trees and O'Connell recalled 'the scene was romantic, and would have been pleasing, if we had not been so utterly in the dark as to the purpose of the journey'. They were soon to find out. The men were taken to opposite ends of the hut by small groups of native women who then began a complicated operation. O'Connell's left hand was raised into the light and the flesh drawn tightly across it. A pattern was traced upon his hand in ink. One of the women produced a small flat piece of wood with thorns pierced through one end that were then dipped in black liquid. The points of the thorns were placed on the marks upon his hand where, with a sudden blow from a stick, they were driven into his flesh. The pain was intense but O'Connell bore it stoically. His friend did not. Keenan 'swore and raved without any attention to rule; the way he did it was profane, but not syntactical or rhetorical'.

O'Connell's torture continued for an hour and a half until his left hand was covered with decorative lines and patterns. Before they left, the women smeared the swollen hand with coconut oil and then patted pulverised coal dust on it. This process was repeated until there was a thick crust of coal dust and oil completely concealing the flesh. (Charcoal was commonly used as a healing agent for the skin.) Later the same afternoon, the women returned and the tattooing continued on his left arm. The next morning his hand had swollen to twice its usual size and the red and tender flesh was blackened and begrimed with charcoal and soot. Keenan, in the meantime, adamantly refused to submit to any further operations. For reasons that were later made clear, his wishes were acceded to and he was spared any further ordeals. O'Connell was not so lucky and over the course of the next eight days he was tattooed extensively over his legs, back, abdomen, hands and arms. At the same time all his body hair was plucked out with sea shells – 'a process which was performed as expeditiously upon my person as the same ground can be cleared of pin-feathers on geese by a dextrous cook'. He described both processes as acutely painful and it took a month before his skin healed and he was able to leave the hut. He returned in triumph to the meeting house 'a bird of much more diversified plumage' than he was a month earlier. Before he could partake in the feast that awaited him, he had to undergo one further trial. He was approached by a daughter of the chief who tattooed a ring on his right breast, another on his left shoulder and two on his right arm, a ceremony that identified the unwitting sailor as her future husband.

O'Connell's wife was fourteen years of age 'affectionate, neat, faithful, and barring too frequent an indulgence in the flesh of baked dogs, which would give her breath something of a canine odor, she was a very agreeable consort'. He obviously adapted to the peculiarities of his wife's diet as he became the father of two 'pretty little demi-savages', a boy and a girl. His elaborate tattooing furthered his island connections and accorded him a higher status than his companion. Keenan was provided with a wife, 'but his unwillingness to submit to the process of tattooing wedded him to a woman of no rank', recalled O'Connell. The Irishman was treated with greater respect. His tattoos were visible evidence of his wholesale acceptance of native life and they told other islanders of his connection to the family of Ahoundel, his chiefly father-in-law. They were 'better than letters of introduction' and provided him with access to other families of wealth and status.

Not all beachcombers were so tolerant of native practices and some were fiercely opposed to any procedure such as tattooing that would leave them marked for life. Horace Holden, the young New England seaman-turned-beachcomber on the Palaus, was terrified at the threat of a tattoo: 'We expostulated against it – we entreated – we begged to be spared this additional affliction; but our entreaties were of no use.' Because he was an unwilling participant, his experience was more brutal than that of O'Connell. He was spread out and tied to the ground while patterns were drawn on his skin. It was then thickly punctured with a little instrument made of sharpened fish bones 'somewhat resembling a carpenter's adz in miniature, but having teeth, instead of a smooth, sharp edge'. The teeth were held within a few centimetres of his flesh and struck repeatedly with a piece of wood, causing them to rebound at every stroke. Because of the resultant inflammation, only small areas could be done at a time, although the operation continued until the entire body was covered. Holden despondently confirmed that 'to this day the figures remain as distinct as they were when first imprinted, and the marks will be carried by us to the grave'. His body hair, including his beard, was also plucked out every ten days – an extremely painful procedure, according to all the afflicted sailors. Holden refused to submit to facial tattooing regarding it as the ultimate disfigurement. He was deeply apprehensive about returning to Europe bearing his exotic experiences visibly on his body. On the islands, however, his options were limited:

> The fashion of wearing a skin so white as ours, seemed to them, no doubt, to be an offence against the taste and refinement of their portion of the world. To go at large without being tattooed, was to carry with us the palpable proofs of our vulgarity; and, to our sorrow, we were afterwards compelled to conform to the custom of the barbarians in this respect.[17]

Actions necessary for survival in Pacific communities were not always understood or accepted in Europe. Many sailors regarded the tattoo as visible proof of their exotic adventures. They were the indelible costume of an erstwhile role now assumed in perpetuity – the nineteenth-century version of a holiday T-shirt.[18] But a social accessory on one side of the beach was seen as a social stigma on the other. To Western eyes, the tattoo was the ultimate marker of beachcomber degeneration. It was indisputable and irreversible evidence of his nativisation, representing the sailor's shameful desire to be accepted on native terms by looking the same as those around him. To be tattooed was not only to become native – it was to cease to be Western.[19] Tattoos were a mark of permanence from a place of passage, and they irrevocably identified those who bore them as 'savages'. Contemporary accounts report that women and children screamed in horror when they passed James O'Connell on the streets after he returned to civilisation, settling in America in 1833. Ministers speaking from the pulpit warned that unborn children would bear his horrific markings if he was seen by pregnant women. O'Connell's tattoos spoke of the savage rites and unspeakable horrors that occurred far from the safety of the civilised world. As a native white man, he symbolised the exoticism of far-flung savage places. He embodied all the misconceptions, fears and prejudices associated with the 'idea' of the Pacific island savage.

King of the Savages

One of those misconceptions was based on a prevalent European fantasy about the white man as king of the savages. That desire was founded on a myth of Western mastery and domination, appealing to men like the beachcombers, who lived outside the limits of European regulation and control. Its roots lay in the belief that white men, with their muskets and their technological 'superiority', could establish a power base for themselves in the midst of heathens. Herman Melville's description of the Marquesan beachcomber, Lem Hardy, encapsulates that gun-toting mythology:

> He had gone ashore as a sovereign power, armed with a musket and a bag of ammunition, and ready, if need were, to prosecute war on his own account. The country was divided by the hostile kings of several large valleys. With one of them, from whom he first received overtures, he formed an alliance, and became what he now was, the military leader of the tribe, and war-god of the entire island.[20]

Melville's white 'war-god' epitomises the illicit appeal of all outlaw characters. Hardy anticipates Conrad's Kurtz, who broke away from tradition by creating a new role and a new 'kingdom' for himself in the wilds of Africa. He was fearless, imaginative and curious – the same traits required by any beach-crossing sailor struggling to solve the mysteries of an unknown culture. Kurtz was an educated and civilised man who used his intelligence and his gun to reign over his dark empire. 'Everything belonged to him', wrote Conrad. There was no one to stop him; he had taken a 'high seat amongst the devils of the land'. His effect on the natives, many of whom had never come into contact with any European, was profound. 'He came to them with thunder and lightning . . . and they had never seen anything like it.'

His displays of might and power forced an obeisance from a primitive people who feared and worshipped him.

Freed from the restraints of Europe, the beachcombers may have harboured dreams of white supremacy in the islands, of building strongholds and establishing themselves as Pacific potentates. But it was a myth of European power and control that was challenged by the political reality of the islands themselves. Although beachcombers were sometimes credited with having influence over the wars and politics of island cultures, their roles in military upheavals have been exaggerated.[21] Real power lay in the hands of the chiefs, and European dreams of island kingdoms remained a fantasy only. Some beachcombers did become trusted and valued advisors and were honoured with the title prime minister or privy councillor. However, those titles still managed to overlook the subsidiary role played by white men, even with muskets. Beachcombers' every course of action depended on native patronage. Warfare was one of the ways they could justify their worth to their adoptive community, and most men were happy enough to oblige. They fought on behalf of their chiefs and were expected to fulfil the same duties as other adult men in the community. When they performed well, they were rewarded with status and influence, but they were not appointed to positions that would give them authority over groups of islanders, as this might have challenged the ultimate authority of the chief. They had no personal power base and could not use their positions to fuel their own militaristic ambitions. They had little or no possibility for independent action, let alone empire building. Chiefs may have relied on the advice of beachcombers from time to time, but they did not have matters decided for them. The only kings on Pacific islands were native ones.

It is true, though, that the role of warrior was an important one in the sailors' route to full assimilation. Edward Robarts cemented his position in the Marquesas by becoming a warrior. The Marquesans were a warlike people and Robarts got plenty of experience beginning with an early skirmish in which he was hit by a stone from a sling. It caught him just underneath his right eye, piercing his cheek and knocking two upper teeth into his mouth. Rather than let the local 'surgeon' probe his wound with a shark's-tooth lance, he decided to let the wound heal itself, leaving himself with a distinctive scar.[22] Despite such injuries, he enjoyed the excitement of battle, and his vivid descriptions of various encounters reflect his enthusiasm for the role of warrior. He describes himself as resourceful and courageous, suggesting that his superior tactical sense brought victory to his own side:

> I took particular remarks of every place either to advance or retreat. I pointed out [the islanders'] errors as they are under no form of order every one acting as he thinks best . . . I made them to understand first for the women and old men to withdraw to a place pointed out, and then dispatch a strong party with plenty of stones and spears to take their post in ambush at a certain place so advantageous to us that it could not fail.[23]

Robarts' plan may have been successful in this particular instance, but his repeated suggestions had little long-term effect on Marquesan battle strategy, which consisted of a relatively inconsequential round of advances and retreats. Petty feuds and raids were frequent but minor, and despite Robarts' assertions the influence of beachcombers like himself on island politics was negligible.

He did, however, fulfil a valuable service as an intermediary, enabling him to present himself as a Great White Man among the savages. In his European life he was a common seaman – a 'little man' in his own estimation. Island life gave him a chance to become something greater than he was. He participated in a number of raids on behalf of his adoptive family and served his chief faithfully. His greatest achievement, in his own eyes, was the service he was able to perform for visiting ships. 'I had the pleasure of Making myself particularly usefull to several ships that touched at this place,' he boasted. He acted as pilot, he provided food and supplies and he facilitated trade with the Marquesans. His role as intermediary was important, as he helped avoid potentially fatal contacts between Europeans and islanders through his local knowledge. When going aboard the ships he was often taken for a native: 'My beard was very long; it coverd my breast, for I had not been shaved for about 3 years. My skin [was] tand with the sun.' His sense of self-importance is obvious:

. . . the thoughts of doing good, which was and I hope ever will be, uppermost in my mind, debard me at present from returning to society; for assisting of the weary navigator was ceartainly of the greatest Importance to commerce, and commerce is the glory & support of nations. I could do more with a wave or beckon of the hand then the force of arms could accomplish. I was little in myself, but my mind was great. I never lookd at a steep Mountain, but I reachd its summit.[24]

For the most part, long-time beachcombers, such as Robarts, made the best of their sojourns on the islands. But even those who achieved a high level of assimilation could never completely forget their old lives. The psychological barriers to full integration were hard to overthrow. Although Robarts had lived happily with his Marquesan friends and family for seven years he was emotionally overcome when he found an old sea chest belonging to an earlier beachcomber. The man in question was William Pascoe Crook, a missionary from the *Duff*, who had been left in the islands early in 1797 in an abortive attempt to convert the natives. Crook spent a lonely year in Vaitahu before moving to Nukuhiva on the other side of the island. The remnants of his stay – an old sea chest, some medicine, a Bible, an old pair of black breeches and a journal full of letters – are all that remained of his two-year sojourn. They were insignificant items in every way, but to Robarts they were powerful reminders of his own status as a forsaken and forgotten European. The sad mementoes reinforced his own loneliness – they reminded him of his displacement from home, from family and from others like himself. Robarts was a typical beachcomber, conforming in all respects to the cultural practices and beliefs of his hosts. He made the best of his unforeseen situation by creating something worthwhile out of his island experiences. But his journal revealed that his triumphant metamorphosis from European to native was not without its own particular sort of sacrifice:

This discovery [of the sea chest] gave me a great deal of unesiness. I could not tell what to think. By the date of some of his papers he had been abscent about eight months. At times I was verry unhappy, Sometimes I thought he had died; other times I thought he had been murdered . . .

Often I would weep in some secret place. How much did I regret the loss
of the company of this good young man.

Living with natives, learning their language and becoming tattooed
was not about a descent into savagery. Nor was it a joyous abandonment
of the European self to the savage pleasures of the primitive. That
obsession reveals more about Western fascination for those, like
Conrad's Kurtz, who are seen to have exceeded the boundaries of
civilised behaviour. Going native required an acceptance of the
reality of another way of life. It demanded an abdication of one's own
ideological beliefs, a suspension of judgement and an awareness of
a connection between the rituals, ceremonies and beliefs of diverse
cultures. In his narratives, the beachcomber often began by focusing
on the bizarre and foreign aspects of island culture. As his knowledge
and experience deepened, he changed direction. He began instead
to highlight the similarities, the commonalities between people and
cultures. He became aware that the native stranger is not other,
merely different. Sailors-turned-beachcombers became relativised by
experiencing life as it might otherwise be lived. A sailor in Fiji wrote
of drinking kava: 'Disgusting as this beverage was to me at first, my
repugnance gradually wore away and after a while I could drink it
with as good a relish as I can now swallow a glass of beer.'[25]

Castaway sailors did not discover their heart of darkness in the
Pacific. They were participants in a complex cultural performance
whereby they adopted specific roles, learned new languages and wore
costumes appropriate to their adopted identities. Their continued
safety depended on their ability to observe, learn, imitate, participate
in and integrate into the life surrounding them. All castaways had to
recognise and negotiate new representations of power and prestige,
and adopt unfamiliar realities as their own. They had to become
something they were not – and they had to do it convincingly. For
beachcombers such as Edward Robarts, James O'Connell and Will
Mariner, the transformation from European to native was a most
dangerous form of theatre. It would prove to be their greatest
performance.

CHAPTER SEVEN

Drama and Role Play in the Life of the Beachcomber

All the world's a stage,
And all the men and women merely players;
They have their exits and their entrances;
And one man in his time plays many parts,
His acts being seven ages.

WILLIAM SHAKESPEARE, *As You Like It*

White men who stepped ashore on Pacific island beaches in the late eighteenth and early nineteenth centuries were confronted by indigenous cultures rich with dramatic shows of power. Many aspects of island life and culture were marked as significant precisely because of the theatre that accompanied them. Processions, speeches, gift-giving and name exchange all formed the backbone of many intercultural confrontations. These displays were highly formal and stylised representations of native might and local authority. Their performance in a specific place and at a specific time differentiated them from the routines of normal everyday life. The drama of those moments made an impact on all who witnessed them. All sailors described the rituals, ceremonies, dances and so on which inevitably preceded their acceptance into island communities. Jackson's adoption ceremonies, Lamont's pehu or rites of welcome and O'Connell's tattooing rituals were all instances of the highly theatrical nature of island cultural life. Arrivals and departures, births and marriages, warfare and death were similarly acknowledged in specific moments of drama that were extremely significant to the community as a whole. They were life-changing events. They signalled a movement from one state of being to another and were marked as such. Their drama and their show were a reflection of their importance.

Theatre on the Beach

When William Bligh and the men of the *Bounty* arrived in Tahiti in 1788–89 they were fêted and celebrated. Plays, dances and dramas were performed for their benefit. Gifts of feathers, cloaks, livestock and food were offered and accepted. Speeches were given and ceremonial exchanges were made by both sides. The islanders demonstrated their wealth in people, canoes, land and produce. As the natives of the land, they graciously bestowed their bounty on the strangers from the sea. The new arrivals, in return, performed a theatre of their own. Bligh made arrangements to welcome the young king and his cohorts on board ship. The islanders arrived in a flotilla of canoes laden with gifts. The king was carried on the shoulders of his servants and received homage from gathered crowds. His arrival on the *Bounty* was marked by the firing of the ship's guns

> at which they [the natives] appeared much amazed & always stopd their ears & fell down as soon as they saw the Flash, and a Pistol was to all appearance as much dreaded as a four pounder. Mr Bligh took the opportunity at such times, to shew them the effects of round and Grape Shot which to them appeard Wonderful, and they always exclaimed in amaze when they saw the shot fall, scarcely giving credit to what they saw.[1]

Bligh's performance was a dramatic representation of European might, power and authority – a demonstration of cultural superiority based on technological advancement. He ensured that the European presence was imbued with amazement, wonder and terror. His methods were different but his aim was the same. All cultures represent themselves to others through theatre – through ceremonial gestures and ritualised actions. The visitors' plays of power, status and hierarchy, their signs of authority, were mirrors of the natives' own staging. Pageantry, ritual and performance were the same on both sides of the beach and instantly recognisable across cultures.

Fletcher Christian knew the value of such representations. When the mutineers took control of the *Bounty* they evicted Bligh and his officers. They placed them in a boat loaded with clothes and provisions, and set them adrift to find their own way to land and justice. The mutineers then returned briefly to Tahiti where Christian performed an unexpected act. He wanted to make an impact on the natives. He wanted to show the cohesiveness and discipline of his band of men. The mutineers had to be taken seriously; they needed to display their worth and value in some important, unmistakable way. They were on the cusp of a new life and they wanted to start out right. Ironically, Christian decided to reconstitute the very sense of authority and power that he had repudiated so dramatically in the act of mutiny. So he '[c]ut up the old Studding sails to make Uniforms for All hands, taking his own for edging, observing that nothing had more effect on the mind of the Indians as a uniformity of Dress, which by the by has its effects among Europeans as it always betokens discipline especially on board British Men of War'.

He then took his band of men to search for a safe haven. The island they initially chose, as described in Chapter Three, was Tubuai. This was where they would build their island base. They would call it Fort George in a nod to their sovereign and their past lives. Before they could begin, however, they needed permission from the local chief. James Morrison told the story. We 'went on Shore where we were met by the Chief and some of the friends who presented Mr Christian with two young Plantain trees, and two roots of Yava by way of a Peace Offering'. The gifts were accepted. The sailors then marked out their territory '& the Ground being Measured out for the Fort possession was taken by turning a Turf and hoisting the Union Jack on a Staff in the Place'. Two forms of theatre are being enacted here – the transfer of power by way of a peace offering from the native chief ceding the land to Morrison, Christian and crew; and the accession of power and territory displayed by the token turning of the turf and the raising of the flag. Both parties demonstrate their agreement in symbolic terms. Both recognise and respond to the drama inherent in the delicate cross-cultural negotiations taking place.

The *Bounty* mutineers numbered twenty-five men. They had their ship, their guns, their provisions and the company of their comrades. They were well placed to make a theatre of their island comings and goings. The shipwrecked sailor faced a much harsher reality. His arrival, accidental and unplanned, brought with it a loss of traditional authority, as recognised by another shipwrecked sailor, James Oliver:

> Officers and crew, who, a short time previously, were connected with a noble ship, and greatly cheered by the near prospect of bidding farewell to the Islands, were now sitting together on the matting-floor, dejected and weary, with torn garments, pale and down-cast faces, and dependent for mere subsistence on the uncertain benevolence of savages. Especially was I embarrassed to see him, whose orders I had faithfully endeavoured to obey, who had exerted his utmost skill to save the ship, now reduced to the same hard lot with his men.[2]

Lost ships and destitute captains signalled the end of institutionalised authority and its attendant plays of power. It was a fact of maritime life that when 'a merchant ship is wrecked, all authority immediately ceases, and every individual is at full liberty to shift for himself'.[3] Without the traditional forms of authority that structured their lives as seamen, sailors had to find new roles to play. Shipboard life was over and a new drama was about to unfold on island shores. The sailor was no longer an unwilling co-star in an institutionalised world but the main performer in the drama of his own life. New places and new opportunities offered him a chance to become involved in a theatre of a different kind.

Beachcomber Performance

On island shores the beachcomber became involved in the most vivid experience of his life. As a sailor he had often witnessed the dramatic displays of power and prestige shared between nations but in his new-found state as a castaway he could claim no such authority. He was denied the comfort of familiar rituals and rules that helped him know his place. He was bereft of the traditional markers that would demonstrate that place and status to others. Going native required him to become a performer in the theatre of a foreign culture. Unlike ritualised displays of power which are predicated upon a disjunction between outer show and inner reality, the beachcomber's role was highly personal. His convincing adoption of a native persona was continuous, ongoing and vital to his survival. It was not time-bound or restricted to specific occasions. It would last as long as he remained on the islands.

Performing on that level could not be done lightly – it involved the 'whole person, all the senses all the emotions, memory, a sense of presence, co-ordination of mind and body'.[4] It was hard work; it was risky and dangerous. It was not a reflex, a quick, automatic or habitual response to a particular circumstance. Anthropologist Victor Turner believes that any performance is 'highly contrived, artificial, of culture not nature, a deliberate and voluntary work of art'.[5] His definition aptly describes beachcomber experience. Their decision to go native was not a spontaneous response to the lure of a native lifestyle or a willing repudiation of the constraints of civilisation. It was a carefully controlled, theatrical and self-conscious process – a painstaking performance on which their lives depended:

> When the individual does move into a new position in society and obtains a new part to perform, he is not likely to be told in full detail how to conduct himself, nor will the facts of his new situation press sufficiently on him from the start to determine his conduct without his further giving thought to it. Ordinarily he will be given only a few cues, hints, and stage directions, and it will be assumed that he already has in his repertoire a large number of bits and pieces of performances that will be required in the new setting.[6]

The beachcomber's novel situation allowed him very little familiarity with socially recognised signs and accepted modes of behaviour in island societies. His learned skills from Europe might not, and often did not, carry the same significance. It was extremely difficult for him to navigate safely through such murky waters. An ideal performance occurs when an actor is totally at one with the experience he attempts to portray: 'Because the very best that can happen is to have the actor completely carried away by the play. Then regardless of his own will he lives the part, not noticing *how* he feels, not thinking about *what* he does, and it all moves of its own accord, subconsciously and intuitively,' argues performance theorist, Richard Schechner.[7] While it might have proved best for his long-term survival if the beachcomber could adapt to his native role in this 'ideal' fashion, it almost never occurred that way. Performers, while being someone or something else, do not stop being themselves at the same time. Performance is dangerous for the performer – he is both subject and object of his own play. He is a self split up the middle – a psychological displacement that manifested itself in episodes of illness and despair.

Traditionally, the beachcomber was not taken in by his own routine. He did the best he could, in movement, actions, dress, language and mannerisms, but he never allowed himself to become completely transformed into the character he pretended to be. His performance was usually only a means to an end. It ensured his continued safety until his eventual escape. If his life was not in imminent danger, his performance could often enhance his personal status. It could improve his standard of living by gaining him increased power and respect. He was quick to realise that, regardless of his actual situation or his

E. H. Lamont, who was cast away on Tongareva (Penrhyn Islands) in 1853.

personal feelings, his outward manner would dictate how others reacted to him. Shortly after arriving on the island of Tongareva, E. H. Lamont adopted a conscious strategy of 'difference' – a policy of non-integration by which he hoped to distinguish himself from the other sailors and claim a greater degree of personal status. 'I sat down on the log of a cocoa-nut tree, and tried to mark out a line of conduct for myself,' he wrote. 'I was convinced that the proper course to pursue was to associate with them on such terms as to impress them with the idea of their inferiority and at all risks to keep firm in any difficulties that might arise.' He did not have long to wait. The natives ordered the sailors to carry coconuts to the village but Lamont refused:

> such work would have humbled me in the opinion of the natives, and if I commenced to labour for my own food I should be obliged to continue it . . . If I were obliged to do what I had no great capacity for, I should sink to the lowest scale in the estimation of the natives. At present I was evidently considered a superior being, and while so regarded could easily maintain my supremacy, and, if necessary, increase it.[8]

The world of the island offered him freedom from his shipboard persona and he grasped it eagerly. His performance met with a great deal of success: 'The influence I thus exercised seemed to make considerable impression on the natives,' he wrote. It led to his adoption by a family of higher rank than the other sailors and allowed him to become affiliated, through marriage and adoption, with a number of prestigious island families.

Often the effort required to create the right dramatic effect meant that the sailor was not fully implicated in his performance. In other words, he was so busy *playing* the role that he was not actually *living* the role. He was not at one with the part he had adopted (or been forced to adopt) but was constantly working at it as something outside of himself and something that took a great deal of effort to maintain. But outward show was not enough. There had to be some sort of corresponding inward acceptance of the role he was playing, otherwise discrepancies would surface and danger would ensue. A native audience would be quick to spot any disparity between fostered

appearance and reality – a delicate and fragile reality that could easily
be shattered by minor mishaps. John Jackson is a case in point. He was
given a position of honour among the Fijians and was made a personal
attendant of the king. However, his role as subservient minion was
hard to maintain. On a number of occasions he forgot to prostrate
himself in the presence of the king. It was an affront noticed by all
around him and Jackson found himself in immediate danger of being
killed for his disrespect. He was saved by the actions of the king himself
who, having a real affection for his pet sailor, tied a piece of tapa around
his neck and declared him taboo. His mistakes were forgiven and his
life preserved as long as he wore his sacred marker. He was forced to
rigorously monitor his role as a real native. However, his increased
efforts merely served to reinforce the degree to which those actions
were purely performative.

Although the psychology of performance proved stressful, the
beachcombers were ultimately successful. They survived by a
masterful blend of outward conformity and inward acceptance of their
unprecedented need for role playing. As they became more at home in
their native worlds, they became less cynical about the parts they were
to play. The gap separating the sailor from his role began to narrow, as
demonstrated by those men who voluntarily submitted to the ordeal
of tattooing. Their decision to adopt such an irrevocable marker
of difference demonstrates the true level of their transformation.
They were not just undergoing a change of appearance but, in some
important way, experiencing a change of being. Certainly, it was often
seen that way by European society which remained disgusted with the
sailors' degeneration. It meant something else to the sailor himself.
He had identified with his native role to the degree that he agreed
willingly to become like the men around him, on a permanent basis.
His outward show was a visible symptom of his inner acceptance of
another cultural reality.

Renegade Roles

But the role playing necessary for sailors to live successfully as
natives resulted in further condemnation from their contemporaries.
Theatre invokes a world of indeterminacy – a world where things are

not necessarily as they seem. It threatens notions of stability based on an immutable correspondence between external sign and inward reality by making a virtue out of being insincere. Western theatrical conventions associate 'acting' with make-believe. The words used to describe theatre, acting and performance are all nuanced towards the emptiness of signs and insincerity of actions.[9] Representation is linked to the worlds of illusion in which people play roles, put on acts, portray different characters and construct different realities. Its intention is to deceive, beguile and delude. The essence of the actor's role, for instance, is transformation – he aims to turn himself into something or someone else. Performers, therefore, are not necessarily who or what they appear to be. Like a confidence man or trickster, an actor plays a role that is somehow different to his true self.

In Western society, performances take place in privileged spaces and at specified times. These are deliberately distanced from those times and places set aside for work, sleep and so on. Theatre suspends everyday reality. It allows people to stand aside from habitual patterns of thinking. It does not simply reflect existing social systems but it critiques and evaluates the social life from which it stems. It challenges the habitual models or patterns of behaviour traditionally assumed to be inviolable and unassailable. It permits new parameters to be specified, old structures to be challenged and new roles to be negotiated. Recognising social behaviour as a form of performance is a challenge to society. Because it is not a natural event but a model of collective and individual human choice, human behaviour is subject to revision. It has the capacity to change. There is danger in this sort of social freedom which has the power to disrupt the stability of any community that sees itself as unchangeable. It offers groups and individuals the chance to become what they once were or, more importantly for castaway sailors, the chance to become what they never were, but wished to be. Life as an ongoing series of performances mounts an overt challenge to social conditioning. It threatens established Western social hierarchies which, in the period under discussion, would have rigidly defined the sailor first by his lower status in society and second by his place in the lower echelons of the ship.

French existentialist philosopher Jean-Paul Sartre said: 'There

are indeed many precautions to imprison a man in what he is, as if
we lived in perpetual fear that he might escape from it, that he might
break away and suddenly elude his condition.'[10] There is danger in
the ability to assume roles and play parts other than those assigned
by birth and society. Many of the beachcombers did just that. They
stepped outside their designated roles and availed themselves of the
freedom to construct new identities and play new roles. In doing so,
they demonstrated the dramatic nature of all societal interaction. The
actions of the castaway sailor exposed the fragility of class, status and
other socially imposed hierarchies of control, and revealed deep-seated
fears of social anarchy.

The beachcomber was a renegade performer. As an artist, an
adventurer and performer, he was more like a trickster figure. Neither
one thing nor another, he found himself free to become something
else entirely. Dr Long Ghost, Melville's beachcombing companion in
Tahiti, revelled in that freedom. As he boasted: 'I'll put up a banana-leaf
as physician from London – deliver lectures on Polynesian antiquities –
teach English in five lessons, of one hour each – establish power-looms
for the manufacture of tappa – lay out a public park in the middle of the
village, and found a festival in honor of Captain Cook!' The freedom
of the performance situation allowed for novelty and creativity to
emerge in each new situation. It was a heady sort of liberty and it was
embraced by many of our sailors. 'When the captain called out, "Every
man for himself," he abdicated his authority,' recalled one shipwrecked
sailor. 'We were free! from the caprices of numskulls. We could see
now the whole extent of our misfortune, and we set about at once
taking advantage of every favorable circumstance.'[11] Such autonomy
was often frightening after life in the highly institutionalised society
of the ship. But it was also rich with possibility.

Lamont, for instance, took advantage of those 'favourable
circumstances' by presenting himself as a doctor on Tongareva, where
he providentially cured a local girl of a headache by blowing on her
forehead: 'The cure caused quite a sensation, and thenceforward I was
looked on by many, especially the women, as a "tangata kiche" or spirit
doctor – a belief which, I must confess, I was unscrupulous enough
to turn to my benefit on many future occasions.' James O'Connell

took on a similar role. He taught the islanders how to find their pulse, something they perceived as magical if not supernatural, and thereafter was often asked to predict the outcome of various illnesses. He believed that an affirmative response, confidently pronounced, would usually give the patient confidence to recover: 'by caution in pronouncing judgment, and care in forming it, my word, as I gained experience, was considered with the islanders life or death to the patient'.

Beachcomber role playing in this instance is grounded in a perceived medical authority and in a technologically advanced knowledge of the human body. But it was a knowledge that the sailors were happy to capitalise on, even if it required them to play a part for which they were traditionally unqualified. John Twyning wrote:

> For some time past I had possessed a medicine chest, which I had obtained from a Whaler, and I always took care to keep it well supplied. I had therefore been in the habit of applying the simple plasters, &c. it contained, to such of the natives that met with any accident, and with such success as to make me somewhat famous as a leech.[12]

On Hoorn's Island (Futuna) in 1839 Twyning was involved in several skirmishes between rival tribes. One battle was particularly vicious and resulted in at least forty casualties, one of whom was the chief. He had been pierced by a spear which had entered his right shoulder and had embedded itself in his back. As the islanders were not able or willing to lay their hands on the sacred body of their chief, in the belief that such a transgression would be punished by their gods, they waited expectantly for Twyning to perform the operation. His reputation as a medicine man was about to be tested.

First he broke off the barbs that jutted a full finger's length from the body of the spear. Then he made a wider incision at the point at which the spear entered the body of the chief. This enabled him to withdraw it without tearing the surrounding flesh. He cleaned the wound with water and covered it with a soft cloth. The chief was delighted. Twyning's success led him back to the battlefield. All afternoon and late into the night, he was employed taking pieces of spears from the wounded. His method was preferred to the native one, which was to twist the spear round and round 'till the barb had torn away the flesh that resisted its being drawn out backwards'. His labours continued the next day: 'I was employed . . . setting and splintering the broken legs and arms, and after that I had to take out the spears and musket balls from the dead bodies,' he recalled. The natives' belief that Twyning was a doctor (an illusion that the sailor was happy to promote) ensured his continued safety and survival. It was the reason, as he admitted, that 'so many pains had been taken to spare my life'.

Metamorphosis

Island life offered many men an unlooked-for opportunity to transcend their humble seagoing origins. John Young, for instance, was forty-six years old when he first came to Hawaii in 1789. He was the boatswain on an American trading vessel, the *Eleanora*, and was anchored in Hawaii, waiting to rendezvous with another ship. Bored with the inactivity on board, he decided to go ashore, but was unexpectedly left there when his ship sailed without him. His first few days were fearful and uncertain. He was without native patronage and without European companionship. Eventually he was taken by the natives to Kealakekeua Bay where he was relieved and surprised to meet up with another castaway, Isaac Davis. The two men became close friends and both figured prominently in subsequent Hawaiian history.

The castaways were offered patronage by the young chief Kamehameha, who shrewdly took advantage of their superior knowledge of firearms. They offered assistance, fought by his side, and became trusted advisors and valued warriors. As their prospects improved, they turned their backs on Europe. Their return home would only expose them to 'the vicissitudes of a life of hard labour, for the purpose of merely acquiring a precarious supply of the most common necessities of life . . . which for some years past, had not occasioned them the least concern'.[13] It was a pivotal decision. As the years progressed, and with the support of their chiefs they became wealthy and powerful men. In 1800 Kamehameha appointed Young as Governor of the large island of Hawaii with supreme authority. He was the chief's viceroy, his trusted lieutenant and controller of all trade that passed through Kawaihae Bay. From lowly sailor, to plantation owner and governor of the island, John Young transformed himself. He courted the chiefs and priests; he made himself indispensable to the king. Along with Davis he became a close personal friend of Chief Kamehameha and benefited greatly from his patronage and support. Their prestige increased the more they were able to serve the interests of the Hawaiians. Both sailors grasped the opportunity to become greater than birth and status had initially decreed. As one commentator remarked, 'Surrounded by barbarians, they did not suffer themselves to sink to the level of the barbarians, but rather to have risen above their former selves, as being made great by the great obligations thrown on them and accepted.'[14]

Young lived a long and productive life, dying peacefully in 1835, forty-six years after his arrival in Hawaii. Davis's history was more tragic, as his close friendship with the king led to his early death. In 1810 he uncovered an assassination plot and while he was able to warn the king, who subsequently survived, he himself was eventually poisoned by those same assassins. Young's death, occurring much later, was marked with all the pomp and ceremony accorded to a high chief. The penniless and destitute sailor had become a great man in his adopted society. He had recognised the opportunity for self-fashioning that was offered him, and he had grasped it with both hands. His metamorphosis was complete and spectacular. He became the man the Hawaiians wanted him to be: loyal, courageous, hard-working, disciplined and committed to the interests of the island people. It was a performance that greatly enriched his life and it enabled him to bequeath a legacy of power, prestige and influence to his many native children, descendants of whom can still be found in Hawaii.

Another sailor to be left behind by his captain was David Whippy, a young man who set sail from Nantucket to the Pacific in 1819.[15] In 1824, he was left in Fiji to collect a cargo of sandalwood. But his ship never returned and Whippy was forced to make a life for himself, at least temporarily, in Fiji. Like Young and Davis in Hawaii, he welcomed the opportunity to transcend the limitations of his previous life. He committed himself to his island hosts and worked hard on their behalf

– mediating with visiting ships, establishing favourable terms of trade, and acting as ambassador between rival Fijian chiefs. He was given the honorary title 'Mata ki Bau', which designated him an official ambassador for the chief Bau in the heated political rivalries with chief Rewa in the late 1830s. From sailor to beachcomber, to ambassador and then settler, Whippy transformed himself again and again, depending on the political and economic climate. His value to Europeans as well as Fijians was recognised in 1846 when he was appointed honorary vice-commercial agent, a post he held for the next ten years. It was an appointment made on instructions from the American president, probably on the recommendation of Charles Wilkes of the United States Exploring Expedition that had visited Fiji in 1839. The sailor became a respected and wealthy man, a patriarch of his own extended native family. He owned vast tracts of land, over 3600 hectares, and became a planter, sugar trader, shipbuilder and cattle rancher. His legacy lives on in concrete terms. Modern visitors to Fiji, who sign on for one of the many island cruises, will find that their schooner was most probably built in the thriving shipyards of Fiji's famous boatbuilding family, Charles Whippey & Sons, of Suva.

The experience of the beachcombers like Young and Whippy highlights the theatrical nature of self-construction in all societies. No other group of people had been so rudely or so completely transplanted from their own world to one so different in every way. The adjustments they were forced to make emphasised the dramatic nature of everyday social reality – a knowledge that was universal and deeply discomforting. Their narratives describe just how hard it was. They write of the difficulties inherent in the everyday and mundane representation of one self to another. They reveal deep anxiety about performing a new self in an unknown society, where traditional markers and signals are redundant. They show that the only way to survive is to enter wholeheartedly into the theatre of self-invention and self-creation offered by a new life on foreign shores.

Their lives as sailors had prepared them well. Representations of power, rituals of obedience, and adherence to a specific role in their shipboard lives awakened them to the drama of everyday life. Mimicry, role playing and improvisation were valuable skills employed to make the best of island life. They became second nature to men whose success or failure on those islands was often a matter of life or death. A number of them were certainly not above utilising those skills for their own ends, as beachcomber William Lockerby demonstrated. In order to gain an advantage over the islanders, he constructed an elaborate play on the mysterious powers inherent in the notion of tapu. Lockerby (whose journal was subsequently to cause so much consternation for his family) had been left at Highley Bay in Fiji by his captain with instructions to stockpile large quantities of sandalwood. Hearing of a substantial supply further inland he travelled to the site to negotiate with the owner. The owner wanted one large whale's tooth for the wood, something that Lockerby was unable to provide. Desperate to complete the ship's cargo he told the islander that the white man's god or 'Callow' wanted the wood to be paid for in iron. The Fijian refused to capitulate and Lockerby was forced to extemporise further. He took some long grass and bound it around several breadfruit trees. He then piled stones before a pond of fresh water that lay to the side of the hut, telling the islander that 'whoever should eat of the bread fruit would die, and that the same fate would meet the person who should wash himself in the pond'. Before he left, he predicted that the owner's family 'would be sick before the day following at noon'. This was decreed by the white man's god, argued Lockerby, who was angry at the conflict over the disputed wood. His threat had an unforeseen consequence. When the owner and his family fell ill the next day the village was thrown into a panic:

> When I entered they all rose and made a most lamentable cry, promising the Callow of the ship all their wood and everything they had. I was now sorry I had worked so much on the minds of these simple creatures . . . After a good deal of persuasion I was prevailed upon to take off the taboo, and receive a lot of wood as a present to the ship's Callow . . . I then drew my hand over the faces of those who had been sick, on which they stood on their feet.[16]

His conscience got the better of him. On receipt of the wood he presented the man and his family with large quantities of iron and beads 'of far more value to them than a whale's tooth, if they could have understood their own interests', he claimed.

Life on Pacific islands offered the beachcombers a chance to play a different role than the one set aside for them in European society. Their successful acceptance of those roles was manifested upon their return to Europe. It could be seen in their tattoos, their darkened skin and, in some cases, their public demonstrations of native costume and savage dances. These were visible markers of a role apprehensively undertaken but successfully performed. The truly unsettling aspect of their transformation lay at a deeper level. The performative aspect of beachcomber experience revealed the extent to which reality, appearance and identity are only a constructed illusion. The beachcomber who performed and played roles by which he was accepted into island society exposed the social construction of identity and status, in any society. He suggested that behind the roles played and the masks worn there may be nothing, no individual unique self. Character, rather than being fixed and unchangeable, was something that could be repeatedly erased and written afresh. The fluid and shifting identity of the beachcomber, his ease and success at crossing cultural and social boundaries, suggested that while the world might not be a stage, life was certainly a masquerade.

CHAPTER EIGHT

On the Margins and in Despair

Try to go back to the savages, and you
feel as if your very soul was decomposing
inside you. That is what you feel in the South Seas,
anyhow: as if your soul was decomposing inside you.

D. H. LAWRENCE, *Studies in Classic American Literature*

The continuous role play and the cultural adaption required of the beachcomber on island shores carried its own particular burden. When he began to live as a native, the sailor became a marginal man. He was no longer a European and yet not fully a native. He had decided, by a mixture of fate and misfortune, to live in two societies and to participate in two different cultures. And he became a stranger to both. He was an in-between person; he occupied the margins between civilisation and savagery, between culture and nature. He was poised in psychological uncertainty between two divergent social worlds and he encompassed in his experience and in his soul the anxieties and disharmonies of both. Those disharmonies caused acute mental tension.[1] They affected his mental and physical well-being. They resulted in psychological distress that often manifested itself as a mysterious and unfathomable physical illness. They literally made him ill. The experiences of Herman Melville serve as a paradigm for many other instances of mental maladjustment. His story is worth telling.

July 1842 was a very important month for the American sailor. He had been at sea a long time. It was eighteen months since he had signed on a whaling voyage to the South Seas from the port of New Bedford. His trip was an adventure of sorts; it was an excursion into the life of a common working seaman undertaken by the son of a gentleman. His family were prominent New Yorkers of Scottish and Dutch descent. Their pedigree was impeccable, even if their financial status was less exalted. Melville could count revolutionary heroes and New World explorers among his many relatives. As a young man, he had been well educated, even working for a while as a country schoolteacher. He was clearly meant for better things, but fate intervened. The death of his father and the financial difficulties faced by his mother, sisters and brother turned his thoughts towards the sea. He would follow his uncles and cousins and try life as a sailor. On the way he would become financially independent. He would make a voyage of his own and 9 July 1842 was the day it would begin. As his ship moored in the extreme western end of Taiohae Bay in the Marquesas, his thoughts were in turmoil. The past months had been hard ones. A brutal captain, low rations, substandard conditions and a disgruntled crew made the ship a volatile place to be. In front of him, just across the line of breakers he saw the answer to his troubles. Breadfruit and hibiscus trees, groves of coconut and myrtle, kingfishers and parrots appeared as a feast of colour to his sea-weary eyes. He decided to desert.

Mutiny was the reason for Melville's departure and mutiny, in one form or another, informed all the actions that followed. He left the discipline and structure of the ship and the world it represented. He struck out alone and searched for another reality, a more palatable and agreeable one, on foreign shores. Melville regarded himself as a loner. He was different to the rest of the crew. He had a different history and subscribed to a different dream. He was searching for something of his own, something that he believed he could find in the Marquesan hills and valleys. Although friendly with his shipmates, he did not keep company with them. On the ship and on the shore he kept his distance. There was only one other in whom he recognised a similar spirit. Richard Tobias Greene (Toby) was also twenty-one years old,

Richard Tobias Greene (Toby), Melville's companion on the Marquesas.
Although Toby left the Marquesas before Melville, the two sailors eventually
contacted each other, years later, after their return to America.

and 'active, ready, and obliging, of dauntless courage, and singularly
open and fearless in the expression of his feelings'. He would be
Melville's companion in desertion. He would share his adventures on
the journey to the valley of the Taipi. Toby would stand beside him,
a fellow American among the islanders, until he managed to escape,

never to return. Melville would then have the rest of his adventure, alone, among the native strangers.

Melville and Toby were renegades. They abandoned their duties, their obligations and their loyalty to their country of origin. Their decision to desert arose from a desire for romantic adventure. They sought liberty, knowledge, danger and new experience. They romanticised the beach and constructed a mythic landscape which would be severely challenged by the harsh reality of Marquesan geography. Freedom was elusive and it was not long before obstacles of one sort of another were placed in their way.

By the mid-nineteenth century, the Marquesan beach had become politicised. Melville's South Sea paradise was already tainted by the political reality of an armed protectorate. The French were in residence: their armed ships lay in the harbour and their soldiers were camped on the shore.[2] This was not the virgin beach of Melville's dreams. But he looked past it, towards the rugged interior of the island. It was there he would find the paradise that flourished in his imagination. He dressed for his journey: new trousers, serviceable shoes, heavy jacket and a hat. He took with him a handful of broken biscuits, several pounds of tobacco and a few yards of cotton cloth. Toby had sewing utensils, a razor case and a roll of calico. They hoped to survive on the natural bounty of the islands and to trade with the islanders. They wanted nothing that would encumber them or delay their speedy escape across the beach. As soon as they were able to, they separated themselves from their shipmates and headed for the safety and anonymity of the rugged hills. There they would be safe from the French and from the consequences of their desertion.

Their plan was facilitated by heavy rain, which obscured their departure, although it made their journey into the interior arduous and time-consuming. Because they were runaways, they were unable to take the easier paths that led around the beach. They were forced to head straight for the steep ranges that flanked the harbour settlement. As the days passed, they found themselves fighting to clear a path through thickets of cane and tangled undergrowth. They soon became lost in the inhospitable valleys and hills. Nights were long, cold and miserable. Their meagre supply of food ran out and they became disoriented among the jagged peaks and steep waterfalls of the island. They were hungry, tired, thirsty and more than a little disillusioned with their adventure. After many long days, they stumbled across a verdant settlement nestled between the hills. 'Had a glimpse of the gardens of Paradise been revealed to me', wrote Melville, 'I could scarcely have been more ravished with the sight.' The valley spread out before them. It was surrounded by grassy cliffs, criss-crossed with sparkling waterfalls. It was silent except for the sound of the water and the cries of the birds. Trees, fruit and flowers added their colour and fragrance to the beauty of the landscape. Small thatched huts were dotted throughout the luxuriant foliage. Melville and Toby had finally found the sanctuary they had been searching for.

The sailors were to spend four weeks with the Taipi natives – a period that is lengthened to four months in Melville's narrative, *Typee*. Once the excitement of their unexpected arrival had passed, they were welcomed into the community. Adopted by native families, they spent their days with other young men wandering the hills and exploring the far reaches of the native settlement. They were given food to eat, clothes to wear and women to entertain them. Melville became enamoured of a beautiful native girl called Fayaway: 'The face of this girl was a rounded oval, and each feature as perfectly formed as the heart or imagination of man could desire', he rhapsodised. The sailors should have been content – their escape was successful, the valley beautiful and the women affectionate – but Melville was ill.

His mysterious ailment began during his trek over the mountains. June to September is the rainy season on the Marquesas and Melville spent many long, wet nights in the hills, exposed to the elements. Not surprisingly, he awoke one morning to find that his leg was extremely swollen and very painful. He was chilled and feverish and assumed he had been bitten by some sort of tropical insect. However, his leg refused to heal, even after he had been taken in by the Taipi. It caused him ongoing distress, rendering him completely lame for periods at a time. 'Indeed my malady began seriously to alarm me', wrote the sailor, 'for, despite the herbal remedies of the natives, it continued to grow worse and worse.' Nothing seemed to ease his discomfort. Despite the beauty of the valley, and the loving attention of his hosts, Melville 'continued to languish under a complaint, the origin and nature of which were still a mystery'.

His island paradise became as poisoned as his leg. He felt himself to be cut off from the rest of the world. The Taipi, according to myth and legend, were ferocious cannibals and he became desperately anxious about his long-term safety. He was helpless, incapacitated and unable to move freely. The malady seemed to worsen day by day, leaving him prostrate with pain and deeply depressed. It dawned on him that he had exchanged one form of captivity for another. The suffering sailor soon fell 'prey to the profoundest melancholy'. Forsaken, lonely and ill, Melville resigned himself to his fate. Escape was impossible; he ceased pining for his old life: 'I gave myself up to the passing hour, and if ever disagreeable thoughts arose in my mind, I drove them away.' His health then took a turn for the better. Miraculously, his leg healed, the swelling disappeared and the pain subsided overnight. There were now no barriers to his enjoyment of the pleasures of the valley. His physical and mental sufferings were gone: 'I flung myself anew into all the social pleasures of the valley, and sought to bury all regrets, and all remembrances of my previous existence in the wild enjoyments it afforded.'

Melville's 'wild enjoyment' continued until he was threatened with a tattoo. He was under sustained pressure from the Marquesans to undergo the same treatment as the other adult men of the village. It was an issue central to their culture and close to their hearts, but it horrified the sailor. His powerlessness reminded him of his captive status and reinforced his lack of independence and free will. 'It was during the period I was in this unhappy frame of mind that the powerful malady under which I had been labouring – after having almost completely subsided – began again to show itself and with symptoms as violent as ever', he recalled. He plunged again into desolation and despair and decided to escape. On hearing that a ship had moored in the harbour looking for fresh supplies, he begged and pleaded with his captors to take him to the shore. They refused, so with the aid of a handmade walking stick he began to limp and hobble his way to the sea. A benevolent islander, who recognised the sailor's desperate desire to re-unite with his countrymen, helped him along the way. His departure came at a cost, however. A large roll of cotton cloth, numerous bags of powder and a musket were needed to procure his liberty. Even then, he was still physically restrained from reaching the waiting ship. Although he did finally make it on board, his departure, like that of other sailors, ended in violence:

> Even at the moment I felt horror at the act I was about to commit; but it was no time for pity or compunction, and with a true aim, and exerting all my strength, I dashed the boat hook at [an islander]. It struck him just below the throat, and forced him downwards. I had no time to repeat the blow, but I saw him rise to the surface in the wake of the boat, and never shall I forget the ferocious expression of his countenance.[3]

D. H. Lawrence analysed Melville's discontent with native life and searched for the cause of his mysterious ailment.[4] According to Lawrence, the problem lay in the landscape itself. His Pacific is a vast repository for the sensual-mystic dreams of previous civilisations. It 'holds the dream of immemorial centuries. It is the great blue twilight of the vastest of all evenings'. It echoes with glories of a past so long forgotten that even its present inhabitants are unaware of it. His vision encompasses the beauty, ease, peace and timelessness of the islands, but recreates it as an archetypal form of dreaming. Lawrence's understanding of the South Seas was romantic and mythic rather than geological or historical. His Pacific induces forgetfulness. It is a place of lassitude and lethargy. He hears the names of the islands – Samoa, Tahiti, Nukuhiva – as the sounds of a dream, a dream to which Melville and others like him were remorselessly, but fatally, drawn:

> The truth of the matter is, one cannot go back . . . we cannot turn the current of our life backwards, back towards their soft warm twilight and uncreate mud. Not for a moment. If we do it for a moment, it makes us sick.[5]

Melville became ill, argued Lawrence, because island life was a torture to him and to men like him. Instead of idealism and attainment, it offered only silence, nullity and stasis. Lawrence believed that Europeans like

A native habitation in Nukuhiva, Marquesas. This dwelling is
similar to the one shared by Herman Melville and Toby Greene
during their sojourn on the islands.

Melville, dedicated to the ideals of progress and enlightenment, would
never find peace in the islands. He foresaw problems with a life of
unlimited ease. (As with many other writers, Lawrence subscribed to
the myth that islanders never work.) Lawrence's Pacific symbolised the
beauty and grandeur of the past. It was a timeless and static beauty
that could offer little but malaise and despair to a modern psyche
focused on the present.

Real and Marginal Natives

The reality is somewhat simpler. The beachcombers were always
marginal natives. Despite the length of time they spent on islands and

their personal level of absorption and assimilation, they were never fully accepted by their native communities. The adoption ceremonies they participated in did not decisively resolve their ambivalent cultural status. The sailors were still regarded as white strangers who worshipped different gods and who adhered to their own often alien and mystifying set of rules. When told of the inappropriate behaviour of a visiting sailor, the chief of Tonga remarked, '[W]hat can be expected of a papalangi (foreigner)?'[6] Their status as outsiders deprived them of participation in important social and cultural rituals and ceremonies. It denied them total acceptance and left them stranded on the periphery of island communities.

Unlike real natives, the beachcombers had very little moral autonomy. A real native could behave in ways he thought were right; he was granted a level of personal independence that allowed him to have opinions, to act, to become involved and play a part in the activities of the community.[7] Marginal natives were constantly protecting themselves from the dangerous, if not fatal, assumption that they were entitled to the same social and moral freedom as true natives. They were not always able to act spontaneously, or to say or do exactly what they wished. Unaware of a great many social taboos, they lived in a state of constant trepidation and personal danger. William Mariner, captured by natives in Tonga, made the disastrous mistake of sneezing at the outset of an important expedition. He was completely unaware that in native terms this innocent act committed the expedition to fatal results and placed him in serious danger. One young chief was so incensed that he attempted to kill the sailor on the spot. He was held back by others and after a period of contemplation, Finau, the king, 'resolved that as [Mariner] was a foreigner, and had different gods, his sneezing was not to be considered of any consequence'. Mariner was extremely shaken and decided to head inland to his plantation and remove himself from harm's way. Although he was eventually reconciled to the young chief, it was a lesson in cultural sensitivity he never forgot.

Underneath all positive experiences and personal achievements was the awareness that danger was always present. Many sailors described the 'continual suspense in which we lived whether of falling into the hands of friends or enemies, of which there were twenty to one in favour of the latter'.[8] They wrote about 'melancholy and distressing thoughts [that] would prey upon the mind at times, and gain such an ascendancy over the drooping spirits, as those who have not experienced the like, can only conceive of'.[9] There were a number of explanations for this continuing sense of vulnerability and unease: the volatility of the natives; their intertribal vendettas, which could bode ill for the Europeans living among them; the native desire to possess any objects owned by the Europeans; the possibility of unwittingly transgressing native boundaries; and the shifting, and to Europeans often mystifying, loyalties of various island groups. On the islands laughter and play could change to violence and death in an instant and for reasons often not understood by the sailor. It was a precarious existence, lived in the knowledge that danger was always present. It manifested itself in an extraordinarily high incidence of ill health and mental anguish.

Personal Suffering

John Twyning's accounts have proved helpful on many aspects of the beachcomber experience – most particularly in his writing about his shipwreck in Tonga and his attempts at assimilation. Because of his twenty years in the Pacific, he was equally informative about the mental and physical cost of living as a marginal native. Twyning was physically damaged by his experiences on islands. 'The hardships I had suffered', he wrote, 'have rendered me incapable of doing any labour whereby I might earn my daily bread.' His first illness occurred on Lakembo (Lakeba) in the Fiji group about four years after his arrival in 1829. There were no warning signs and no logical explanation for his sudden decline. He simply woke one morning to find that he had lost the use of his limbs. He hoped it would be temporary but he continued in a state of paralysis for six long months until he 'was reduced to skin and bone'. He feared he was going to die. He called his friend and business partner John Jones to come and help him prepare for death. Jones was horrified by his friend's condition. Twyning recalled, 'I shall never forget his looks and expressions of pity and commiseration, when he first witnessed the deplorable state of weakness to which I was reduced.' Jones cleaned and washed the ill man and then fed him a mixture of taro and coconut milk. He also moved him to a different part of the island, hoping the change of air and atmosphere would help him recover.

The journey added its own complications, however. The two men set off in a canoe manned by the retainers of the local chief. They were plagued with bad weather and strong winds which blew the canoe onto a reef. Unable to use his legs, Twyning was left lying in the water at the bottom of the vessel while the rest of the crew jumped overboard. In an effort to save him from drowning, the chief 'took up his club to knock my brains out'. Fortunately, he was rescued by Jones who, with great difficulty, managed to get him safely to shore. Once there, he made a slow but eventual recovery and continued with the bêche-le-mer trading business established by himself and his partner.

He relapsed again in March 1840 with another mysterious ailment. This time it manifested itself as 'a violent inflammation in my eyes, and . . . a severe attack of rheumatic gout in the chest'. No medical assistance was possible. Twyning could not speak and lay in a hut, gasping for breath. Determined to do something to ease his suffering, he decided to drink a large glass of turpentine. While his rheumatic pains ceased immediately, and did not return, he warned his readers not to follow his example as his impromptu cure almost killed him: 'I was reduced very low; and the inflammation in my eyes continued very bad for several months'.

A year later, in 1841, Twyning was living with his wife on Hoorn's Island, maintaining a base for his trading operations. But these were turbulent years and the island was politically unstable. Despite themselves, resident white men were drawn into local wars and political disputes. There were bitter rivalries between different chiefly factions and the constant presence of whaling ships and the resultant economic pressures were adding to the turmoil. A Catholic mission had been established on Hoorn's Island and when one of its priests was brutally murdered the situation quickly became unstable. The priest had encouraged a number of islanders to break a local taboo, assuring them that their gods would not exact punishment. The king objected to this overt challenge to traditional authority and ordered the execution of the priest. After the execution the island grew increasingly volatile and the lives of all foreigners were endangered. The king then contemplated 'whether or not, all the white men resident on the island should be put to death' so the news of the priest's death would be contained. Twyning's health, never very good, got rapidly worse. He again lost the use of his legs and remained in that state for several months.

Before the end of 1841, while lying on his mat, he looked upwards towards the roof of the hut and a piece of matting fell into his eye. His eyes became inflamed and developed a growth which left him completely blind for six years. He had to be led around by his little daughter or by a dog. By December of that year his health was in even more serious decline. 'I was in great distress', he wrote, 'having the dropsy, the rheumatism, and was blind.' A large part of his distress was caused by the death of his wife. She fell ill in September 1842 and lingered for just over a year before she died. He was still suffering from blindness and he remembered, 'I used to run against the trees, often hurting myself severely.'

In 1845 he left Hoorn's Island and returned to Lakeba with his daughter. He remained there for nine months, living with the support and patronage of the local chief. It was during those months that his daughter, his 'eyes in the darkness', became seriously ill. He was devastated: 'She appeared to me almost to be a part of myself . . . and when she sickened she could not bear that anyone should touch or do any thing for her but myself. She could not walk, but I used to carry her in my arms to take the air.' When she died, Twyning had nothing left to live for: 'My guide and companion was gone, and I fretted so much I could hardly set one foot before another.' In desperation, he searched for a ship that would take him away from the islands. His thoughts turned towards his native land, although it was another three long years before he was able to gain a passage and return to Plymouth. Although his sight eventually did return, it was not surprising that he was permanently incapacitated upon his return to England in 1848.

Physical Distress

Inflammation of the legs, partial loss of sight, mysterious swellings and general debilitation were common ailments among Europeans living on island shores. As Lamont remarked about his life on Tongareva, 'Since my arrival on the islands I had scarcely ever been well.' In many ways his situation was more favourable than most. He was lucky to find himself with the company of other white men on the island. Despite the natives' reputation for ferocity and violence, the white men were welcomed into the community. Lamont was treated well, took three native wives and was given assistance when he decided to build a boat. He spent a great deal of time exploring the remoter parts of the island group and travelling to other communities. He was eventually adopted by the chief, Mahauta, became known as his son, and was accorded respect and influence due to his noble family connections. However, the sailor suffered during his captivity, favourable as it was. As the months passed, his shoes and clothes fell apart and his feet in particular became severely infected. He found himself unable to walk because of the 'points of shells that had broken in my feet'. He was ill, depressed and prey to fits of melancholy:

> Living in peace and plenty, 'monarch of all I surveyed', I should have
> been perfectly content, but for the constant yearning for home. Thoughts
> of absent friends, of my business, and of my future in the world, carried
> my mind away in discontent from a lot often envied by my comrades in
> bondage. I still wandered to the beach morning, noon, and night, in the
> hope of beholding a white sail nearing our island prison.[10]

A degree of illness could be expected as a physical reaction to a dramatic change in diet and climate, as seen in Twyning's case. But the copious examples of mental distress, together with the degree and range of bodily malfunctions, suggest a psychological cause. In the majority of cases, illness and debilitation can be understood as a physical manifestation of mental distress. It reflects the anxiety inherent in the state of marginality. The act of assimilation produced a conflicted individual, one who had to make his way in a world where traditional relationships between European and native were turned upside down. The beachcomber's disabilities left him physically dependent on the charity of his hosts, and his overall sense of mental and physical well-being was severely compromised. His lack of independence, coupled with the severe restraints placed on his freedom of movement, manifested itself in despair. Island life might have been idyllic, but not for those men who lacked true freedom of movement: 'I think, however, we might have lived a few days among them tolerably well,' commented a Marquesan castaway, William Torrey, 'had not the idea of our being obliged to do so, with no means of getting away, been so terribly impressed upon the mind.' After twelve months on the islands, Torrey lamented the loss of European company: 'This deprivation, change of diet, and the probability of our being forever doomed to dwell among them, tended much to impair our health.' John Jackson faced a similar situation in Samoa. During his captivity, he 'gave way to melancholy, and lost all appetite, and was disagreeable and morose, hated everybody, and even myself'.

Mental Anguish

The life of a white native on Pacific islands was not an easy one, although perhaps few sailors suffered to the extent of Samuel Patterson. Patterson was the American 'mendicant' author mentioned earlier who attempted to make a living selling the story of his hardships to an uncaring public. His story of personal suffering warrants closer inspection. As a poor child in a poor family, Patterson had very few prospects, and the history of his early life follows a pattern shared by the majority of seagoing young men at the time. He would sign on for a voyage and spend long months at sea, only to return to port and rove about 'with the sailor boys until my money was gone'. Each homecoming was an occasion for great joy for his mother, who never knew where he had gone or if he would ever return. Returning from one long voyage and only thirteen years old at the time, Patterson made his way to his village and knocked at the door of his family home. '[My mother] came and opened it, and on seeing her son who she thought was lost, she stepped back, sat down, and gave vent to a flood of tears, then, after embracing me, she told me the many night's sleep she had lost on my account', he remembered. Reunion with his mother would awaken his conscience. He repented his profligate behaviour and constant wandering – a way of life that he immortalised in a burst of poetry:

> I rang'd the world, I cross'd the seas,
> In hopes my restless breast to ease,
> By pleasures yet unknown:
> To all amusements I have run,
> That's found beneath the daily sun;
> Till weary I have grown[11]

Those sentiments would last as long as the search for an outward bound ship and the cycle would begin again. It was a life lived for the present and one that lasted as long as the money that fuelled it. It looked no further than the end of one journey and the inevitable beginning of the next. Given Patterson's lack of skills, education and prospects, it was the best he could hope for. He obviously enjoyed his freedom from a land-locked existence. He was a familiar face in the taverns and inns of Providence and New York – favourite places for signing on the ships that came to his home town of Rhode Island.

Patterson was an unsettled and rootless individual, a typical rover. He would as happily commit himself to a journey to Africa as he would sign on a short trip to New York. His voyages were dramatic affairs. He was a troublesome and wayward young man with a fiery temper and little personal control or forbearance. Frequently at odds with his workmates and his superiors, most of his working life was marked by disputes and disagreements. He was guilty of a foolish sort of bravado, which manifested itself in a tendency to step outside limits and challenge all forms of petty authority. As a common seaman, Patterson's life was one of hardship and adventure. He was washed overboard several times, escaping death by drowning and attacks by sharks. He narrowly avoided being marooned by one captain for insubordination and was beaten and flogged by another for disobedience. The furious officer 'flew at me in a rage with a rope and beat me until he was tired', recalled the sailor, 'and then catched up a hand spike and struck me over the head and left me speechless'. In

Havana he caught yellow fever and almost died and on another voyage he was placed in irons at the mercy of a despotic commander.

In 1804 he sailed to Hawaii and discovered an island already familiar with European religion, culture and trading practices – an island where European currency formed the basis of all transactions. He continued travelling between America and the Pacific until he was shipwrecked in Fiji in 1808 and decided to remain there when his captain and some of the crew left on a canoe to try and find a ship. 'I then reflected on my past conduct, especially in disregarding my mother, and leaving her as I had done. I retired to a cocoanut tree, and sat down under it and gave vent to a flood of tears', recalled the repentant sailor – shipwreck and destitution again providing an age-old impetus for a re-evaluation of one's life.

Patterson spent four months living with the Fijians before being rescued by the *Favorite* of Port Jackson. Although he was given protection by the islanders and fed and housed, his health suffered from his cultural dislocation. He lived as a commoner and wrote, 'I was in a poor, lingering and debilitated state of health; some times I could eat the produce of the country, and sometimes I could not relish it, and almost starved for food.' His low status meant that he was often treated roughly by the Fijians, who would beat and kick him when he unwittingly transgressed their social boundaries. A shipboard accident had left him lame and his affliction worsened during his time on the island. He continued to grow weaker with each passing day until his limbs completely gave way. He was placed in a shabby hut on the edge of the village and left to fend for himself. For about five weeks he lay on a hard mat spread on the ground, naked and without any additional covering. Unable to work, dependent on native charity and goodwill, his situation was pitiful:

When it rained the water would pour upon me in streams, and the ground under me become mud, and the water around me be half deep enough to cover me. In this situation I was often obliged to lie, being unable to move or help myself. Night after night without any human being near me I have spent thus lying in the water and mud; while peals on peals of thunder, seemingly shook the very foundations of the earth . . . as though volcanoes

were bursting in every direction around me. When the storms ceased, and
the water dried away from my bed, by day my naked emaciated body was
bitten and stung with numerous insects, which constantly, on all days,
never ceased to devour me. I was nearly blind with soreness of eyes, the
use of one leg entirely gone, and distressingly afflicted with the gravel;
which were my principal complaints, together with a general weakness
through the whole system.[12]

To make matters worse, Patterson recalled that the men would come
and feel his legs telling him, 'white man, you are good to eat', while
the women added their own form of indignity by checking to see if
he was circumcised. '[W]hen they found out that I was not, they
would point their fingers at me and say I was unclean', recalled the
miserable sailor.

As the days slowly passed, Patterson began to improve. His eyes
got better and a small degree of strength was restored to him. With
his companion Noah Steere he made plans to escape using a stolen
canoe. Unhappily, it was full of leaks and broke in two as they were
attempting to launch it. Their activities on the beach alerted a group
of natives, who informed the chief. He was furious that the sailors
had tried to leave without permission and attacked them with his war
club. Throwing themselves on the sand and begging for their lives,
they were eventually forgiven and were led back to their huts. It was
there, in the depths of despair, that Patterson tried to hang himself
– unsuccessfully. Weeks later as his health worsened, he was given
permission to take a canoe and head towards a ship anchored in the
harbour where the chief demanded a quantity of 'knives, beads, scissors
and whales teeth' in exchange for his freedom. The transaction was
completed and Patterson continued his sea-bound existence, albeit in
a state of physical decrepitude.

I was an object of pity; the use of one leg entirely gone, so weak that I was
not able to stand, and my body burned with the scorching sun in such a
manner, that I was blistered from the crown of my head, to the soles of
my feet; even the rims of my ears were blistered.

My shipmates brought me a shirt, and pair of trowsers: and they brought us a bottle and gave us a drink of grog, and a chew of tobacco. I looked round, and thought if there was any heaven, I had got to one, in being out of the hands of savages, and on board of an European vessel.[13]

Fabric of Disintegration

Patterson's life in Fiji was briefer and more brutal than most. But even those men with long-term island experience continued to suffer their own version of despair and personal hardship. Their distance from home and their innate sense of personal dislocation could often be charted by the disintegration of their original suit of clothes. European dress would slowly and inevitably be modified by the practicalities of island living. Jackets, knives, scarves and hats were usually appropriated by the natives shortly after arrival and the sailors were forced to improvise some sort of apparel to protect themselves from the elements. They wore hats made of pandanus leaves and went barefoot after their shoes had worn out. They held up their trousers with native fibres or adopted the short pareu, a cloth tied around the loins as worn by the natives. Melville wrapped himself in a long tapa cloth that dropped from his waist to his feet and protected his upper body from the sun by a piece of cloth worn as a poncho. Mariner was a bizarre spectacle. When rescued he was wearing 'a turban round the head, and an apron of the leaves of the chi tree round his waist'. Another sailor described his piecemeal and patchwork appearance: 'My hair was now very long, my beard thick and bushy. My trousers were in a very dilapidated condition, only kept together by the help of my fish-bone needle and bark thread.'[14] Their clothing reflected their marginality. Not quite one thing or another, the beachcombers symbolised the trauma of a life lived on the borders of two cultures.

Beachcombers were both part of the community, yet not part of it; they were subject to the whims of the natives, and hostage to any unforeseen change of circumstances. While dress and daily behaviour were easily changed, moral or psychological adjustments were much harder to make. There was no period of orientation that would prepare them for the uncertainties of acceptance into another culture. Some sailors crossed the beach without a backward glance. They had discovered within themselves a psychological compatibility with a native way of life and were keen to change the course of their future in quite dramatic ways. But the majority feared going native. However much they outwardly conformed, they found themselves involved in a constant psychological battle to resist 'the lure of the native'.[15] The majority of castaway sailors were obliged to conform rather than psychologically predisposed to do so, because of their absolute reliance on the islanders in all aspects of their new life.[16] Regardless of their apparent levels of assimilation, they still thought of themselves, first and foremost, as American or British sailors.

Because of this, they lived with an indefinable sense of isolation from those around them. They were constantly aware of their own precarious position, their own inferior status in communities with different rules and rituals. Their European behaviour often carried a different significance in their new societies. On Samoa, for instance, John Jackson unwittingly transgressed Samoan protocol in 1840 when he stole a pig intended as a sacred offering. He was hungry and mistakenly believed that his popularity would ensure his forgiveness. He was soon disabused of that hope when he noticed 'a man whispering to the chief, and, although I could not hear what was said I judged, by black looks and side glances, that my doom was sealed'.[17] Anticipating the worst, Jackson waited until the chief's attention was directed elsewhere and ran for his life. He hid in the bush for the rest of that day and the night that followed. When he was sure he was safe from pursuit, he cautiously made his way to a small village on the other side of the island where he, and his transgression, were unknown.

Personal and social dislocation characterised their lives as natives. John Twyning's overriding memory of his twenty years in the Pacific is imbued with fear. He was never sure if the natives 'would not take the fancy into their heads to slaughter us at no very distant day'. When he finally managed to obtain safe passage on a Europe-bound ship he felt an enormous relief. He was 'extremely thankful to Almighty God, that we were out of the power, that for some time had been exercised in an arbitrary manner over mind and body'. That lack of autonomy together with their status as marginals took a great toll on the sailors. Despite their best intentions they were unable to abandon completely their own social and personal histories. The majority of beachcombers were not able to turn their backs on the men they had once been. Melville was one of them. As Lawrence wrote in his analysis of Melville:

> There on the island, where the golden-green great palm-trees chinked in the sun, and the elegant reed houses let the sea-breeze through, and people went naked and laughed a great deal, and Fayaway put flowers in his hair for him – great red hibiscus flowers, and frangipani – O God, why wasn't he happy? Why wasn't he?[18]

The lure of home, combined with the precarious nature of their island existence, adversely affected the beachcomber. 'The necessity of conforming in many respects, to the manners of the natives, made us, besides other reasons, desirous of leaving the island,' wrote James Oliver in 1830. Most beachcombers regarded themselves as temporary residents and planned to return to their old lives as soon as they could. Those men held as captives were continually on the lookout for an opportunity to escape, while others left after deaths in their island families, or with the arrival of missionaries. Ill-treatment at the hands of the natives was another common reason and even those who deserted became disillusioned, ill or bored, and eventually made the decision to return home. As one sailor wrote:

> Hope now revives that I once more,
> Shall see my long'd for native shore.
> And all the powers of science fail,
> The raptures of my soul to tell.[19]

Decisions to leave were often spontaneous. Archibald Campbell, suffering from his multiple amputations, was nevertheless living a contented life in Hawaii as a favoured guest of King Kamehameha in 1810. He had been given a twenty-four-hectare plantation and fifteen retainers to work it. His future seemed secure, until he was overcome by sentimentality on hearing that there was a European ship in the harbour: 'When I learned this, I felt the wish to see my native country and friends once more so strong, that I could not

A violent encounter in a Polynesian society. Seemingly random acts of native brutality increased the beachcombers' sense of vulnerability.

resist the opportunity that now offered.' He requested permission from Kamehameha, who was anxious to know if the sailor had any complaints about his treatment: 'I told him I had none; that I was sensible I was much better here than I could be anywhere else, but that I was desirous to see my friends once more. He said, if his belly told him to go, he would do it; and that if mine told me so, I was at liberty.' Campbell's decision, however capricious, was a stand against fate. It was his last opportunity to wield a degree of personal control over the direction of his life.

James O'Connell caught sight of a ship in 1833, six years after his arrival in Ponape and, like Campbell, was overwhelmed by thoughts of home: 'George [Keenan] and I bounded about for joy, skipping up the hill, as if our feet could not serve us fast enough.' The sailors had to prevaricate, though, in order to escape. They asked the chief for the loan of a canoe to take a short trip round the island, promising to return. O'Connell was torn between his love for his family and his desire for freedom: '[M]y heart smites me now, as I recollect the gratified expression of my wife's countenance upon receiving the assurance [of his return].' The pull of civilisation was too hard to resist: 'No civilized person however theorized and philosophized though he were into contempt for the shackles of civilization, could content himself with innocent, unsophisticated, natural men forever', he argued. But his escape was full of hazards. The islanders became suspicious and chased O'Connell and Keenan across the beach. Jumping into their canoe they managed to push off from shore only to find themselves pursued by angry islanders who capsized the boat. As he tried to re-enter the canoe, O'Connell wrote that 'the Indians commenced beating us with the flat sides of the paddles when ever we showed our heads'. When they finally managed to regain their boat and steer through the reef, it was swamped again, washing them overboard. It was not until twenty-four hours later that they were able to get close enough to be taken on board ship. Feeling guilty about his desertion, O'Connell sent gifts to his wife and father-in-law, but decided to stay on board 'afraid to trust ourselves on shore again'.

The islanders were possessive of their white men and did not want to lose them. They made the sailors' departure as difficult as possible, often sabotaging their attempts to leave. Instances of passive and active resistance to their departure were reported by all sailors. Lamont particularly suffered through a number of abortive attempts to leave Tongareva. His popularity was such that the islanders were reluctant to let him go. They refused to carry him across the coral and they hid their canoes so he could not escape by sea. He was rarely left alone and was never able to travel without an escort. The story of his escape from island captivity is a typical one. It began with the appearance of an American whaler moored off shore – a highly emotional moment for the castaway. 'While I was doubting the truth of the report, a wild shout from the crowd dispelled all uncertainty, and a stately ship, her tall spars crowded with white sails, appeared in sight', Lamont remembered. He was overcome with the realisation of his most ardent wish. With steely determination, he made preparations to leave the island. His native hosts, however, were equally determined to prevent him. Lamont went down to the shore with his pistol loaded – resolved to reach the ship or die trying – and tried to force his way on board a canoe heading for the open sea. When the chief refused to stop for him, Lamont threatened to shoot. His time among the islanders had left them with a healthy respect for his temper. Lamont assured them that he would pull the trigger if they went without him: 'Alarmed for his own safety, the chief ordered the canoe to put in, and I sprang on board.'

The canoe drew closer to the ship. 'I took off my shirt', wrote the desperate sailor, 'and, fastening it to the end of a spear, waved it to and fro. Joyful sight! The vessel hove to, having observed the signal.' But Lamont's trials were not yet over. Two women from his adoptive family were becoming distraught at his possible departure. Calling out his name and shouting to the men in the canoe to turn back, they plunged into the water. There was no time to lose. Lamont drew his knife and threatened to attack the men if they attempted to slow down. He promised them riches in exchange for his freedom. The ship, he assured them, held vast supplies of knives, fish-hooks and axes. They would be well rewarded for their trouble.

The whaler had moored just outside the reef. The crew lined the decks armed with cutting spades and boarding knives, the tools of the whaling trade. Muskets and cannons protruded through the open cabin windows in a display of might and hostility directed at the flotilla of approaching canoes. Pulling close to the ship, Lamont called out loudly in English and a line was thrown from the ship. At that point he found himself pinioned from behind, as one of the islanders grabbed him by the arms, refusing to let him board. Again, he resorted to violence:

I contrived with the strength of despair to wrench my pistol hand from his embrace, when I placed the muzzle over my shoulder in the direction of his face at which he was fain to release me in such a hurry that he fell prostrate in the canoe.[20]

The ship was the *John Appleton* from New Bedford; Captain Isaac Taylor was the commander. When Lamont finally stepped on board he found himself trembling from head to foot. He was so overcome by the reality of his rescue that he had to lie down and gather his emotions before he was able to speak. Like many sailors before and after him, Lamont realised that it was easier to enter the islands than it was to leave them. The sailor's personal relationships with various islanders, together with the obligations and regrets it gave rise to, complicated his easy departure. It tainted his island sojourn with an inevitable legacy of betrayal and ingratitude for the kindnesses and compassion that he had been lucky to receive. Along with O'Connell, Mariner, Melville and many others, Lamont did make it back across the beach to safety, drawn by the lure of home and the memories of the life he had once known.

Beachcomber experience demonstrates that the problem of successful cultural adjustment lay with the sailor and not with the islands. It was not the age, history or mythical antecedents of the Pacific that challenged the sailors; it was their own struggles with the problems of assimilation in societies and places so far from their own. While life in the Pacific was undoubtedly different, it was not necessarily better. Their responses to that life revealed more about their threatened sense of self than about the reality of their island experience. Despite their best efforts they were not always able to discover the paradise they were searching for, as Samuel Patterson acknowledged:

> O happiness! at which all men do aim,
> How few know more of thee than just the name.
> Alas, how eager is poor mortal's chase
> In search of thee, in every land and place:
> They talk of thee, and yet they know thee not;
> Ah, few there be that find the happy spot.[21]

Assimilation took a physical and mental toll on the visiting European. The complicated rituals and ceremonies and the alien way of life demanded a fundamental re-evaluation of deep-seated ethical and moral beliefs. It was a mind-shift too radical for most men to make. Survival depended on successful integration, but the depth of integration that was required resulted in divided loyalties and a clash of ingrained values. This was particularly apparent when the sailors came face to face with that most feared and abhorred native practice – the act of cannibalism.

CHAPTER NINE

Too Close to Cannibalism

These savages are cannibals and eat the bodies of their own malefactors, and those of their prisoners.

SAMUEL PATTERSON, *Narrative of the Adventures and Sufferings of Samuel Patterson*

John Jackson, infamously known as Cannibal Jack, was no stranger to the Pacific. He was a nineteen-year-old sailor from Essex, England, when he first saw the islands of the South Seas. The blue lagoons, coral reefs and golden palms enthralled the Englishman, who was never to return home. He spent nearly fifty years on the beaches and sands of the Pacific until his death in 1891. Jackson was an extraordinary beachcomber. Also known as William Diaper, under which name he wrote his partial autobiography, he was the 'king of all wanderers' – a restless and unsettled individual who roamed the South Seas, signing on ships, deserting, living with islanders, assimilating to native life, and then moving on again. His beachcombing life began when he was kidnapped in Samoa in 1840 by islanders who wanted their own resident white man. After staying with them for several months, he eventually obtained passage on board a ship travelling to Fiji. He spent the years that followed wandering throughout Tonga, the Solomon Islands, New Caledonia and southern Vanuata before he settled again in Fiji from 1860 to the 1880s. The last ten years of his life were spent in Vanuatu and the Solomons.

Jackson was the archetypal odd-jobbing, beachcombing, border-crossing, culturally transgressive sailor who spent his long life exploring new worlds on the other side of the beach. The life he found on the islands was the only one he needed. He never looked back to his European past. Instead, he created a new and colourful existence for himself; one that would be heard in the tales told and the stories written about the early days of European–Pacific encounter. The one-time sailor embraced the freedom, opportunity and excitement of his new world. He spoke a number of native languages; his editor, the Rev. J. Hadfield, who met Jackson when he was an old man, mentions at least four, including Samoan, Tongan, Fijian, and several dialects of New Caledonia and the Loyalty Islands.[1] A man of passionate temper and insatiable curiosity, Jackson was a restless and independent individual who was a familiar sight to many Pacific travellers.

His island life was a unique and atypical combination of assimilation and non-conformity. Jackson was tattooed, linguistically proficient and a favourite of many native chiefs and warriors, but his naturally defiant nature seriously impacted on his long-term safety. He transgressed form and ritual, broke taboos and was known to have personally insulted and abused powerful priests and chiefs. His thoughtless actions often placed him in grave danger and resulted in repeated expulsions from town and village. His hot-headed responses to the vagaries of island living dictated the course of his travels, forcing him to move from place to place to avoid reprisals. 'I was in a very bad humour', he wrote on one occasion, 'and if it is true that passion is the whetstone of courage, I must have been all my lifetime a very courageous man, because the whetstone has been in incessant use with me now for nearly seventy years.'

He was a survivor, however, as his longevity suggests. Island life demanded adaptability and resourcefulness, both of which he possessed in abundance. He fought, he drank, he argued and caroused his way around the islands. His passage was marked by numerous sexual liaisons:

My acquaintances, who, by the by, seem to know as much of my antecedents as I do myself, have long since declared that I am the reputed father of

38 children, and 99 grandchildren, and so, that being the case, I shall in a very few years more be the great-grandfather of 999 – perhaps 1,000 – great-grandchildren, and if I live long enough for this to become a *fait accompli* . . . I think I shall then be entitled to gratulate [sic] myself on not having lived . . . in vain.[2]

He was the ultimate opportunist: 'As things cropped up appearing advantageous to me, so I embraced them.' He became a jack of all trades. He repaired muskets, built boats, distilled and sold liquor, transcribed sermons for the missionaries, collected tortoiseshell and traded in Fijian artefacts. 'I neglected nothing with which I could make money', he boasted, 'not so much for the love of it – as I did not at that time any more than now worship it – as for the amusement it gave me in accumulating it.' His island life was a far cry from his home on the farm in Essex. He lived with exotic peoples, he fought alongside their warriors, he drank kava and ate baked dogs and taro. There were very few aspects of native life that Jackson did not embrace and enjoy, with one noteworthy exception.

Witness to Horror

On Fiji, sometime between 1840 and 1842, he was a horrified spectator at a cannibal feast. He had been living with the Fijians for several months and had fought with them on a number of occasions. Until then he had never seen any evidence of cannibalism. After participating in a raid on a neighbouring village Jackson was one of a group of warriors who returned to the village bearing the bodies of their slain enemy. When the men threw the corpses into a clearing at the centre of the village, Jackson did the same. A native 'orator', a local character employed for the purpose, then made his appearance. He approached the bodies, stood gazing down at them and then launched himself into a frenzy of verbal and physical abuse. He kicked, prodded, mocked, taunted and ridiculed the dead warriors in a ritual meant to further humiliate the vanquished. Jackson realised that something unusual was about to take place. He watched the debasement continue as several young girls joined in and performed 'a most lewd kind of dance, touching the bodies in certain nameless parts with sticks as they were lying in a state of nudity, accompanying the action with the words of the song'.

The bodies were taken to a special site dedicated to the preparation of food, located at the side of the square. A heap of human bones whitened by the weather marked the spot. Next to it stood the bure kalou or sacred hut of the priest surrounded by a small grove of ironwood trees. The entrance was shrouded by long pieces of tapa in different colours, screening the priest who sat inside. Jackson described an old man with a white beard down to his waist and fingernails nearly two inches long. To the sailor he seemed a figure of horror, as he presided over a table 'constructed of human bones' and held chopsticks made of the same material. Two human skulls, used for drinking angona (the local liquor), lay on the table. Several more lay strewn about the floor. A rack was suspended from the ceiling above the priest's head. It held a selection of arms and legs specially set aside for the use of the gods, 'no one thinking of disturbing them or anything else belonging to this sacred place', according to Jackson. The priest was a man of great power in the village. The ensuing ceremony would take place under his watchful eye.

Outside in the square the preparations were under way. The fire was kindled and the stones heaped high upon the flames. The tafa tamata or butcher began cutting up the bodies using a medley of knives, shells, hatchets and bamboo, 'the latter being preferred for cutting through flesh'. The king, however, was impatient to begin

and not choosing to wait till it was properly prepared, told the butcher just to slice off the end of the noses, and he would roast them while he was getting the other parts ready. The butcher did as he was ordered, and handed the three ends of the noses to his majesty, which he grasped hold of very nimbly, and put on the hot stones to warm a little, not wishing to lose any time. The first he hardly let warm through, but while he was eating it, the second got a little better done, which he quickly demolished.[3]

Jackson sat close by. The king noted his interest and thought he was longing for a taste. 'His generous feeling overcame his love of this diet,' recalled the sailor, '[and] he immediately offered me the last nose he held between his thumb and finger.' Jackson was repelled. He refused to sample the human flesh, despite repeated pressure from the natives around him, telling them that 'this kind of work was not always believed when spoken of in my country'. In a spirit of conciliation he did agree to sample some turtle flesh being prepared at the same time and was given several leaf-wrapped packages to eat. Inside, he was appalled to discover a 'package of human flesh' – easily identifiable because it was 'darker and yellower' than the flesh of the turtle. He threw everything away: 'I took care not to eat anything but vegetables till I was certain all the human flesh was devoured.'

Jackson may have been a nativised white man but, he assured his

'The Banquet', a staged postcard showing Fijian men preparing for a cannibal feast, 1885–91. It is a sight described by many beachcombers who claimed to have witnessed instances of native cannibalism.

readers, there were still some borders that he refused to cross. 'I had gone beyond the bounds of an Englishman,' he wrote, 'to be even a spectator of such a scene.' For Jackson and other beachcombers like him, cannibalism was the main stumbling block on the road to full assimilation. In Jackson's narrative, it is identified as the ultimate boundary between himself and the islanders. He was not the first author to insist on such a division. The sailor was heir to a long-standing literary and philosophical Western tradition that used cannibalism, among other things, to define the savagery of others. Throughout all ages and to the present day, the accusation of cannibalism functions as a marker of total and irrevocable difference between one community and another. It serves an ideological agenda by enabling one group of people to define themselves as civilised specifically in opposition to a non-civilised other.[4] For the Westerner, cannibalism effectively divides the European from the non-European, the human from the inhuman. It separates those who eat each other from those who do not. The cannibal is placed outside the boundaries that define acceptable human behaviour and is denied a common humanity. The European understands himself as Christian, enlightened, educated and progressive, specifically in contrast with the savage, heathen figure of the cannibal. Instances of Western participation in cannibalism therefore are always downplayed or denied. Undoubtedly there would have been occasions whereby sailors were unwitting or unwilling consumers of unidentified food at native feasts. But even those who knowingly participated would never have admitted that fact to Western audiences.

Those who lived beyond the bounds of the known Western world and those at an earlier and more primitive stage of human history were often accused of being cannibals. Anthropophagy was believed to have been practised by those who were less civilised and who had not been exposed to the progressive enlightenment of humanity in general. Both prehistoric Europeans and non-Western man were believed to be cannibals. Both lacked the requisite benefits of history and culture and both were deemed to occupy the same degenerate, savage, pre-civilised state. While the physical and geographic aspects of the New World may have been idyllic, the inhabitants of those lands were not. The 'savage nature', it was argued, 'still feasts on the flesh of its prisoners – appeases its Gods with human sacrifices – whole societies of men and women live promiscuously, and murder every infant born amongst them'.[5] The cannibal who lived in distant lands was a reflection of Europeans 'as we once were' – he represented the historic state of savagery out of which European society had raised itself.[6] To participate in cannibalism was to revert to the chaos and disorder of the past. In the Western philosophical tradition, it heralded a return to the savage state.

Theory versus Experience

To philosophers and writers such as Rousseau and Montaigne, the cannibal had other, more mythic, resonances. They saw him as the epitome of purity in a corrupted modern world. Untainted by artifice, intellect or imagination, he was an ideal, untouched, natural man, living in a world of natural simplicity. Montaigne saw the difference between 'us' and 'them', but in an interesting reversal of traditional ideology, he idealised the cannibal and demonised the European. In his childlike state of grace, the cannibal highlighted those values of Western society deemed despicable or unworthy. He was honest and spontaneous in a world of artifice and hypocrisy. Montaigne relativised cannibalism, arguing that it was not as horrific as the worst excesses of civilisation. Western examples of warfare, death and torture were the true face of barbarism:

> I am not sorry that we should here take notice of the barbarous horror of so cruel an action, but that, seeing so clearly into their faults, we should be so blind to our own. I conceive there is more barbarity in eating a man alive, than when he is dead; in tearing a body limb from limb by racks and torments, that is yet in perfect sense; in roasting it by degrees; in causing it to be bitten and worried by dogs and swine . . . than to roast and eat him after he is dead.[7]

His relativist approach to the otherness of others and his disinclination to view cannibalism as the greatest horror inflicted by humanity upon its own species, was a view echoed by many of the later beachcombers.

It was to become a defining feature of their narratives. They, too, questioned the savagery of the cannibal by a comparison to the barbarity of Western practices, but they differed from Montaigne on a fundamental level. Montaigne's was a purely theoretical response to the myth of primitivism. He had never travelled to places newly discovered and had never met any native people, cannibal or otherwise, in their own habitats. His information was gained by talking to 'a man in my house that had lived ten or twelve years in the New World'.[8] His intellectual reaction to the idea of the cannibal was typical of those who idealised and wrote about new lands and alien people without ever leaving home.

The beachcombers were afforded no such luxury. Their experiences took place on islands long reputed to be home to man-eaters. They were grounded in the reality, not the theory of anthropophagy. They were faced with the living practice, not engaged in a theoretical debate:

> I shall never forget the observation of one of our crew as we were passing slowly by the entrance of this bay [Taipi] in our way to Nukuheva. As we stood gazing over the side at the verdant headlands, Ned, pointing with his hand in the direction of the treacherous valley, exclaimed, 'There – there's Typee. Oh, the bloody cannibals, what a meal they'd make of us if we were to take it into our heads to land! but they say they don't like sailor's flesh, it's too salt. I say, maty, how should you like to be shoved ashore there, eh? [9]

Throughout the last quarter of the eighteenth century the peoples of the Pacific, with the exception of the Maori from New Zealand, were not generally assumed to be cannibals. Their reputation began to change after sensational reports from Fiji told of cannibal feasts and inhuman rites. The Marquesans also came to be feared. 'Every dark crime wh[ich] contaminates the mind, sweeps from the heart every tender and noble feeling, stains the polluted soul of the Marquesan', wrote missionary Robert Thomson in the 1830s. '[H]aughty and vindictive; cruel and ungrateful, he stands forth a most revolting character, a living blot on Natures brow. Mercy is a stranger to his bosom and his

hand is often wet with blood.'[10] By the mid-nineteenth century, South
Sea islanders in general were seen as stereotypical cannibals lying in
wait for the unwary European. A group of shipwrecked sailors cast
ashore in Fiji in 1829 were representative in their common fear of
a 'fate worse than death'. The frightened castaways, in no condition
to defend themselves, were taunted, abused and threatened by large
numbers of naked Fijians holding clubs and spears. One particular
sailor was singled out for special examination. He was led away from
the rest of the crew and carefully studied: '[F]irst they opened his
bosom, then pulled off his jacket and waistcoat; and lastly stripped
him to the skin. We really felt as though they were going to butcher
him,' recalled a terrified companion. It was with great relief that the
sailors finally realised 'it was *his shirt* they wanted'.[11]

Fact or Flights of Fancy

To beachcombing sailors and the Western societies they left behind,
there was no notion more repelling and enthralling than cannibalism.
It was a forbidden act, surrounded by the most potent social and
cultural taboos, and, predictably, examples of it were deeply intriguing.
The beachcomber-authors were well aware of this. They recognised
the appeal of the exotic and the terror of the unknown. They all
promised, in one form or another, to titillate, amuse and educate their
readers. The narratives tell of men killed in battle; they describe the
cutting up and preparation of bodies and the methods of cooking. They
always include details of the feast that follows. There was already a
fair amount of literature in circulation that frequently indulged itself
in hyperbolic flights of fancy on the subject of cannibalism, often
without having a basis in reality.[12] Imaginations worked overtime
on the more ghoulish aspects of the practice, as the missionary-poet
William Henry made clear:

> Just now a *human victim* fresh arrives,
> And the sage Priest plucks from it both its eyes,
> And on his blood stain'd hand doth rudely place,
> And them present before his Sovereign's face.

His royal mouth the Sovereign opens wide,
The priest obsequious doth the morsel guide
Quite near his lips; then gently turning round,
Doth cast the eye-balls on the sacred ground.[13]

Such works were written to shock and scandalise rather than inform and educate the Western reader. They were highly sensationalised treatments of a compelling topic utilising the standard tropes of cannibalism – the depraved participants, the dismembered corpses and the hellish feasts. The authors of such adventures understood the expectations and demands of a nineteenth-century readership – a readership primed for tales of degradation and horror from savage countries. Beachcomber-authors were subject to those same impulses and influences, but they claimed a different authority.

To gain true knowledge and become an authentic commentator, an author had to cross the boundary that separated romance from real-ism, that divided imagination from actual experience. Beachcomber accounts were based on their first-hand, eyewitness experiences of native life. They gain their power and force from the author's proxim-ity to the events described. Beachcomber-authors claim for themselves the authority as well as the notoriety of having been on the spot. Their personal experience is used as incontestable evidence of the truth of their tales. 'I had seen so much of their dark ways', wrote one sailor in Fiji, '[so] I thought I would witness all I could, till I saw an opportunity of getting off the islands.'[14] They insist upon the truth and accuracy of their personal experiences. Whether that truth is historically verifiable is a matter of ongoing debate. The ideological impulse that underlies many accusations of cannibalism throws a taint of suspicion over many 'first-hand' accounts. European attempts to define the other as less than human via participation in cannibalism often reveals more about Western culture than it does about the indigenous people themselves. The veracity or otherwise of any report on cannibalism is inseparable from the prevailing ideologies in place at the time. Beachcomber-authors were undoubtedly products of their age, but they insistently define themselves as the primary authorities for their own texts. They have their own tales to tell about cannibalism.

Fijian artefacts made from human teeth and bone. These macabre mementoes were collected by sailors and taken home as evidence of their native experiences.

Shocking Tales

William Lockerby was a young man when he sailed from Boston as first officer on board the *Jenny* on 2 June 1807. It was a journey that took him to Port Jackson, New South Wales, calling at several islands in the South Seas. He was away from home for a long time and his family feared the worst. They presumed he had been press-ganged on board ship and was either missing or dead. His disappearance had occurred shortly after his marriage, but his young wife refused to wear mourning. She could not imagine his death. She believed she was too young to become a widow. For many years she waited, believing that her young husband would return from wherever he was. Three years and seven months later, Lockerby did in fact return to his native land, and he had a terrifying story to tell. Along with a small group of sailors, he had been marooned in 'the Cannibal Isles' by his captain in 1808 and had lived with the natives until he could effect his escape.

He recorded his adventures in a journal written shortly after his return home, but the younger members of the family were unable to read it. Older family members were reluctant to allow them access to the more sensational elements of Lockerby's island life. They were also hesitant about exposing one of their own to public scrutiny. Old-fashioned prudery ensured the narrative remained in private hands, under lock and key. It was eventually sent to a publisher in 1850, although the subsequent loss of the manuscript meant that it remained unpublished and unread. Lockerby had made another copy for his parents, still safely guarded by the family. It was that manuscript that was finally published in 1925. Although Lockerby was one of the first Europeans to write about the early days in Fiji, his story was not read by many of his descendants until nearly a hundred years after it was written.[15]

In it he describes his journey to the Pacific in search of sandalwood. The *Jenny* and its crew traded successfully up and down the Fijian coastline, exchanging ironwork, beads and cloth for quantities of native hardwood. Lockerby was left on shore organising the collection and loading of the wood when his ship inexplicably sailed without him. He was marooned with four other men, deserted and forsaken in

Fiji: 'I was left among a race of cannibals, far from every object that was near and dear to me, and possessing but very faint hopes of a vessel calling at such a simply dismal corner of the Globe that might carry me and my unfortunate comrades again into civilized society.' Realising that he would need patronage and protection, he approached the King of Myemboo with whom he had a cordial working relationship. Explaining his situation and asking for protection, Lockerby was adopted by the king and treated with a corresponding level of honour and respect that continued throughout his stay. He was able to travel freely, was welcomed into all homes and villages and was a frequent spectator, and sometimes participant, in a variety of island ceremonies and celebrations. Because of his royal connections, there were few aspects of Fijian life that were not open to the sailor. He was an avid witness and diligent recorder generally, but his journal is particularly valuable because of its detailed description of cannibalism. His account of a massacre that occurred in Fiji is a paradigm for similar stories from a variety of other beachcomber narratives.

In 1808, the sailor was part of a small group of white men travelling in a convoy of 150 war canoes. They were en route to a nearby island to mount a surprise attack on an enemy village. The battle, which lasted for three full days, was successful and the victorious invaders prepared to return home. On their way back to the beach, they discovered 350 women, children and old men seeking sanctuary from the carnage. Wholesale slaughter followed. Women and children were knocked down with clubs and lanced with spears. The children were chased and shot down with arrows. They were then dragged by their hands and feet over the rocks to the canoes which lay about 250 metres from shore. Anyone who escaped was pursued by the warriors and beaten by their clubs. 'The scene of horror that I and my comrades here witnessed, who were all the time naked, with death pictured in our countenances, surpasses conception, and it is impossible for me to convey to the minds of the reader an adequate idea of this terrible scene of human misery,' recalled Lockerby.

The battle turned into an orgy of cannibalism. It was a commonly held contemporary belief that the Fijians were cannibals and that war casualties were almost invariably eaten. In his journal Lockerby records that forty-two dead bodies were cut up and cooked either in the ground upon hot stones covered with green leaves and earth, or cut into pieces and broiled on the fire. No part of the bodies was wasted. The head was held over the fire to singe off the hair before it was cleaned with shells and placed with the rest of the body. Feet were burned till the skin of the soles peeled off. Intestines were cleaned in water and then roasted and eaten. Lockerby is an apologetic author. He knows his readers will find 'such details as these disgusting, but still they may show into what an abyss of dreadful depravity these poor wretches are sunk'. Although he was forced to eat yams cooked in the same pot, he refused the human meat. Not all the white men were so lucky. A fifty-year-old prisoner had been 'cut up and divided among the chiefs, who made a hearty breakfast of it. Some of my companions, I am sorry to say eat a part of it involuntarily, mistaking it for pork, as it was cooked and resembled it very much'.

William Endicott, third mate on the *Glide*, had a similar tale to tell. His account was written after his return to America and sent to the *Danvers Courier* in his home town in New England. Dated 16 August 1845 and entitled 'A Cannibal Feast at the Feejee Islands, By an Eye Witness', Endicott's story is an intriguing one. It concerns an event that took place sometime in March 1831 in the region of Macuata in the northern part of Vanua Levu, twenty years after the scenes witnessed by William Lockerby. He was working on board ship when he heard that the local men were bringing back the bodies of their dead enemies and planning a grand 'soleb' or feast. He decided to attend – as an observer only – confessing that he 'had a strong desire to see the manner in which [the natives] prepared and ate human flesh'.

Endicott arrived in the village just in time to witness the arrival of the vanquished warriors. They were tied on poles about three and a half metres long, each pole supported by six men. As Endicott recounted later, 'They were bound with wythes [flax cords], by bringing the upper and lower parts of the legs together and binding them to the body, and the arms in a similar manner by bringing the elbows to rest on the knees, and their hands tied upon each side of the neck.' The victorious warriors, all in a state complete nudity, began

William Endicott was shipwrecked off Vanua Levu in 1831. Endicott
was perhaps most famous for the gruesome descriptions of cannibal feasts
that he claimed to have witnessed in Fiji during his time as a beachcomber.

to dance. 'They were painted in a most frightful manner,' Endicott
recalled, 'each one attempting to outdo the other in the most loathsome
obscenity and savage appearance.' He was soon surrounded by over
a hundred dancers, chanting their war songs and gyrating to the
beat of the drums. While the dance continued, Endicott turned his

attention to the preparation of the bodies. There was a bizarre pattern to the dismemberment that followed. First the right hand was cut off, then the left foot, right elbow and left knee, until all the limbs were separated from the body. Entrails and vital organs were taken out and cleaned for cooking. The flesh was cut through the ribs to the spine which was broken apart enabling the body to be separated into two pieces. An oblong piece of flesh was removed 'commencing about the bottom of the chest and passing downwards about eight inches, and three or four inches wide at the broadest part'. This was set aside for the king. The head was removed last:

> [It] was thrown towards the fire, and being thrown some distance it rolled a few feet from the men who were employed around it; when it was stolen by one of the savages who carried it behind the tree where I was sitting. He took the head in his lap and after combing away the hair from the top of it with his fingers picked out the pieces of the scull which was broken by the war club and commenced eating the brains.[16]

The rest of the flesh was neatly wrapped in fresh plantain leaves and placed in the earth oven over hot stones. Endicott gave no further details: 'I shall not here particularize. The scene is too revolting.' He returned to the feast many hours later when the food was finally cooked. He was the sole European present at an event 'seldom witnessed by civilized man'. His sense of obligation to his readers forced him to record what he termed, the islanders' 'excessive greediness for human flesh and their savage thirst for blood'. Endicott was handed a package wrapped in plantain leaves. He reluctantly opened it to discover part of a foot 'taken off at the ankle and at the joints of the toes'. He threw it aside and refused to eat it, but needed an excuse if he was not to antagonise his hosts. He argued that it had been kept too long before being cooked. The king was not impressed. He pointed out that white men kept their salted meat for much longer periods of time. In the king's view the sailors' salt beef was 'the most unhealthy and loathsome food that could be eaten'. Endicott refused to enter the debate, as he explained in his account: 'I had no desire to discuss the question of diet with this old savage and cannibal, knowing that I could not convince him of the base impropriety of eating human flesh.' Despite his repulsion, Endicott was determined to obtain 'some relic as a remembrance of the scene I had witnessed'. He asked for, and received, a souvenir of the grisly occasion in the form of a pair of sail needles, made from a bone of one of the devoured victims.

Endicott and Lockerby were demonstrably disgusted by the activities they witnessed. They were both young men from another world. Their sea voyages had taken them far from the comforting security of home. The books they had read and the tales they had heard proved totally insufficient for the harsh reality of Pacific life. They could never have imagined they would come face to face with cannibalism as a living practice. It was the stuff of nightmares. Like other sailors, they tried to make their repugnance known, often at considerable risk to themselves. John Twyning, for instance, saved the life of a native enemy sentenced to be eaten. The distressed islander had pleaded for his help and Twyning 'hid him where they could not find him, and thus saved his life'. When returning from battle, Lockerby threw corpses overboard in order to prevent them being eaten, risking the wrath of the Fijians and jeopardising his own safety by doing so, while others attempted to promote more civilised codes of behaviour. John Jackson, whose own relationship to cannibalism was problematic, tried to convince a Fijian chief that his actions were blasphemous: '[I] made him comprehend the disgust we had to these practices, but could not by any means instill into him the wickedness of them.' He encouraged the Fijians to bury the bodies rather than eat them. He believed it was possible to re-educate the people, but a young chief disagreed, saying it 'would be impossible for me or even himself to do away with that practice as it was an old established rule from time immemorial throughout the Feejees'.

Tainted with Suspicion

Beachcombers were the archetypal boundary crossers, literally and metaphorically travelling to places denied to others. Their voyage from civilisation to savagery brought them perilously close to the practice of cannibalism. It was a proximity that compromised their integrity, threw doubt upon their moral fibre and made their European contemporaries distinctly uneasy. The Russian explorers who came face to face with Jean Cabri on the Marquesas needed no encouragement to assume the worst. The white man's copious tattoos and native costume damned him in the eyes of the visitors. They had no doubt that his character was as tainted, marked and degenerate as his ink-stained skin. Cabri's obvious adoption of *some* aspects of Marquesan culture condemned him to participation in *all* native practices. The Russians were extremely suspicious of the beachcomber

> who had indeed lost all appearance of an European education, [and] asserted that he had never eaten the enemies whom he had taken, only exchanged them for swine ... Notwithstanding this, I am disposed to think that a man, who had in other respects incorporated himself so entirely with the natives, who might be said to be both morally and physically transformed into a savage, who himself confessed that he went out hunting on purpose to catch men, and exchange them for swine, and thought this an excellent pastime, – I cannot help, I say, being much disposed to think that such a man was very capable, when he had caught his prey, of eating it in company with his new brethren.[17]

Cannibalism was seen as doubly horrific if practised by a white man. No other act had the same power to condemn the European so irrevocably as other. Cannibalism was quite simply the point of no return in any act of going native. To Westerners, a white savage was bad enough, but a white cannibal was unthinkable. Cannibalism denied the perpetrator any place in an ordered, structured Western society. It placed him outside the realm of all that was deemed to be cultured and civilised. In the case of the beachcomber, it certainly denied him the status of legitimate author. He had forfeited his proper position of authorial detachment and was in danger of being implicated in the very acts he was describing. In the eyes of his readers, he had become indistinguishable from those he wrote about; he had moved from privileged observer to degraded participant.

John Jackson was a case in point. He was a scandal on island beaches. Europeans were unimpressed with the 'long-bearded, grimy old beachcomber' that confronted them, regarding him as little better than

a 'drunken loafer and an outcast'.[18] The growing missionary presence
was aghast when he appeared before them wearing 'neither shirt nor
trousers', remembered Jackson, 'only just a fathom of thin white calico
round my loins'. In fairness, his editor, the Rev. J. Hadfield, is less
critical. Despite Jackson's ragged clothing and dishevelled appearance,
Hadfield described him as a 'man of distinguished bearing' and 'shrewd
intelligence'. But neither his supporters nor his detractors were
comfortable with the darker rumours about his island acculturation.
His nickname did nothing to reassure them. The sailor himself
explained the origins of his infamous nom de plume:

> I suppose the reader will expect an explanation of how I, in the first place,
> came in possession of that somewhat disgraceful-sounding sobriquet of
> 'Cannibal Jack', and which I have since taken as my *nom de plume.*
>
> Well then, as it is now a long time ago since I first commenced
> scribbling – some forty years – and among the rest, I named one book
> *Jack the Cannibal Killer*, thinking perhaps as everything is in a name, that
> it would have the greater circulation, but instead of remaining at that, it
> was, by some means or other, altered, and 'Cannibal Jack' became indelibly
> fixed upon myself.[19]

The name obviously stuck. His beachcombing account was given the
title *Cannibal Jack: The True Autobiography of a White Man in the South
Seas* by Hadfield in 1928, who realised the potential for sensationalism
in the sailor's life. Jackson, then known as William Diaper, denied
being a cannibal, but his editor was not convinced: 'I trust I am not
traducing his name if I suggest that in spite of this disclaimer it was
the accepted opinion in the Islands that he had been addicted, as no
doubt were not a few white men, to such practices.'[20] The use of the
word 'addicted' is revealing. Europeans link cannibalism with appetite
and desire – a desire that, once indulged, is regarded as insatiable.
It is an appetite that unleashes an infinite capacity for debasement
and perversion. It traps the cannibal in an instinctual and oral stage
of development from which there is no progression and no escape,
according to our mendicant author, Samuel Patterson:

The greediness of these people, and all cannibals, for human flesh is astonishingly great; and perhaps there is no evil habit so hard to be eradicated as this inhuman one: it has been shown, that even after the practice has been renounced, and the persons Christianized, still a lurking hankering appetite has remained a long time.[21]

If the beachcombers were to be taken seriously as authors, they had to bury the spectre of cannibalism. Their presence at the events they described certainly empowered their texts. Unfortunately, it also endangered their credibility. How far did they go? Were they spectators or participants? Did they truly succumb to the dangerous 'seduction of appetite'? It was a dilemma faced by all sailors who wished to claim the authority of a first-hand, unmediated experience of actual, lived events. All those who document cannibalism take great pains to separate themselves from the events they describe. They work hard to ensure that their personal integrity remains unquestioned. They are keen to tell their stories and bear witness to the act of cannibalism, but they need to assure their readers of their non-participation. While the cannibal may be regarded as a figure of degeneration, disruption and disorder, the sailors – as travellers, natives, witnesses and authors – may not.

They reinforced their non-cannibal status by indulging in some literary sleight of hand. As always, Melville showed the way. On the Marquesas he and Toby were convinced that their hosts are about to indulge in a cannibal feast. They saw the warriors return from battle carrying long poles on which were lashed 'three long narrow bundles, carefully wrapped in ample coverings of freshly plucked palm-leaves'. Primed with previous stories of South Sea cannibals, they had no doubt as to the contents, although Melville was honest enough to admit that the 'thick coverings prevented my actually detecting the form of a human body'. Far off in the valley, the sound of the drums could be heard. Consumed by curiosity and full of terror, they slowly and carefully made their way towards the Ti – the sacred meeting place of the men of the tribe. Unnoticed by the crowds, Melville approached a large wooden trencher and lifted the covering. His worst imaginings were fulfilled. Before him lay the 'disordered members of a human skeleton, the bones still fresh with moisture, and with particles of flesh clinging to them'. The event that prompted such agonies of anticipation had already taken place. The sailors arrived too late to witness the actual feast itself. They had to content themselves with the sight of the leftovers, with brief and hurried glimpses of the remnants of the feast. [22] They were separated from the gory event by the passage of time. They could only describe the aftermath. They saw too little and for too brief a time. As a literary strategy, the distance provided by the sailors' late arrival was effective. It acknowledged their presence but distanced them from the act itself. The mere suggestion of the dreaded event proved more than enough for both sailor and reader. It left the full horror to the workings of the imagination, an imagination more than able to supply the missing details.

Jackson's presence at many of the cannibalistic scenes that he described raises disturbing questions about his own status as a possible cannibal. To deflect suspicion he adopted a strategy of physical distance throughout his narrative. This is particularly noticeable in the later chapters where he pointedly removed himself from the scenes he described. He can usually be found, he told us, at 'the top of a rock at the back of the square' looking 'down on all their proceedings'. Other sailors did the same. John Twyning told of a mass slaughter that occurred during his stay on Wallis Island: 'We, white men,' he wrote 'withdrew ourselves from amongst them [the natives], and retired to a rising ground at a short distance.' The physical distance between the white men and the carnage confirmed their status as non-participatory witnesses. Twyning observed from afar 'the most savage slaughter . . . that I had ever witnessed' while effectively removing himself from any charge of involvement. He was present at the scene but peripheral to it; 'we stood firm, about twenty yards from the horrid scene' watching a 'female, wallowing on the field of slaughter, and drinking the blood as it issued from the wounds of a dying man'.

The sailors are not only removed from the carnage, but are physically superior to it. They stand above and beyond the heinous activities taking place. The testimony of a non-participatory witness is always preferable to one who is too closely involved. In the minds of readers he has retained the necessary objectivity and distance needed to identify himself as credible and authoritative. The sailors positioned themselves on the margins of the action. They watched it from afar; they were on the edge, at the borders, looking down, as opposed to their customary level of personal involvement.[23] One sailor described the death of an enemy chief, whose heart was cut out of his body and 'presented to the chiefs on a large plantain leaf. Whether it was eaten or even tasted I cannot say, as I was not present at the disgusting ceremony,' he wrote.[24] Physical distance is used to separate witness from deed – it divides the European from the act itself. As a strategy of caution it symbolises an ideological remoteness. It signals a massive separation in enlightenment, civilisation and humanity that is presumed to exist between the author and the savage he observes.

The White Cannibal

But despite their literary tactics, the notion of the white cannibal was a pernicious one. A native cannibal was regarded as the epitome of untutored and unredeemed savagery. A white cannibal was something else altogether. He represented the degeneration of civilisation. He was a horrific symbol of regression and debasement. His very existence drew attention to the fragility of ideological divisions between European and native. He had the capacity to destroy the carefully constructed boundary between 'us' and 'them'. A white cannibal was a figure of chaos with the power to disrupt law, civility and an ordered world. He signalled an inverted moral and spiritual universe. Even worse, he exposed the savage impulses that lay just beneath the veneer of civilisation. In societies such as Europe, carefully predicated in opposition to a non-European other, he was a potent emblem of pure anarchy.

European or Western cannibalism, however, is an historical fact. It is often described as 'survival cannibalism' – an act committed by those who find themselves in life-and-death situations. It was a common, if unpublicised, reality of seagoing life, for instance. It occurred when men were separated from their ship, adrift on unknown oceans and forced to confront the imminent and immediate possibility of death. By eating their dead or dying companions, they were able to survive for a while longer in the hope of eventual rescue. It was a horrific act, but one that arose from the desperation of specific, unrepeatable circumstances. One graphic example will suffice.[25]

In 1819 the whaleship *Essex* set sail from Nantucket on a two-and-a-half-year voyage to hunt sperm whales in the South Pacific. She had a crew of twenty-one men, mostly young and nearly all from Nantucket, sailing under the command of Captain George Pollard, Junior. They were hardy, intrepid individuals, men who understood the dangers and hazards of the whaling industry and who were well aware of the precarious nature of a seagoing life. The *Essex* became famous, or infamous, for one particular incident literally unheard of in the annals of maritime lore and history. It was a story told wherever sailors gathered, wherever men took to the sea for their livelihood. It was an event that would inspire a young American sailor to write one of the greatest stories of the sea. The book was *Moby Dick* and its author was our American beachcomber, Herman Melville. His story of Captain Ahab's pathological pursuit of an enraged White Whale who attacked and sank a ship became a classic and was based on the history of the *Essex*. It was a history bequeathed to us by Owen Chase, first mate on the *Essex* and one of the few survivors of the disaster. His account, *The Wreck of the Whaleship* Essex, was the inspiration for *Moby Dick*, but truth, in this case, was certainly more marvellous than the fiction it inspired.

The *Essex* was whaling in the waters between Chile and Peru and was more than 1600 kilometres from the nearest land. Its crew had taken over twenty-five whales and had 800 barrels of the precious oil stored in the hold when the ship was unaccountably struck by a whale. The huge sperm whale had surfaced approximately ninety metres away when it turned and headed directly for the ship. It rammed its huge head into the bow with such force that the wood cracked, splintered and buckled. Water gushed into the hold and before the crew could grasp what had happened and before repairs could be made, the whale turned back and deliberately struck a second time. There was a resounding crash and within ten minutes the ship had filled with water and was lying on her side. The men scrambled for the whaleboats, taking with them ninety kilograms of hard bread and 295 litres of drinking water. They could do nothing but watch in dismay and disbelief as the ship quickly sank beneath the waves. Their legendary ordeal was about to begin. 'I have no language to paint the horrors of our situation,' wrote Owen Chase as he cast off from the sinking ship and headed into the unforgiving ocean.

Twenty-one men in three whaleboats charted a course for the nearest known land, the west coast of South America. It was a journey that was to take over three months and was to cause an unparalleled degree of personal suffering. Each day every man received a biscuit weighing a little over six ounces and half a pint of fresh water – a diet that was abysmally below their daily needs. The men were unanimous: although it was barely enough to keep them alive, they would not ask for more. Their meagre allowance would enable them to eke out the bulk supplies of food and water. Survival was a hope, not a certainty. They did not know when they would reach land and their supplies had to last. They would survive by fighting their cravings.

Time dragged on. The boats were buffeted by winds and lashed by rain. The men shivered uncontrollably and lay in wet and stinking clothes at the bottom of the boats, too weary to sit upright. It was worse when the wind dropped. Hours lengthened into days as their boats lay becalmed, drifting helplessly across slow and silent seas. The men lost hope. Their rations were halved. They grew thinner and steadily weaker the longer they searched for land. They began to starve to death. In the long weeks that followed, twelve men succumbed to starvation, illness, depression and despair. Their companions could do nothing but witness their agonies and watch them die. 'He lay in the greatest pain and apparent misery' wrote Chase of a dying comrade, 'groaning piteously until 4 o'clock in the afternoon, when he died in the most horrid and frightful convulsions I ever witnessed.'

All bodies had previously been committed to the sea but as the level of suffering increased, other options now had to be considered. The agonies of the living demanded a sacrifice from the dead. Chase suggested that the body of their comrade be kept for food. There was only three days' provision left and the ocean stretched endlessly before them. If salvation was to come it demanded some form of human endeavour. Nobody objected to Chase's suggestion. Another, more horrifying ordeal now lay before them. The men prepared the body to prevent it from spoiling: 'We separated the limbs from the body and cut all the flesh from the bones, after which we opened the body, took out the heart, closed it again – sewing it up as decently as we could – and then committed it to the sea.' They ate the remainder over the next few days, making sure that no morsel was wasted. It satisfied their bodily hunger. What it did to their minds can only be imagined. 'The painful recollection . . . brings to mind, at this moment, some of the most disagreeable and revolting ideas that it is capable of conceiving', Chase recalled. 'Humanity must shudder at the dreadful recital,' he wrote. 'I have no language to paint the anguish of our souls in this dreadful dilemma.'

Five men survived. They had travelled more than 3200 kilometres on their uncharted voyage to the South American continent before they were finally picked up by a passing ship. They had spent over ninety gruelling and harrowing days at sea and were in a pitiful state. The horror of their history was indelibly etched on their bodies and minds. Shrunken limbs, cadaverous faces, sunken eyes, and bones jutting through the skin told the true cost of their journey. In all, seven dead men were eaten by those who lived through the voyage. The survivors had spent three months at sea, suffered the most appalling experience, but had lived to tell their tale. They all returned to their home town of Nantucket where they were received quietly back into their community. Their story was told by Chase in 1821. It was a tale that had been told before. In a community whose entire livelihood depended on dangerous long-distance whaling voyages, disasters at sea were a fact of life. Instances of survival cannibalism were not unknown but remained relatively undiscussed. The men from the *Essex* were never asked to account for their actions.

All five survivors eventually returned to the sea. Owen Chase, in particular, became a successful whaling captain and made a number of profitable voyages to the Pacific. He was a changed man, however, from the twenty-one-year-old who had made his fateful voyage on the *Essex*. Like the other survivors, he never spoke of the shipwreck, even to his family. His ordeal remained buried in the past but its memory never died. As the years passed he was plagued by recurring pains

Owen Chase, first mate of the ill-fated *Essex*, in later years.
He never fully recovered from the horror of his experiences and
by 1868 he was judged insane.

in his head from which he could gain no relief. He was also haunted by a fear of starvation. After his death at the age of seventy-one, his family discovered a hoard of crackers and other food hidden in the attic of his home.

White cannibalism on the islands could not claim the same sympathy. It was seen as something else entirely. It was a submission to one's basest, most degraded urges – a surrender to animal-like appetite and behaviour. White cannibals profaned the most hallowed laws, codes and taboos at work in all moral societies. In the eyes of their contemporaries, the beachcombers as possible cannibals could never be fully trusted. There was sufficient ambiguity and threat in their lives and in their texts to cause unease in a number of readers. William Torrey's description of his enforced participation in a cannibal feast on the Marquesas exemplifies that disturbing element of transgression:

> those feasts [in which] we were compelled to partake, [were] greatly against our wishes; yet had we been unconscious of what the feast consisted, I think we would have called it a most delicious morsel; and should any of my readers sit down to a dish nicely prepared, without knowing what it was or supposing it something different, I think they would join with me in declaring it of the richest flavour.[26]

Even as the beachcomber insisted upon the boundary between self and cannibal in his text, his existence as a white native placed that same boundary under threat. A beachcomber such as John Jackson challenged the exclusivity of all ideological categories. His notoriety, his life history and his status as a semi-savage were to haunt him perennially. When he worked his passage between islands by signing on passing ships, he found himself to be an unpopular figure. His reputation had usually preceded him. He was an isolated man, shunned by other sailors and forced to skulk about the ship. He came out only at night in order to avoid their derision. His supposed depredations were written on his physiognomy: 'The cold feline expression of his eyes was anything but agreeable', wrote the captain, who described Jackson as a 'strange looking fellow . . . somewhat below the middle height'.[27] Julian Thomas writes of an infamous beachcomber known as 'Jack', whom he saw in Fiji in 1880. He was repelled by the old, unkempt and dishevelled individual and by his notoriety among both natives and Europeans. Thomas is in no doubt about the true nature of his ultimate depravity: '[T]here was a dispute as to whether he had been a convict', he wrote, 'but there was no mistake as to his anthropophagy.'[28]

The beachcombers' proximity to cannibalism was one of the most dramatic features of their narratives. To readers of all ages, the fascination and horror symbolised by the figure of the cannibal ensured that the sailors' graphic descriptions of cannibalism and dismemberment were unforgettable. The extent to which their descriptions were based on prevailing ideologies, or influenced by the expectations of their audience, can never truly be known. All sailor-authors insisted upon the veracity of their experiences and their presence at the scenes they described, even to the detriment of their own status as civilised Europeans. The inventive literary strategies they utilised to proclaim and guarantee their innocence never entirely succeeded in cleansing them of the taint of cannibalism. The more admirable and resourceful aspects of their lives as natives were overshadowed by that suggestion of depravity. Because there is no way to judge the true extent of their immersion into the darker side of native life, the white-man-turned-cannibal remains one of the most destabilising and disturbing figures from the early days of European–Pacific encounter.

CHAPTER TEN

Voices from the Beach

In character, after about five years' residence with them, I pronounce them hospitable, sagacious, and benevolent.

JAMES O'CONNELL, *A Residence of Eleven Years in New Holland and the Caroline Islands*

The beachcombing sailors' experience of native life was one that was rarely equalled by any group of travellers before or since. For the most part, it was an experience that began in loss, despair, fear and uncertainty. Wrenched from the security and comfort provided by their home nations, wrecked or marooned white men were particularly vulnerable to the vagaries of unknown worlds. The fact that they survived and, in many cases, prospered under such inauspicious circumstances was a testament to their resourcefulness and adaptability. It was also a reflection of the flexibility and tolerance of the native communities that absorbed these unlooked-for strangers from the sea. The welcome and support offered to many unfortunate sailors by islanders throughout the Pacific was as welcome as it was unexpected. On islands associated with violence, death and cannibalism, the sailors found friendship, comfort and love. It was a gift they repaid in the only way they could – through the stories, tales, narratives and memoirs that they left behind. In their words and images they vividly portrayed the culture of the islands and brought to life many of the people they met.

The most memorable of these was Finau, King of Tonga. Finau 'Ulukalala was broad-shouldered, well built and at six feet tall towered over his subjects. His bearing was manly, his posture erect, his stature imposing. His hair was jet-black and curly, his nose aquiline and large. Like the majority of islanders, he had large, strong and even white teeth. Although a big man, he was fit and muscular. His limbs were 'well set, strong and graceful in action'. His people always knew when he was near. He moved quickly and imperiously throughout his domain, his loud voice and booming laughter constantly signalling his presence. His intelligence and humour shone through eyes described as 'large and penetrating'. It was not hard to know what he was thinking. All emotions registered themselves in his fine-boned and articulate face, mirrored in the smiles and frowns that flitted across his expressive features. He was warlike in stature and appearance. He was heroic in his aspect and actions.

But he also had his faults. His unstable temper and vengeful nature were legendary. When he became angry, his rage was terrible and he instructed his chiefs to hold him down until the worst of his violence had passed. Although he inspired great confidence and loyalty from his supporters, he struck awe and terror in the hearts of his enemies. He was politically ambitious and highly astute. He did nothing without a purpose and that purpose always served his own interests. His decisions were regarded as acts of fate; once made, they were enacted swiftly and without hesitation. Those who disobeyed him had good reason to fear the consequences. Yet when brute force failed to achieve the desired ends, Finau had other weapons at his disposal. When he spoke, people listened. His eloquence and rhetoric were recognised by all. Many of his enemies refused to listen to him in case they were persuaded to a course of action prejudicial to their interests. As the sole and absolute monarch of his small island kingdom, Finau 'Ulukalala was a force to be reckoned with.

William Mariner is the sailor responsible for providing so much information about the Tongan king. This fifteen-year-old castaway lived with the Tongans as a member of the royal household for over four years from 1806 to 1810. The brutal massacre (described in Chapter Five) that followed the arrival of his ship, the *Port-au-*

Prince, in Tonga is not easily forgotten. Twenty-six men, including the captain, were slaughtered. Mariner was one of the fortunate few who survived that horrific introduction to native life. The young Englishman's arrival and subsequent sojourn in the kingdom of Tonga was to have far-reaching consequences. He was little more than a boy when he arrived. At such a young age, he had few ingrained preconceptions and prejudices, while his complete dependence upon the islanders for all aspects of his survival resulted in an extremely high level of assimilation. He was an impressionable young man who responded wholeheartedly and unselfconsciously to Tongan life and culture. His editor, Dr John Martin, believed Mariner to be ideally suited to the task, being 'endowed with the principles of a good education, of an active and observing mind, of a retentive memory, of an ingenious and ingenuous turn of thought, of a disposition to inspire confidence in others'.

Mariner told us a great deal about his native 'father', the king. Bereft of his own family and far from home, Finau's islands became the sailor's world. In that world there was no more important or imposing figure than that of the king. He was a larger-than-life character, 'gifted by nature with that amazing grasp of mind which seizes every thing within its reach'. Finau was extremely eager to learn as much as possible about the wider world beyond his shores. Insatiably curious and highly intelligent, he spent many hours with Mariner as the sailor explained the concepts of reading and writing, the uses of money, the intricacies of politics and warfare. He was fascinated by methods of government and very keen to understand the English system. He puzzled over the use of a compass and the concept of gravity and was particularly interested in Mariner's account of the solar system and its implication for seasonal change and ocean tides. Finau was an engaging individual at the height of his capabilities, almost too large a personality for the small stage on which he played out his life. He certainly thought so:

> Oh, that the gods would make me king of England! There is not an island in the whole world, however small, but what I would then subject to my power. The King of England does not deserve the dominion he enjoys.

Possessed of so many great ships, why does he suffer such petty islands
as those of Tonga continually to insult his people with acts of treachery?
Were I he, would I send tamely to *ask* for yams and pigs? No I would come
with the *front of battle; and with the thunder of Bolotane* [Britain]. I would
show who ought to be chief. None but men of enterprising spirit should
be in possession of guns. Let such rule the earth, and be those their vassals
who can bear to submit to such insults unrevenged![1]

An extraordinary man, Finau was an 'admirable politician' and one
who 'hated to see oppression in others'. He would 'frequently take the
part of the oppressed, against those who were punishing them harshly',
according to Mariner. The young sailor's portrait of Finau does not
ignore his faults, his vindictiveness, bad temper and his capricious
abuse of power. But his admiration and gratitude to the Tongan
king, who always treated him fairly and kindly, permeates his entire
narrative. Mariner learned early to value Finau's nobility of character.
When the king decided to make use of the cannons from the wrecked
ship against a number of his enemies, he solicited the help of the other
marooned sailors from the *Port-au-Prince*. They showed him how to
prime the guns and transport them to the battle site. Finau opened
fire against enemy forts in Vava'u harbour, effectively destroying their
walls and barricades. The sailors urged him to employ his superior
power and demolish the fort and everyone in it. The king refused.
He would not fire the guns directly against other men believing that
'these guns gave him too great an advantage'. He preferred to 'receive
their attack, and fight them upon equal terms'.

Finau, the man who had ordered the capture of the *Port-au-
Prince* and the slaughter of a large part of its crew, was more than a
bloodthirsty savage. The sailors who survived fared much better than
they expected. Mariner in particular was welcomed, supported, given
patronage and incorporated into the royal family with all the honour
and respect due to someone in that position. He was treated as a valued
member of Tongan society and travelled throughout the islands as a
special favourite of the king. He repaid that kindness. In the stories he
told his editor, Mariner brought the Tongan king to life. His wives,
warriors, friends and subjects all feature prominently in his narrative.

A chieftain of Tongataboo. This is a figure that would have been
familiar to all Tongan beachcombers such as George Vason, the
ex-missionary from the *Duff*, and the fifteen-year-old William Mariner.

They were central to his island experience and they remain at the heart of his personal account. While the sailor himself is the primary witness and sole source of all information, he is nevertheless marginal to his own life story. It is the Tongans who hold centre stage. The men and women that peopled Mariner's island are fully drawn, highly complex and individual characters with all their accompanying flaws and inconsistencies. They are not the depersonalised and unthinking savages featured so frequently in many other writings, but complex and intriguing examples of humanity.

The voice of Mariner's *Account of the Natives of the Tonga Islands* is that of Dr John Martin. It is his vision that shapes the story with its aura of romantic primitivism. But the narrative belongs to Mariner and he makes sure that the focus of his story remains with the Tongans. He includes many native songs, myths and histories as told to him by the islanders. Via his editor, he makes an honest attempt to reflect Tongan culture. The islanders had their own stories to tell; they had their own complex society and history. Although he was a young and naïve sailor, Mariner understood the Tongans to be the primary actors in their own life stories. He shows them to be as human and humane as their European counterparts.

Finau, in particular, stamps his personality on Mariner's account in the same way he imposed himself in real life. His successes and failures, his friends and enemies, his political subterfuges and personal intimacies are all documented faithfully by his adopted English son. He was an historical personage, infamous in his day, and documented by many European travellers, writers and explorers. But it is in Mariner's book that he can be truly known. No other European lived with him so intimately and knew him so well. Mariner's royal connections gave him an unparalleled insight into tribal politics, political machinations, royal subterfuges, as well as an intimate acquaintance with everyday royal life. Their relationship was one of love and respect on both sides. Mariner refers to Finau as 'patron, father and protector', while Finau gave the young beachcomber the name of his favourite son 'Togi Oocummea'. From time to time, vessels passed through Tongan waters and on one occasion Mariner asked for permission to leave. His request provoked a great deal of discussion among the chiefs. A number of them wished to keep him, but Finau was of a different mind. Mariner heard him say, when he thought the sailor was asleep, 'Poor *papalangi*! what a distance his country is off! Very likely his father and mother are now talking about him, and comforting themselves by saying "perhaps tomorrow a ship will arrive and bring our son back to us."' On this occasion Mariner was refused passage by the visiting captain who had no room for extra passengers or crew. When he finally did leave Tonga, his departure was a mixture of luck and determination. Although many Tongans did not want him to go, Mariner was adamant. He was eventually sent on his way with Finau's blessing and laden with gifts for the journey home.

Affectionate Relations

Of course, Mariner was not the only beachcomber to form close personal connections with his native hosts. While it was politically expedient to be associated with a powerful native family, there are many instances of true affection between white man and islander. William Lockerby knew before his arrival in Fiji that the islands were 'inhabited by cannibals'. Reflecting on the time when he was first marooned, he vividly recalled his fear and despair at the workings of fate: 'I was left among a race of cannibals . . . and possess[ed] but very faint hopes of a vessel calling at such a simply dismal corner of the Globe.' Lockerby's eyewitness experience of cannibalism, described in Chapter Eight, was the cause of his greatest personal fear: 'Never do I think of this awful and perilous moment, with death and the thought of being mangled and devoured by these savages', he wrote, 'without feeling sensible of the interposition of the Divine Being in preserving my life.' But Lockerby gained a deeper understanding of island culture. He became enmeshed in personal relationships and established a more permanent relationship with those around him. He began to see beyond the stereotypes to the individuals beneath. 'During that period their conduct towards me, and their general character, as much as I could observe of it, make me consider them in quite a different light than in that of cannibals.' He developed strong personal feelings for the king who always 'answered me more like a father than an uncultured savage'. As he wrote his journal hundreds of kilometres and many years away from the islands and their people, he remembered the comfort, support and acceptance offered to him, although he arrived as a friendless and powerless sailor. He reviewed his earlier assumptions about the nature of his 'cannibal' hosts: 'I question much', he wrote, 'whether the unfortunate stranger if thrown destitute among the peasantry of our own country would have been treated with equal kindness.'

The depth of his affection was particularly visible upon his departure. His months in Fiji under the protection of the king had been happy ones:

> I could not help feeling considerable pain on parting with them. From the good old King I had received kindnesses which I should remember while I live with gratitude. Left as I was on his island without the least means of subsistence, to the mercy of the lower class of natives, who might have plundered me of the few articles I had left, and even deprived me of life, he not only supplied me with food when there was a great scarcity all over the island, and granted me his protection against the insults of his people, but he taught me by his advice how to acquire their goodwill.[2]

Despite his determination to return home, Mariner was similarly distraught when he finally left Tonga after four years as a captive, feeling 'all the sweet bitterness of parting from much loved friends'. His depth of emotion was reciprocated and an 'abundance of tears was shed on both sides'. As Mariner saw the islands disappear behind him, he was overcome by a sense of loss. He was turning his back on a place and a people that he would never forget. His native home, family and friends were now consigned to his past, leaving him overwhelmed by 'sentiments which he never before had felt to such a degree'.

Neither Mariner nor the other beachcombers were prepared for such a response. Their landfalls were often traumatic and their introduction to native life traditionally uncertain and fearful. But they were constantly, and happily, surprised at the kindness and solicitude offered them by 'rude' natives. It was a hospitality that contrasted quite dramatically with their expectations. It shook them out of their complacency and challenged their traditional assumption of European superiority and civility. They were forced to revise their earlier beliefs:

'I have never met a more truly conventional people, always considerate for the feelings of others', wrote Robert Coffin in Fiji in 1855, 'yet they were cannibals.'[3] It was not expected that cannibals would be as considerate as 'conventional people' but native savages did not always conform to European expectations. James Oliver, another castaway sailor, could attest to that. The kindness and support he received in Fiji after his shipwreck in 1830 was as welcome as it was unexpected. It also provoked an unflattering comparison with the lack of compassion shown him by the American consulate in Hawaii during his journey home: 'Thus was the American seaman . . . asking in vain for that aid which the cannibals of the Fijis had not denied him', he recalled.

The beachcomber's unparalleled position on the borders of two cultures enabled him to explore the gaps between the rigid black and white divisions that permeated nineteenth-century ideology. While the sailors were not believers in a primitivist ideal (their experiences of shipwreck and captivity put paid to that), they also refused to label their hosts as mere savages. In their stories, they insisted on a more complicated, less judgemental reality. They were able to portray the islander neither as idyllic primitive nor as unredeemed savage, but as something in between. Living as natives made cultural relativists of the beachcombers. It was demonstrated by their narratives, which emphasise the interconnectedness of people and cultures. By means of their familial and tribal ties, they forged a unique cross-cultural relationship based on closeness and comparison rather than distance and difference. It was not long before their initial fear and contempt was replaced by an unexpected trust and fondness.

Their narratives focus on the friendship, loyalty, care and kindness, which were passed both ways across the beach.[4] When Horace Holden left the Palau Islands in October 1832, he wrote that '[T]he rude kindness of the natives had so entirely overbalanced their faults that, on parting with them, we experienced emotions of regret, and were quite overpowered with a sense of our obligations to them for the many favours which they had bestowed upon us.' The hospitality that the sailors found in the islands was civilisation by another name. 'Some people claiming to be civilized might take a lesson from the humanity of these people [the natives] to shipwrecked mariners,' remarked the tap-dancing Irishman James O'Connell after his acceptance by the Caroline Islanders (Ponapeans). When his initial fears of cannibalism and death proved unfounded, he assured his readers that '[T]he conduct of the natives to us was all that uncultivated kindness and hospitality could prompt.' Because beachcomber narratives were fundamentally democratic in origin and in conception – they were the written accounts of the forecastle – they insisted on the reality of their experiences even in the face of prevailing ideologies. It was an approach that often revealed shortcomings in traditional European behaviour and beliefs.

Again, the exploits of the youngest castaway prove informative. Mariner and fellow crew members repeatedly found themselves hungry and underfed in their first few months in Tonga. Although they were sometimes invited into native homes to share a meal, more often than not they were neglected and were reduced to stealing the barest rations in order to survive. When informed of their hunger, the king was amused at the stupidity of the sailors who were unaware that they could go to any house where a meal was being prepared and without invitation partake of food and drink. He asked how food was obtained in England and was extremely surprised when told that every man provided for himself and his family, that friends were fed by invitation only and that strangers were seldom invited. He laughed at what he called the ill-natured selfishness of the white people:

> After this, the generality of the natives made this selfishness, as they considered it, of the Europeans, quite proverbial; and when any stranger came into their houses to eat with them, they would say jocosely, 'No! we shall treat you after the manner of the Papalangis; go home, and eat what *you* have got, and we shall eat what *we* have got![5]

Myths and Preconceptions

European assumptions and expectations continued to be challenged throughout the Pacific. When Herman Melville first arrived in the Marquesas as a twenty-one-year-old sailor, his imagination was in full flight. His islands were a contradictory mix of myth and reality.

They were picturesque and perilous. They offered sanctuary as well as savagery. Like all sailors, his response to the Pacific and to the primitive was to mix the real with the unreal, the fact with the fiction, the reality with the myth:

> The Marquesas! What strange visions of outlandish things does the very name spirit up! Naked houris – cannibal banquets – groves of cocoanut – coral reefs – tattooed chiefs – and bamboo temples; sunny valleys planted with bread-fruit trees – carved canoes dancing on the flashing blue waters – savage woodlands guarded by horrible idols – heathenish rites and human sacrifices.[6]

His expectations focus on the beauty of the landscape and the savagery of the people. He would find evidence of both in the weeks that followed. Melville's story of his time in the valley of the Taipi has already been dealt with in Chapter Eight. Now we must return to the moment of his arrival. His first sight of the islands after six weary months at sea fulfilled his expectations. He sailed around rock-bound coasts that lay at the foot of lofty cliffs stretching in jagged peaks towards the sky. Thickly wooded valleys, separated by spurs of mountains, swept down towards the sea. As he neared Nukuhiva, he was rewarded with glimpses of blooming valleys, deep glens, waterfalls and balmy groves. The natural glory of the harbour left him at a loss for words: 'No description can do justice to its beauty', he wrote. But he is also alert to the darker side of island life. Even before visiting the Marquesas, he had heard 'some revolting stories in connection with these savages', including the capture, bloodshed and murder of European crews. The cannibal Taipi, in particular, enjoyed 'prodigious notoriety all over the islands', their name inspiring terror in islander and European alike.

It was the Taipi that Melville was most afraid of, and – as already recounted – it was the Taipi whom he was fated to meet. After a sleepless first night pondering his possible fate in his cannibal community, the sailor woke to see a Marquesan warrior in full regalia standing in his doorway. The warrior's name was Mehevi and he was an imposing sight. On his head he wore a semicircle of long, brightly

Pahutiki 'Wrapped in Images'. The tattoos displayed by this Marquesan
chief are similar to those described by Melville.

coloured tropical tail feathers, arranged to stand upright from a
central crown of guinea heads that he wore strapped to his forehead.
Around his neck he wore several enormous necklaces of boars' tusks,
polished like ivory, and reaching down to his waist. Two whales' teeth
hung from his ears, while a dark coloured tapa cloth, decorated with

braids and tassels, covered his hips. Bracelets and anklets of human hair completed his outfit. He held in his right hand a four and a half metre-long spear, sharply pointed at one end and flattened like an oar blade at the other. However, his most impressive adornment was his tattoos, which covered every limb. His entire body was stained dark blue and black by the intricacy and profusion of his decoration. Lines, curves and figures covered his body like fine lacework, but it was his face that was most startling to behold. Two broad stripes originated from his forehead, obliquely crossed both eyes and ended below each ear. There they met another line that swept along the lips to form the base of a triangle. From inside that triangle two black eyes stared at the terrified sailor.

In his dress, bearing and deportment, Mehevi fulfilled the stereo-type of the primitive savage, at least from Melville's perspective. What Mehevi thought when he gazed at the stranger before him can only be imagined. Certainly, the white man could not be accounted for in any traditional Taipi value system. He was an uninvited stranger with no signs of rank, no influential friends and no possessions. The peculiar visitor with his pale skin and water-coloured eyes could have no expectation of any support or favour. But that is what he received. Despite Melville's trepidations, his fears were soon put to rest. The chief of the Taipi, for that was Mehevi's true status, was a humane and magnanimous individual. He was to prove a generous host to Melville and his companion Toby. They were housed, fed and welcomed into the small community where they were provided with clothes and food, instructed in the correct method of eating, provided with native companions and shown the most restful and scenic places in the valley. Mehevi insisted that his foreign guests enjoy every amenity offered by the village. He was also adamant that they remain captive. Any dissatisfaction on their parts, including their repeated desire to travel to the coast in search of a ship, made him extremely angry. He was not a man to be crossed. He was absolute ruler of his small community and demanded the same fealty from native and European alike.

Despite his lack of independent movement and despite Mehevi's heavy-handed tactics, Melville recognised in the savage king a true leader of men. His nobility and personal stature were particularly evident at a gathering of island chiefs. His breeding, carriage and actions all defined him, at least in the eyes of the sailor, as the greatest of the chiefs, the head of his clan and the true sovereign of the valley. Mehevi was not just a savage leader, but a man of dignity worthy of the many titles bestowed on him. The young sailor attributed to the older man the noble traits of the barbarian with the redeeming graces of a civilised being. This was not the sort of individual he expected to find among the cannibalistic Taipi.

Melville's expectations of the islanders had been formed by his reading and by discussions with other sailors. He was aware of opinions such as those expressed by Richard Armstrong, who spent eight months attempting to establish a mission in the Marquesas in the 1830s. The Marquesan, according to Armstrong, was 'unaccountably mean in his dealings, filthy in his habits and conversation, savage in his temper, a cannibal by education, ungrateful for favors, cruel to his enemies, treacherous to his friends'.[7] Melville, too, presupposed the cannibal tendencies of the Marquesans. Although his 'first-hand' evidence was too slight and circumstantial to provide verifiable proof, he lived in constant terror of cannibalism during his time on the island. It was a fear that was all the more potent for being unrealised. Melville and Toby were particularly alarmed because of the high value that was placed on them and at the level of their hosts' watchfulness. Their permanent state of anxiety and dread coloured all their relationships and resulted in a number of misunderstandings.

One night the sailors awoke to find the small village deserted. The islanders had gathered in a grove just outside the settlement where the flames of a fire could be seen. As they struggled to understand what was happening, they saw a number of dark figures moving to and fro in the shadows. Others capered about between the flames looking, as Melville described it, 'like so many demons'. They discussed the disturbing development. Toby believed the fire had a specific purpose. It is 'the fire to cook us, to be sure, what else would the cannibals be kicking up such a row about if it were not for that?' he asked his companion. 'For what do you suppose the devils have been feeding us up in this kind of style during the last three days?' he added. 'Depend upon it, we will be eaten this blessed night, and there is the fire we shall be roasted by.' There was a ghastly inevitability in the sailors' minds concerning the cannibalistic tendencies of the natives which proved to be quite unfounded. The flames heralded a midnight feast to which all were invited, but as participants, not as the main course.

The humane treatment received at the hands of the islanders demanded a change in perception. Melville, a man who was always alert to the contradictions and paradoxes of his experience of native life, was faced with yet another conundrum. The hospitality and benevolence of the Taipi contrasted vividly with their reported status as depraved cannibals. It also confused the erstwhile uncomplicated division between the native cannibal and the civilised European. Like many sailors before and after him, Melville became something of an island philosopher. He began to question his earlier beliefs about the nature of cannibalism. He puzzled over whether 'the mere eating of human flesh so very far exceeds in barbarity' the punishments and tortures 'which only a few years since [were] practiced in enlightened England'. He realised that civilisation breeds its own form of savagery. War, violence, murder, torture, imprisonment and slavery are just some examples of what he termed the 'remorseless cruelty' of modern society. The islanders that Melville met were not the bloodthirsty ogres he had read about. They had their own social structure and political order, their own fidelity to important cultural and religious ceremonies. The peace and tranquillity experienced in the valley and in the everyday behaviour of the Taipi forced an inevitable and disturbing comparison with the Western world.

> The fiend-like skill we display in the invention of all manner of death-dealing engines, the vindictiveness with which we carry on our wars, and the misery and desolation that follow in their train, are enough of themselves to distinguish the white man as the most ferocious animal on the face of the earth.[8]

Those men who lived with islanders empathised with native culture to a much greater degree than those who chose the security of the ship. Melville, like Montaigne before him, disputes the barbarous nature of cannibalism by a direct comparison between the practices of

Europe and the Pacific. His personal experience forced him to question prevailing ideologies and to challenge the assumed superiority of the cultured European. The general tenor of native life in the valley of the Taipi caused the sailor to reconsider his earlier prejudices. 'In the altered frame of mind to which I have referred', he wrote, 'every object that presented itself to my notice in the valley struck me in new light and tended to strengthen my favourable impressions.'

He did not go as far as David Porter, commander of the USS *Essex* and visitor to the Marquesas in 1813, who, in a burst of romantic primitivism, wrote that 'a more honest, or friendly and better disposed people could not exist under the sun . . . We find them brave, generous, honest, and benevolent, acute, ingenious, and intelligent.'[9] Porter's affirmation of the islanders would prove to be extremely short-lived, however. In 1814, he returned to challenge the Taipi by making a territorial claim for an American empire in Nukuhiva. His ambitions were laid to rest by a native ambush and by the successful guerilla tactics of the islanders. In retaliation, Porter burnt every house belonging to the 2000-strong population, killing whom he could.[10] Melville's writings had less drastic consequences for the native people. Instead of attacking them, he turned his pen upon his own culture. It was not a case of substituting one prejudice with another, however. Melville challenged the simplicities of both the primitivist and anti-primitivist doctrines.[11] He came to understand that Mehevi and his people were neither noble primitives nor unredeemed savages but, like all people, somewhere in between.

It was a realisation that resonated with the beachcombers. Their own 'in-between-ness' responded to the 'in-between-ness' of others. It was a defining feature of their island lives and it became a defining characteristic of their narratives. They were ambivalent about easy categorisations. Although they were heirs to both the primitivist and anti-primitivist point of view, they trod a middle path. Their texts reflected that level of ambivalence, presenting the islander at different times as disgusting and depraved, as well as noble and virtuous. Of course, their perceptions were never wholly objective or disinterested. They were inevitably influenced by personal circumstances and by individual states of mind. They depended on whether the beachcomber viewed his time on the islands as a refuge or a torment.

All sailors arrived with imaginations primed by stories of cannibals and savages. Their first steps on island shores often verified those expectations. However, their dependence on the charity and goodwill of the islander showed them a different side to the infamous savage. He was more considerate, kind-hearted and civilised than they first thought. As the beachcomber became part of an extended family, the native was seen as an individual rather than a type. Like all individuals, he was a mixture of the appealing and the unattractive, the good and the bad. He simply had a different way of sharing the same values as the sailor. The things they learned did not shake the sailors' belief that all pagan religion is insincere. They did not completely eradicate their belief in the superiority of their own culture and the paganism of others. Even Melville, that great cultural relativist, was unable to live contentedly in his island paradise among people he so obviously admired. But native life did make the sailors uneasy about their previous assumptions. It forced them to query the true nature of the savage and to question the supposed benefits of European civilisation.

Missionary Values

The first of their revisions concerned the South Seas missionaries. These were ordinary men of humble origins and plain and simple learning, driven by religious passion and by a sense of calling. They were chosen because of their 'basic Christian experience and zeal' and they worked in many different ways for the glory of God.[12] Some used their hands and were engaged in building and farming. Others were fledgling authors, compiling ethnographies and writing dictionaries. Many were overwhelmed by what they saw as the evil that surrounded them in these savage lands – an evil that challenged them on personal and professional levels.

They fought hard against the lure of island life, fearing they would lose sight of 'justice, truth, goodness, and mercy' and 'rush with impetuosity into crimes destructive to others and themselves'.[13] They battled hard to support their brethren, improve the lot of the heathens and maintain their faith. Life on the islands was far from easy and temptations abounded. The lapsed missionary George Vason fought a constant battle to withstand the allure of island living. His missionary 'brothers' believed that by going native he had 'not only offended God but . . . betrayed his colleagues'. It was a fall from grace they worked hard to avoid. However, moral defection and ill health played a significant part in the pattern of mission life. These idealistic and fervent men were a long way from home, living in small European communities cut off from others. They were even more at sea in the troubled waters of island culture than the beachcombers. Unlike the sailors, they had to maintain their sense of distance, their separate status. They had to lead by example if they wanted to redeem and civilise the native people. After all, the islanders were expected to rise to the level of the Europeans, not the other way round. The missionaries were lonely, confused and beleaguered by the complexities of a culture so unlike their own. No wonder that in the early days their successes were negligible. An example from Tonga illustrates the fate of their efforts to convey the evangelical message:

> The king and several other chiefs at the Tonga islands appeared quite surprised when Mr Mariner informed them that the object of the missionaries had been to instruct them in the religion of the white people. They had thought that the latter came to live among them merely from choice, as liking the climate better than their own.[14]

The missionaries, as we have seen, were no friends of the beach-combers. Their writings were one of the primary sources of negative information about the beach-crossing sailors, generally emphasising their lawlessness and licentiousness, depicting them as morally as well as socially degenerate. But the sailors struck back in their narratives. They challenged the missionaries' role as local representatives of European culture. The men themselves, as well as the social and religious order they embodied, were found wanting.

The beachcomber narrative that achieved the most notoriety on this account was Melville's *Omoo*, published in the spring of 1847 to great anticipation and acclaim. After his escape from captivity among the Taipi, the American was taken on board the *Lucy Ann* (called the *Julia* in his account) and sailed to Tahiti, arriving there on 23 September 1842. The crew was denied shore leave, and refused to carry out their duties on the ship, an act of mutiny that resulted in imprisonment. They were taken ashore, placed in the local jail, and left there until the ship sailed without them three weeks later. The departure of their ship turned the sailors into beachcombers and they were left to fend for themselves. They found themselves destitute and penniless, relegated to the fringes of both Western and island society. They had no money, no support, no duties or obligations to others. Melville spent six weeks in Tahiti and on Moorea (extended to three months in his narrative) and his account of those weeks as a wandering sailor in Tahiti can be found in *Omoo*, which takes as its title the Marquesan word for 'rover'. His experiences confirmed his earlier views on the dubious advantages of civilisation.

Melville's Tahiti was not the native island paradise it had once been. It now bore the marks of Western civilisation. The missionary presence, in particular, could be seen in the prevalence of Christianity, in the existence of a Tahitian Bible and in the changed dress and behaviour of the natives. Native clothing was forbidden, as were all forms of indigenous decoration. Many sports and other pastimes were banned along with a number of cultural and pagan ceremonies. Melville believed that the 'denationalizing' of the Tahitians, as he called it, had an unforeseen consequence. 'Supplied with no amusements, in place of those forbidden, the Tahitians . . . have sunk into a listlessness, or indulge in sensualities a hundred times more pernicious, than all the games ever celebrated in the Temple of Tanee', he argued. He was unhappy with the religious, moral and social status of Tahiti after fifty years of European influence. His comments, while derogatory of European culture, were also highly critical of the efficacy of the Polynesian missions as a whole. When faced with diseased, starving and dying natives he gave vent to his frustration and despair. 'The missionaries may seek to disguise the matter as they will', he argued, 'but the facts are incontrovertible . . . the devoutest Christian . . . must go away mournfully asking – "Are these, alas! the fruits of twenty five years of enlightening?"'

Polarised Viewpoints

The ideological investment of nineteenth-century society in the missionary endeavour meant that Melville's claims generated a very lively public debate. Reviewers on both sides of the Atlantic were divided equally between those who agreed with Melville in principle and those who accused him of malicious and unchristian behaviour.[15] The severest criticism came, not unexpectedly, from denominational presses in New England. They were scandalised at Melville's overt anti-missionary bias and at his criticisms of the wider evangelical project. They disputed his claims by drawing attention to his own disreputable island activities. His identity as a beachcomber, as the omoo, or wanderer, of the title, disqualified him as a reliable witness. The same complaints had been made about the earlier *Typee*. Critics were disturbed by the author's predilection for native life. They distrusted his fraternisation with the natives, his liaison with Fayaway and his celebration of Taipi culture. Immorality abounded, both in the things that Melville experienced, and in his enjoyment of them. He had compromised his integrity with his beach-crossing behaviour. He was not a man to be taken seriously.

One man was particularly incensed with Melville, his book and the claims he made in it. Edward Lucett was a Pacific traveller and merchant, resident in Tahiti from 1837 to 1849. In his *Rovings in the Pacific*, published in 1851, he claimed to have met Melville in the 'calabooza' (the local jail). Lucett, who was unjustly imprisoned for a brief time, was attacked by a long-haired ruffian with a knife. He argued, incorrectly, that his attacker was Melville. He was offended at the sailor's beachcomber status and disgusted with his writings. 'Regardless of all truth, gratitude or manliness', he argued, '[Melville] has grossly scandalized by name some worthy men living in Tahiti.' He described Melville as a 'most reckless loafer, caring not a pin what enterprises were ruined so long as he could indulge the gratification of his own propensities'.[16] Other critics felt the same. A number of them highlighted the author's moral irresponsibility, pointing to textual evidence of his 'reckless spirit', 'cool, sneering wit' and his 'perfect want of heart' – all of which identified him as an unworthy and unreliable commentator on missionary endeavours.[17] However,

Melville's observations were corroborated by others. Ironically, Lucett himself supported many of the beachcomber's claims about the worthlessness of missionary achievement in the face of native hypocrisy:

> unfortunately I have seen corroborative testimony in certain instances, [that] instead of improving the native character, the missionaries have superinduced upon their other bad qualities hypocrisy of the deepest dye . . . I conscientiously believe that the moral character of the natives has not been improved by missionary intercourse.[18]

These travellers were not alone in their doubts about the effectiveness, even the necessity, of the evangelical missions. During his long island life, John Jackson met a number of missionaries on a number of different islands. On the whole, he believed that they 'are at base driven by money and are in all important ways uncharitable'. During his residence in Vavao, he claimed that 'there had been one or two, if not more, bad missionaries located there'. Robert Coffin, shipwrecked in Fiji in 1855, could only name two 'that were good and sincere' out of twenty or thirty missionaries in Ovalau during his sojourn there. The anti-missionary sentiment was so prevalent throughout his text that his editor, Harold Thompson, was tempted to delete all references to that subject to protect the sensitivities of his readers.

On the Marquesas Islands William Torrey had his own story to tell.[19] Torrey was born in 1814 in Massachusetts. Endowed with a naturally restless disposition, he left home at fourteen years of age to begin the life of a rover. Relying on fate, chance and the kindness of others, he drifted from place to place. His life was one of solitary independence, defined by continual movement, restlessness and a lack of direction. He was, as he put it, driven solely by his intention to live 'independent of parents and guardians'. A sailor's life was the perfect choice. He became enamoured of the incessant movement, the freedom and the lack of family commitments. The desire to roam, he told us, 'was paramount to all others'. By 1834 he was in Hawaii. From there he sailed past Pitcairn, the home of the mutineers, and then on to Resolution Bay in the Marquesas, where his ship ran aground on rocks on 3 February 1835.

Like many sailors before him, he survived through the grace and favour of the natives. When the captain and the rest of the crew took the next available chance to sail to Tahiti, Torrey and his companion Benjamin Noyce chose to stay behind, preferring to take their chances on shore. Months passed and native life began to pall. The arrival of a European ship was a cause for celebration and an opportunity for escape. The sailors ran to the vessel and asked to be taken on board. Torrey was taken for a native and refused entry: '[T]he scanty allowance of clothes with which I had left the wreck, had long fallen off, leaving me entirely naked, and exposed to the sun's scorching

William Torrey of the Marquesas. The engraving, executed by the sailor, draws attention to the Marquesan tattoos displayed on his forearms.

rays; besides my long beard, and uncombed hair, rendered me in appearance scare less than a savage', he explained. As the months passed, the beachcombers found it hard to obtain a passage on any visiting ship. By the mid-1830s many captains had become wary of the dissolute white men living on islands and refused to take them on board, believing them to be seditious troublemakers.

The sailors, now moderately bilingual, had resigned themselves to native life until another ship anchored in the bay. It was a missionary vessel keen to set up a station on the island. The sailors were anxious to win support from the visiting Europeans and provided them with valuable information and local knowledge to aid the establishment of the mission. This goodwill did not last long. The sailors realised that further European presence might lessen their influence with the chiefs, so they began to discourage the missionaries. Relations became strained and the missionaries lost faith in their beachcomber intermediaries. In particular, Torrey developed a strong personal antipathy to one newcomer, Mr Daylia. He lost no opportunity to sabotage his relations with the native chief. In turn, the missionary became so incensed with Torrey's bad influence, according to the sailor, that he 'threatened to send me to England and have me severely punished. His threats I did not heed very much though I should have been extremely glad to have been sent there.'

A few days later Torrey was physically attacked by the missionary's native servant who confirmed that he was merely following the orders of his master. The sailor confronted the missionary, saying that if 'the treatment he had given me, was an illustration of his preaching, he had better stay at home than go to the heathen, professedly to preach peace and salvation, while he practiced such horrid digressions'. Although the accusation was denied, Torrey's distrust of Daylia was even more pronounced. Without the intercession of the beachcombers, relations between the natives and missionaries continued to disintegrate. Eventually the missionaries were forced to leave. Torrey defends his actions: '[H]ad I not interfered in their behalf', he claimed, 'they would have been killed in the early part of their adventure.'

Torrey's feelings of resentment and dislike were focused on one particular missionary. It was more a matter of personal prejudice than a comment on missionary achievement as a whole. The majority of beachcombers followed Melville's lead. They used their texts to castigate the missionaries for what they regarded as the detrimental effect of Christianity and enforced civilisation on the everyday lives of the islanders. While individual beachcombers approved of the eradication of the more unsavoury aspects of native life, such as cannibalism, they nevertheless criticised the missionary as a harbinger of civilisation generally. The victories they claimed were hollow ones. Religious conversions, for instance, were seen as duplicitous and self-interested and were based solely on the observance of empty forms and meaningless rituals. On Tongareva, Lamont believed that '*Sincerely* honest men, and *truly* virtuous women, are, notwithstanding all the missionaries have done, very rare commodities.' He insisted that adherence to the forms of Christianity did not guarantee true religious sincerity:

> Though Mr Royal [the local missionary] is I dare say a good and straightforward man, we may be permitted to doubt whether the transformation of the natives to Europeans of the modern type is altogether a desirable consummation . . .
>
> The forms of religion are attended to amongst these islands with superstitious reverence, but morality of heart and life is perhaps at a lower standard than on the day when Christianity was first introduced amongst them.[20]

The Voice of the Sailor

Our sailor-authors were not the usual Pacific writers and commentators. They had a different agenda to other travellers. They were men of the forecastle not the quarterdeck. They saw life on Pacific shores in different ways to other men and it showed in their stories. They wrote about the missionaries from the native side of the beach. Their accounts stand as a direct challenge to more favourable official reports, which highlighted the success of evangelism in the islands by stressing both the number and the success of native conversions. The sailors were in a unique position to recognise and report on the visible discrepancy between evangelical theory and practice. By doing so, they endangered the ongoing ideological and economic support required for the operation of the missions. Their words may have been unofficial, but they were potent. They illuminated the reality on the other side of the cultural and racial divide and they provided an inescapable challenge to European complacency on the far side of the world.

With little education, minimal status and no institutional or national legitimacy, the sailors were unlikely candidates for authorship. Becoming credible authors was, in fact, one of the hardest roles they had to play. Nevertheless, they acquitted themselves well. Beachcomber-authors understood native societies to be more than a set of rules and roles. They saw beyond the public performance of society and individuals into the heart of the culture. In the midst of their fear and trepidation, they found friendship and love. They formed meaningful friendships and deep relationships with untutored savages and heathens. The kindnesses they received forced them to critique current thinking on the role of the savage and the superiority of Europe. Their experiences on the beach relativised them, forcing more than one sailor to argue that: 'Human nature is the same the world over.'[21]

Their adventures took place among other people. They were characterised by personal relationships, made under duress, often for too brief a period of time. But those unforgettable relationships were a fundamental aspect of their island life and became an essential part of their stories. All narratives provided copious instances of native forbearance and civility on islands historically associated with violence, fear, darkness and savagery. As William Lockerby remarked on leaving Wallis Island, where he had been shipwrecked for three months:

> Desirous as I was of leaving . . . I looked upon the little town . . . with something like regret; a feeling, which, I doubt not, is often felt in some degree by shipwrecked sailors, on a savage coast . . . after having been treated with generous and unexpected kindness by the rude natives.[22]

The sailors repaid that kindness. Their stories were their gift. They were written to give life to the characters and individuals who lived on those far-flung beaches. By personalising their native friends and hosts, they immortalised them. Mariner's Finau, Melville's Mehevi and William Lockerby's native 'father' are known to us through the sailors' stories. The voices of others are traditionally hard to hear as they speak to us from a past full of misunderstanding and misread signs. Their distance in time and their lack of a written tradition only exacerbates the problem. Many voices were lost in the violence of those early encounters. They were lost in silence, in death and in the victories of others. The strangers who came from the sea, however, captured some of them in the pages of their journals. They took them home to Europe and they gave them life. Being enclosed in the words of others is not the best way to have one's own story heard, but it was better than nothing. The beachcombers heard the sounds of those who had been traditionally silenced. In a small but significant way, they tried to give them back a voice of their own.

CHAPTER ELEVEN

The Return Home

Home is the sailor, home from the sea
And the hunter home from the hill

Epitaph for Robert Louis Stevenson

The stories of the beachcombers should properly end with their departure from the islands. Yet, in one form or another, their beach-crossings continued. The return home was but another journey in a long life of cultural voyaging. It was not an easy one. It took courage and determination for our renegades from civilisation to reconstitute themselves in European terms. In its own way, the return home demanded yet another set of philosophical and cultural adjustments. The sailors had been changed by their island experiences; they were no longer the same men who had once set sail in search of adventure. Their lives as European outcasts and marginal natives left them with a legacy of cultural displacement. It set them apart from their contemporaries and bequeathed a sense of distance that they carried with them to the end. 'I sometimes felt lost among civilized men', wrote one returned sailor. 'Everything seems so different – so strange – among the crowds of houses, vehicles and signs of commerce, that I am led to sigh.'[1] The beachcombers were often out of step with their own society. They were outsiders once again, this time on the margins of a world they had once known well.

They have left few records of that last difficult journey back to respectability. Their own brief moments of notoriety usually ended when they boarded the ships that would carry them home. If they were lucky, their subsequent histories might be recorded as footnotes in the stories of others. Too often their later lives were shrouded in obscurity. Hundreds of white men lived on islands scattered throughout the Pacific and for the most part they remain unknown, their stories untold. The men and their histories were considered too insignificant to command further time and interest. Even those who left us their stories often disappeared into anonymity on their return. They are hard men to locate among the larger streams of time and history. Men such as Herman Melville are familiar because of their later literary importance; others, such as James Morrison of the *Bounty*, because of their connection with historically significant events. Others have to be searched for through the archives of history. We have already heard about the beginnings of the sailors' journeys – now we will follow them home.

Jean Cabri did not want to leave Nukuhiva. He had lived with the Marquesans for nearly ten years and he was happy with his life. He had married (twice), had two children, fought as a warrior, been adopted by a chiefly family, and was completely at home in the native language and culture. His contact with Europeans was limited and sporadic. Like Edward Robarts, our other Marquesan castaway, Cabri was happy to be of service to those Europeans visiting the island, but only when it served his own interests. For instance he had offered his services to the Russian expedition led by Captain von Krusenstern who visited Nukuhiva in 1804. In return he received various goods, weapons and red-coloured clothing that would increase his status in the eyes of the natives. The beachcomber acted as a mediator and facilitator of trade and was an expert on native protocol. The Russians accepted his help, but never fully trusted him. They were both intrigued and horrified with the extent of his nativisation. He was too much the savage for their liking. They suspected that the European in him had been overwhelmed by the native.

Cabri never forgave the Russians for what happened next. As von Krusenstern's ship, the *Nadezhda*, was getting ready to depart, Cabri went on board to say goodbye and to pick up some gifts. He stayed there even as the ship slowly pulled out of the harbour. He was not particularly concerned. He was an excellent swimmer and could easily dive off the ship and swim back to shore at any time. The weather unexpectedly worsened and the *Nadezhda* was forced to make a run for it. There was no time to consider Cabri. All hands were employed on a safe passage out of the harbour and there was no opportunity to provide the beachcomber with either a boat or a plank of wood on which he could make it to shore. Cabri blamed the Russians for the subsequent course of his life.

The beachcomber found himself captive on a long journey to Russia. It was a voyage of discovery for him. As the weeks passed, he slowly reclaimed his European self and began to remember the man he used to be. His memory returned; he could recall the name of his parents and the name of his French village. He could picture scenes, places and faces from his pre-Marquesan life. Von Krusenstern and his scientist and naturalist Georg Langsdorff watched carefully. They assiduously took copies of his ornate tattooing and recorded his intriguing mix of French–Marquesan dialect. They were fascinated by the change in the savage as he slowly made contact with his civilised self. Cabri had left everything of worth on the islands but he still had one valuable commodity – the story of his life. On the decks of the ship, surrounded by amused and curious sailors, he quickly learned to make a performance out of his native experiences. He acted out his life of battle, he demonstrated his savage dances and he told of his native amours. The theatre he made on the ship was just the beginning. For the rest of his life he would be seen as an oddity among his peers – a bizarre cultural phenomenon that would prove endlessly entertaining.

The journey away from Nukuhiva took its toll, however. He was frequently depressed and moody. He spent a great deal of time sitting alone and bemoaning his fate. He suffered recurring fits of depression and despair and refused to leave the ship on their arrival in Hawaii. He was wrapped up in his own memories and lost in the past. He continued with the Russians until they landed at the Russian port of Kamchatka in the Bering Sea, where he finally left the expedition in a bid to make his own way in the civilised world he had left over ten years earlier. It was there he began the long journey that he hoped would one day take him back to the Marquesas.[2]

He made a spectacle of himself. He told his story to all he met and he romanticised it along the way. His spoke of his life among the natives, his exploits as a warrior, his instances of fear and uncertainty and his moments of personal bravery. He performed his life for the enjoyment of others. He was a frequent visitor to the courts of Russia, France and Prussia, where he was handled, examined and studied. He exhibited his tattoos and explained the rituals and ceremonies of his adopted land. He performed his savage acts before enraptured audiences. He manufactured a feather headdress similar to those worn by the Marquesan warrior. He wore arm and ankle bands and decorated himself with flowers and skulls. Like Melville's Mehevi, he would have danced and stamped and gesticulated fiercely to the sound of the drums and the call of the conch shell. He always mentioned the loss of his family and his desire to return to the South Seas. As he spoke, he felt his sorrow anew. The islands, his home and friends swam before his eyes increasing his sense of longing. All were moved by the pathos of his story, with one commentator remarking that his 'misery can better be conceived than described'.[3] Others responded to the romance inherent in the beachcombing lifestyle, identifying the exotic glamour with the sailor himself: 'The animation with which he recited these circumstances, strongly marked the fearless independence of his former life. He spoke with the decision of one whose commands had been unappealable, and all the chieftain commanded in his eyes.'[4]

His success in the courts of Europe did not help him in his bid to return to the Marquesas. He was given presents, fêted, wined and dined, but rarely given the financial assistance that he required. He utilised other skills gifted to him by his time on the islands. For a while he became a swimming instructor to the Russian cadets at Kronstadt, staying with them until 1811. By now he had been away from Nukuhiva for over five years but he had never forgotten his island home and had never successfully reintegrated into Western life. He continued his efforts to raise money by accompanying his performances with a written pamphlet. It always included a small vocabulary and a description of the cultural and religious ceremonies of the Marquesans. It was not just about raising funds. It was the beachcomber's attempt to do justice to the people he had loved and left on the far side of the world.

In 1817, he left Russia and began the massive overland journey, on foot, to France. He headed to Bordeaux in a bid to sign on a ship to the Pacific. Again, he needed money and shelter. He did what he had always done. He made a theatre of his life for a curious public. He wandered the fairgrounds of Le Havre, Rouen, Grenoble and Orleans, exhibiting himself alongside a 180-kilogram 'fat lady' and a three-headed cow. In France he was a curiosity – a stranger among his own people. He was seen as a bizarre combination of European and savage, man and monster. He was a civilised man bearing the marks of a savage. The things that had once made him who he was – a Marquesan warrior, a member of a chiefly family, a husband and a father – were now aspects of ridicule and curiosity. His island connections, his personal honour, his family and his reputation were lost in his status as a European freak. He was no longer the man he had once believed himself to be. He had lost more than his family on that long, hard journey back to Europe.

It was too much for him. The tours, the exhibitions and his life as a curiosity took their toll. He was worn out and sick with longing. He was never quite able to raise the necessary funds for his journey and he died in hospital in Valenciennes in northern France on 22–23 September 1822. But that was not the end of his story. His value as a curiosity did not end with his death. His fame had preceded him and the town officials feared that grave robbers would see monetary gain in retrieving his tattoos and preserving his unique skin. In order to deter the body-snatchers and allow Cabri some modicum of dignity, the authorities made a decision to bury the beachcomber in an unmarked grave between two other corpses, one above and one below. It was an ignominious end for a man who had so proudly borne the chiefly marks of a Marquesan warrior. He was forty-two years old, a returned beachcomber, and an oddity to all who gawped at him. He died alone, more than 16,000 kilometres away from those he had loved.

A Wandering Life

When Cabri left the Marquesas, another beachcomber remained. That man was Edward Robarts, the Welsh sailor who had chosen to live with the islanders in 1798 after his desertion from the *New Euphrates*. As we saw in Chapter Six, Robarts fought on behalf of his adopted family and acted as midwife to his first-born child. He had other stories to tell. He was a contemporary of the Frenchman Cabri, but had little to do with him during his years in Nukuhiva, Taiohae and Tahuata. The two Europeans lived on different parts of the island with different family groups. There was little love lost between them – an antipathy noticed by the visiting Russians, who tried to effect a reconciliation between them, even getting them to shake hands.[5] Robarts stayed on in the Marquesas after the 'French boy', as he called him, had left, but found it increasingly difficult to navigate successfully between rival family interests. Feeling trapped and reluctant to choose one side over another, he thought it best to move his family somewhere else. He decided to make a journey of his own.

Robarts was at work in his small plantation in Nukuhiva when he heard the sound of gunfire. It was the end of February 1806, nearly eight years after his arrival. He ran to the beach and saw the white sails of a ship anchored just outside the harbour. The ship was the *Lucy*, a privateer from England on its way to New South Wales. It needed refreshments and refurbishment and Robarts fulfilled his duties as intermediary and supercargo. He helped the captain navigate the tricky waters of native protocol and provided his services as pilot and interpreter. In discussion with one of the officers, Robarts learned of opportunities available for resettlement in Botany Bay. Settlers were welcomed and land was provided. A bounty of £150 would be provided along with men to help work the land. It sounded too good to be true. Robarts took his wife and child, some hogs, coconuts, plantains and quantities of matting and went on board. The moment of parting was hard. 'I stood for a moment', he wrote, 'and viewd the cottage I had built with my own hands, the spot I had spent so many happy days on, and now I was leaving it with the greatest regret.' His native family was distraught. They held him tight and begged for him to stay. 'I took my leave of my dearest adopted relations with the greatest weight of sorrow. My heart, which some time before was like that of a lion, was now melted with the most tender feelings,' he recalled.

The anchor was raised, the sails billowed and the ship set a course for the open sea. Their journey had begun, but instead of facing towards the future, Robarts and his wife gazed back toward their past. 'Theres the land that gave me breath', said his wife. 'Theres my friends and relations. I forsake them all for your sake.' Despite the promise of wealth and prosperity in a new country, their future was uncertain. Robarts was no fool; he knew the obstacles that faced him: 'I could not but regreet that but the day before I was a great man, and now look at myself – the outcast of fortune, an unfortunate stranger going to a strange land without money and without friends.'

They never made it to Botany Bay. Upon arrival in Tahiti, they were informed by the resident missionaries that without money and influence they would be unwelcome and unsuccessful in the new colony. Robarts decided to stay in Tahiti, where for the next eighteen months he distilled rum for visiting ships. In 1806 it was not a happy place. The Tahitians appeared debauched and unhealthy. Everywhere he looked, the Marquesan beachcomber saw a community debased by its contact with Europeans. The people suffered from the ague and from dropsy. Many were humpbacked and covered with ulcers. 'In short these people are loaded with disorders', Robarts recalled. 'The veneral is also among them very bad.' He signed on a pearl-trading expedition, which took him and his family to the Tuamotus, New Zealand, Fiji, the Palau Islands and finally to Penang, where for a brief time he was happy and successful – he became butler and cook to the sister of Sir Thomas Raffles and worked for that family until the untimely death of his employer's husband. Needing to provide for his growing family (there were now three children and another on the way), Robarts travelled to Calcutta. There he attained a level of notoriety as a man who had married a native woman and lived on a cannibal island. His adventures ensured him some degree of interest and a small amount of local fame. It was certainly enough to encourage him to record his extraordinary life story.

Robarts was not slow to realise that his story was valuable currency. In the small horizon of opportunity offered to him by his life as a sailor, his exotic tale was his most prized possession. It set him apart from other men. His 'long and singular career of an enterprizeing and unfortuneate life' was unique. He would use it to provide for himself and his family and to bring to life the dangers and delights of his time on the islands. However, his writing career, like the rest of his life, was not plain sailing. Although he began his journal in 1810 under the financial patronage of Dr John Leyden, a well-known scholar, linguist and anthropologist, Robarts' manuscript was not finished until 1824. A series of misfortunes and accidental mishaps kept preventing it from being published in the sailor's lifetime, and it was eventually discovered in the National Library of Scotland in 1925. Although its provenance is uncertain, it is likely it arrived there among the papers of James Hare, a man Robarts had also met in Calcutta.

Robarts had always been a resourceful individual – an archetypal jack of all trades. He had been a tailor, midwife, builder, warrior, teacher, distiller, trader, sailor, butler, storekeeper, deserter and beachcomber. He took on yet another challenge when he decided to become an author. It was a difficult role and it was one he was woefully underprepared for. It took him 171 pages of hard labour to tell his story. As would be expected of a sailor-author, his manuscript was an unsophisticated work, full of spelling mistakes and almost entirely without punctuation. It was the story of his life told in 80,000 closely scribbled words.[6] He wrote of a life among the savages in a place still relatively unknown to the Western world. He was an ordinary man to whom extraordinary things had happened. His experiences were unique and he was determined they would not die with him. He would use them to claim an immortality of sorts.

Life in Calcutta was hard. Without the patronage he had enjoyed in Penang, Robarts found himself just another 'poor white' living on the fringes of British colonial society. 'I wandered about like a lost sheep from morng till eveng in scearch of employment. I was drove to the greatest distress', he recalled. He took a number of jobs: working in an orphanage, as a peace officer and as an overseer of the botanical gardens. His post-island life was a series of diminishments that slowly, but inevitably, reduced him to the meanest of men. From 1811 to 1824 his life became a long series of missed opportunities, menial labour and dependence on charity. He was desperate to provide for his growing family: 'My poor children was scenceible of our indigent situation. Their cloths was worn thread bare, and I had not the means to replace them. I was drove allmost to despair.' The glamour of his native life was long gone. The Marquesan warrior and son-in-law of a king was no more. The proud and valued mediator and ships' pilot of Nukuhiva was now a faceless, worn, bent and scarred ex-sailor wandering the streets of Calcutta.

He was not the only one to suffer. His wife Enoaaoata was the sister of Kiatonui, the King of Nukuhiva. She could not have anticipated the course her life would take when she agreed to marry the white stranger from the sea. She had expected to follow the traditions of her people. It was the life she understood and was prepared for. She wanted nothing else. But she left her home and travelled with her husband to worlds she could never have imagined. Her life of royalty, status and privilege changed to one of poverty and despair. She was true to Robarts; she journeyed with him, kept him company and gave him five children, but she never stopped pining for her home. Her children often saw her weeping, her face covered with tears, but she would tell them to keep quiet. She would always wipe her eyes before her husband returned home. She contracted a fever and died, aged twenty-eight, on 19 July 1813. She was far from home and was buried without the rituals and ceremonies appropriate to her status. Her only obituary was an English one. The *Calcutta Morning Post* recorded (incorrectly); 'On the 19th instant, Ena O D Atah, wife of Mr Roberts, the deceased was a native of the Friendly Islands'.

Robarts was bereft. 'This fatal event nearly deprived me of my scences', he wrote in his journal. 'My rest was broke. At times I was in a deranged state.' As the years progressed, he would marry again but his second wife died in December 1823. His misfortunes continued. Of his seven children, six would die. The only offspring to survive would be his second daughter, Ellen. 'I now only have one Daughter left born of my royal bride to sooth my sorrows as I advance towards my grave. She is a fine girl in her 19th year, and, I hope, will be a comfort to me in my later end.' It was for Ellen that he continued to write his journal. It was now his gift to her. His story, begun so many years ago under such different circumstances, now had a practical use. It would be used to 'Court the Patronage of the Generous Public' for the 'wellfare of my only Daughter, Ellen Robarts'.

His life ended as it began – in anonymity and obscurity. He had obtained a position as a police constable in 1822 and every year his name would be mentioned in the East India Register of employment. By 1833 it was no longer included. He was never heard of again. His story, the one that was to save him from a forgetful public, was never published in his lifetime. It took nearly 150 years before it was finally edited for publication by Greg Dening in 1974. Like other beachcombers, Robarts' life was a series of beach-crossings as he moved from one land to another, from one community to another and from one state of being to another. He was always driven by the belief that life should be better than it was. He was a sailor away from the sea, a man with no prospects and no personal wealth and status. His life, after he left the Marquesas, was marked by destitution and despair, pain and loss. As the sailor himself admitted, 'I was born to be unfortunate.'

Return to America

Herman Melville had one thing in common with Edward Robarts. He too knew the value of a good story. He was twenty-five years old the day he began to write about his captivity among the cannibals of the Marquesas. It was winter in New York. The wet streets were deserted and a chill wind swept over the city. In the family home in Lansingburg on the Hudson River, the trees were rimmed with ice. America was a long way away from the Pacific and Melville's footloose days as a wandering beachcomber. There were no more canoe trips on the lake with his beloved Fayaway, no more dusky maidens and no warm tropical sun. Distance did not change Melville's memories. It merely gave him a sense of perspective. He did not forget his terror and anxiety, his dread of cannibalism and hatred of tattooing, but those fears had become muted by geography and by time. He returned to civilisation only to recreate the world he left behind. As he sat at his oak desk in the quiet of his study, he began to write about the people he met and the beaches he had seen – Nukuhiva, Maui, Tahiti, Oahu and Moorea. The names formed a litany of adventure and romance as they rolled off his pen.

He had left America on 3 January 1841 and returned home on 3 October 1844, after nearly four years away. His return was the end of the sea as the centre of his experience. He would never see the islands again and he would never sail again, except as a paying passenger. But the islands were not forgotten. They would fill his imagination with golden images. They would be the well from which his imaginative and literary life would spring. They crowded his mind with their paradoxical combination of dark and light, innocence and evil, romance and terror, and they turned him into a storyteller. The sailors on the ships that carried him home were his first audience. He told them of the cannibalism, terror, bravery and violence of his native life. And, as sailors always do, he spun his tale as a yarn. He exaggerated, he embroidered and he inflated acts of terror and moments of bravery. He coloured his story with exotic people and with personal acts of initiative and daring. He gave his listeners the drama and excitement that they imagined him to have experienced. For the rest of his time in the Pacific and the length of his journey home Melville talked about his adventures. Stories were reshaped, told and retold, reworked and re-presented to different audiences. It was great preparation for a fledgling author.

And he was only just beginning. On his return home, his family and friends also clamoured to hear the story of his adventures in far-off places, and so he began to write. It was a revelation to him. As he explained to his literary hero and friend Nathaniel Hawthorne, 'Until I was twenty-five, I had no development at all. From my twenty-fifth year I date my life.' He added: 'Three weeks have scarcely passed, at anytime between then and now, that I have not unfolded within myself.'[7] His post-island life began with the writing of his first book in the winter of 1844–45. He wrote of Pacific abundance in the bitter cold of a New York winter. It was the beginning of the most productive period in his writing life. His imagination had been awakened by the new worlds he had seen. As a sailor he had had little money and no influence but he had gained a knowledge of the world. He became a student of human nature. On islands and beaches he had been privileged with a unique experience of otherness. He would try to explain the ramifications of that difference to those back home. He had been a beachcomber – he would become a writer. He would tell his stories to as many people as possible.

The successes of *Typee* and *Omoo*, published in 1846 and 1847, turned the sailor into a literary celebrity. Women readers were particularly intrigued with Melville's coy, but unmistakable references to his native amours. His adventures endowed him with an illicit appeal. He had not only indulged in impolite behaviour in the South Seas, but he had then bragged about it at home by means of his books. It was an irresistible combination. His admirers easily transferred the romance of his lifestyle onto the sailor himself. 'His nose is straight & rather handsome', wrote one female reader, 'his mouth expressive of sensibility & emotion.' She added, '[H]e is tall & erect with an air free, brave and manly.' He was consistently seen in terms of his erotic prowess in tropical climes. After meeting Melville in person, the same woman wrote to a friend, 'Mr Typee is interesting in his aspect – quite. I see Fayaway in his face.'[8] The tall, dark-haired, blue-eyed sailor-turned-author commanded a great deal of attention. He was a wanderer, an adventurer, a man who still retained an air of bravado and barbarism.

Between the years 1846 and 1851, he wrote and published five books: *Typee, Omoo, Mardi, Redburn* and *White-Jacket*. He was eager to capitalise on his popularity and needed to earn money. He was now financially responsible for a large household that included his new wife, his mother, his four dependent sisters and two younger brothers. He would eventually add four children of his own. His third novel, *Mardi*, was not a factual narrative like the previous two, but an imaginative exploration of a mythical world with a Polynesian geography. It was an allegory that journeyed uneasily from a physical world to a symbolic one, full of pessimism and despair. It was a voyage that most readers did not wish to make. The book was a critical and financial disaster, but the demands of his family kept him at his desk. Two works in quick succession were then written and published – *Redburn*, the story of his earlier voyage to Liverpool as a young man, and *White-Jacket*, based on his year in the US navy. The return of the writer of *Typee* and *Omoo* was celebrated; faith was restored. Once again Melville was the acclaimed master of stories of the sea. They were works that he disparaged, however. They were produced for money only. At this time he sarcastically referred to himself as 'H. M. author of "Peedee", "Hullabaloo" & "Pog-Dog"'.[9]

The book he most wanted to write lay in his future. Before he could move forward, though, he had to secure his finances. He decided to travel to England to negotiate copyright for *Redburn* and *White-Jacket*, which had already been published in America. He chose not to travel on the steamboats that regularly made the journey across the Atlantic. Instead, he went on a sailing ship. It would take longer but it was a journey back to the world he knew. On 11 October 1849 he boarded the *Southhampton*, a square-rigged, three-deck sailing ship. Melville was a minor celebrity at this stage and his new-found fame ensured he was assigned the only single cabin on the boat although he rarely used it. He could not resist the lure of the sea. Every morning he would climb the rigging, to the amusement of the other passengers. Literary gentlemen were not supposed to act like common sailors, but Melville did not care. He allowed himself to succumb to 'the emotions of being at the mast-head'. His 'occasional feats in the rigging' earned the admiration of his fellow travellers. When storms hit the ship and she pitched and rolled, Melville stayed on deck 'proof against wind and weather'.[10] He spent hours gazing at the water, turning his face to the wind. He was a hero to all those who spent the following days prostrate with sickness and incapacitated by life at sea. Melville took great pleasure in being on the move again. For a brief moment he could visit the glory days of his youth. This time he was not a greenhorn. He would not be ordered about by his superiors on the ship. Freed from the tyranny of that old life, he revelled in his physical prowess. He made a show of the skills of a sailor. He climbed to the maintop and joked and yarned with the other sailors, while down below the other passengers socialised in the formal salon, playing shuffle board and sharing a hand of whist.

On his return to America, he began to write *Moby Dick*, his great masterpiece of the sea. Writing a masterpiece was not easy in a noisy city surrounded by a growing family. The Melvilles moved to an old farm set in the rolling green fields of Pittsfield in the Berkshire Hills of west Massachusetts. The years 1850–51 were the flowering of his literary genius. He had read the works of Nathaniel Hawthorne and was delighted to find that the author was a neighbour, living nine short kilometres away. They began a series of visits and an intense friendship that was to have a profound effect on the younger man. *Moby Dick* was Melville's great cosmic adventure and Hawthorne was his spiritual guide. He dedicated the book to his literary hero, 'In token of my admiration for his genius'. Although the book drew a great deal from Melville's own experience on board a whaler, the *Pequod's* journey had a different agenda. Melville wanted to be more than the author of adventure stories. His new book explored the nature of truth and the meaning of life. It was his attempt at a Shakespearean tragedy set in the American vernacular as represented by the world of nineteenth-century whaling. *Moby Dick* was a work of immense symbolism that moved far beyond the world of whaling. It was a powerful, mysterious and wonderful work of art – an epic, an allegory and a tragic drama.

Most critics were baffled and disappointed. The book was an economic failure and a critical conundrum. Melville's brief career as a writer was deemed to be over and his literary reputation faded as fast as it had bloomed. He had lost his earlier readers, had little economic success, and by now publishers were reluctant to invest in his unpredictable works. He was forced to supplement his income by contributing anonymous stories and sketches to various monthly magazines. He also gave a series of lectures for three years based on a trip he had made to the Mediterranean. He would not talk about his experiences in the South Seas. He told his family he was finished with the Pacific. He did not want to repeat himself and relive those same experiences. He resolutely turned his back on the islands and on the allure and excitement of those early years.

The spontaneous happiness, the excitement of the unknown and the terror of the foreign – those tumultuous emotions that characterised his native life – were not matched in the long life that followed. By December 1866, driven by the overriding need to provide financial stability for his family, Melville obtained an appointment as Inspector of Customs in New York. It was a humble position and an anonymous one. The once-famous author became an obscure civil servant. The literary lion, the toast of the South Seas, was gone. Melville stayed in the Customs house for nearly two decades, retiring in December 1885. He spent his life examining the cargos of ships that sailed into New York harbour, but never travelled on them himself. Elizabeth and he had four children and a large dependent family and their life was proscribed by their obligations to others. He became a private, pondering man, alone with his thoughts and living quietly out of the public eye. Melville's writing was all but forgotten by the public. For the rest of his life he continued to write in snatched moments away from the bustle of his family. After his death, a number of stories were found among his papers. The most important of these, *Billy Budd*, his tale of an innocent sailor persecuted at the hands of evil, was not published until 1924.

Herman Melville died on 28 September 1891. His death was almost unremarked in the local papers. Most made no comment on his passing. The *Press* printed a short piece: 'There died yesterday at his quiet home in this city a man, who, although he had done almost no literary work during the past sixteen years, was once one of the most popular writers in the United States.'[11] Whatever fame he possessed belonged to *Typee* and *Omoo*. It was not a legacy he was proud of as he explained to his friend Nathaniel Hawthorne: 'To go down to posterity is bad enough any way', he complained, 'but to go down as "a man who lived among the cannibals!"'[12] It was his greatest fear and his primary legacy at least until 1938, when he was rediscovered by an American critical movement intent on constructing a national literary canon. *Moby Dick* was then hailed as one of the greatest early works in American fiction. In his lifetime, though, and much to his chagrin, he was always described as 'the man who once lived among the cannibals'.

The Dancing Beachcomber

James O'Connell, the Irish sailor who danced for his life on Ponape in the Caroline Islands, also became an author. He left the islands after five years' residence, arriving in New York in 1835.[13] With the help of an editor, known only as H. H. W., his story was published some time in 1836, shortly after his arrival in America. There is some dispute about the veracity of parts of his account. His early years in Australia, for example, are fraught with mistakes: incorrect dates, names of ships and other dubious claims. His editor argues that these inconsistencies may have been put in place to prevent O'Connell being identified as an escaped convict. His description of life on Ponape, however, is accepted as true. O'Connell's intimate and detailed knowledge of native culture was eventually verified by other, more prestigious authors.

His book was important, but it was not the most significant event in his later life. The beachcomber had discovered something about himself during his years in the Pacific. When he was faced with uncertainty and danger, when he felt trepidation or fear, he responded by creating theatre. He danced, he sang, he played tunes – he negated the terror of the unknown by re-presenting it as drama. In America he found his métier on the stages, in the halls and in the rings of travelling circuses. There he found the freedom to capitalise on his island experiences. It is entirely possible that he was the first tattooed man to be exhibited in an American circus. It was a career that he would follow until his death. Between 1837 and 1843 he performed with a number of travelling shows, benefits, fairs and revues. Billed as the 'Celebrated Tattooed Man and Irish Dancer' O'Connell found fame of a sort. He made a name for himself performing savage pranks, native dances, sailors' hornpipes and exhibiting his tattoos to audiences throughout the states. He also became famous for his egg dance, where he would dance blindfolded with his hands behind his back while leaping about and weaving back and forth between rows of eggs set on the floor.

He was a popular figure. In 1849 it was announced that 'The manager of the Franklin Theatre has at an enormous expense engaged Mr J. F. O'Connell, the "Wonderful Tattooed Man", who will go through a variety of performances peculiar to himself and perfectly original.'[14] He later became a headliner at P. T. Barnum's American circus where he continued to make a theatre of his native experiences. He danced the same dances and performed the same movements that had once saved his life on the islands. While the stakes may not have been so high, the impetus to present himself to others through dance and display had

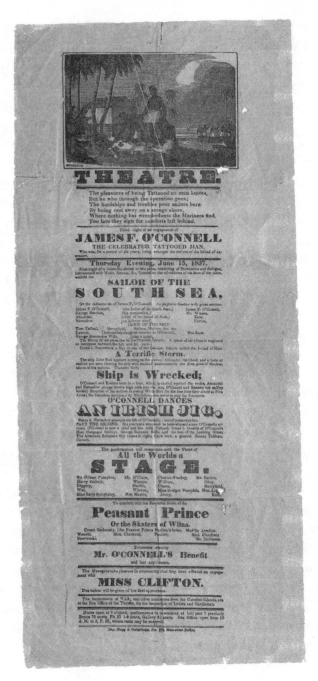

A circus handbill advertising an appearance by James O'Connell
as 'The Celebrated Tattooed Man' on 15 June 1837.

not changed. To the enthusiastic interest of his European audience he would relate the story of his life on Ponape. He would tell of his arrival, exhibit his tattoos and act out his daring escape. By 1850 he was touring with Dan Rice's circus, dancing his way through New Orleans, Cincinnati, Pittsburgh and Memphis, among others.

O'Connell was an actor, dancer, performer and entertainer. The skills that ensured his survival on the islands were called on again in America. He made a life out of being different and that difference was imbued with the romance, adventure and exoticism of far-off places. He was the epitome of savagery and barbarism in the midst of civilised society. The blue, black and red welts of his tattoos covered his face, chest, arms, shoulders and back. They were caused by incisions made with sea shells and then filled with charcoal and berry juice. There is a conundrum here. Traditional Ponapean tattooing is limited to the hands, arms and legs. The extra incisions may have been added later under O'Connell's instructions to increase his exotic appeal. He obviously wished to perpetuate his foreignness. He wanted to capitalise on his otherness, to make of himself a spectacle for others. He must have been successful. Members of the audience described him as grotesque and his fame spread. After every show he was besieged by people wanting to examine him more closely and asking for more information about his savage life. Privately he was moody and withdrawn. In the ring or on stage it was a different story. He was always happiest in front of an audience.

He left his life in a manner unique to him. When he became ill on the road and unable to perform, he was cared for by the other members of the troupe. His illness increased, however, and his situation became hopeless. Nineteen years after he arrived in America, his dancing days were finally over. He died on 29 January 1854, surrounded by his fellow entertainers. He made a specific request – one that was to be honoured after his death. He wanted to mark his passing in the same way he had lived his life. He wanted a joyful tune to be played as he was lowered into the ground. He asked a fellow sailor to dance the hornpipe over his grave.

Trial for Treason

The stories of the returned beachcombers are as diverse as their island experiences and James Morrison has his own unique story to tell. This faithful chronicler of the *Bounty* has already told us much about Fletcher Christian and William Bligh in previous chapters and described life on the islands of Tubuaia and Tahiti in his published journal. His later personal history is also one that is imbued with historical significance. He was one of the men taken back to England to face punishment for mutiny and what happened there is a matter of public record. In 1791 Morrison was living with his native family in Tahiti when he heard of the arrival of the HMS *Pandora* under the command of Captain E. Edwards. Edwards' mandate was clear and he followed his orders assiduously – he would capture the mutineers and would take them home to face justice. He encountered little resistance from the men themselves. Not all the men on shore had been involved in the mutiny. Many felt they were innocent of intentional wrongdoing and gave themselves up. Those that resisted were taken prisoner and led on board ship. Others responded to the call of home. Most of them believed that once their stories were told, justice would be done.

They were soon disillusioned. They were taken on board in view of their native wives and children (there were six already born and others on the way), and immediately placed in chains until they could be imprisoned in a specially built cage. The men called it 'Pandora's Box'. It was 3.3 metres by 5.4 metres and it held fourteen men. They were manacled hand and foot and left in almost total darkness. Morrison described the conditions:

> The Heat of the place when it was calm was so intense that the Sweat frequently ran in Streams to the Scuppers, and produced Maggots in a short time; the Hammocks being dirty when we get them, we found stored with Vermin of another kind, which we had no Method of eradicating but by lying on the Plank; and tho our Freinds would have supplyd us with plenty of Cloth they were not permitted to do it, and our only remedy was to lay Naked.[15]

The prisoners were fed through a small hole, or scuttle, at the top of the box and occasionally had the hoses turned on them when the sweat, vermin and bodily wastes became too offensive. Even then they had to stand upright till the decks dried. In bad weather they lost their footing and fell against each other, often causing severe injury. The only alternative was to lie down in the water, which led to swelling of limbs and loss of mobility. On 29 August 1791 the *Pandora* was wrecked off the Australian coast. It was a death knell to those men manacled to the deck. They called for mercy from the master-at-arms, begging him to leave the scuttle open. 'Never fear my boys we'll all go to Hell together', was his reply. Another guard responded to their plight and threw them a key. In the panic and chaos that followed, four of the prisoners drowned, the remainder making it to the relative safety of the longboats. Their freedom was short-lived, however. They spent the rest of the 1600-kilometre journey home lying in irons at the bottom of open boats. Morrison's protests at his inhumane treatment went unheard. 'Silence, you Murdering Villain, are you not a Prisoner?' shouted Edwards. 'You Piratical Dog what better treatment do you expect?' They remained where they were until they reached England many months later.

The trial that followed their return began on 12 September 1792 and lasted approximately six days. It generated a great deal of public interest and the stakes were high. The mutiny had challenged the established order and the trial provided a chance to reinforce the sanctity of naval law and to punish those that transgressed it. However spontaneous the mutiny may have been, it was regarded as a revolt against constituted authority. It was tainted with the anarchy of the revolution in France that had occurred in the same year. It was a hint of rebellion that the British intended to wipe out once and for all. Only ten of the prisoners had lawyers; the others represented themselves. Morrison was one of them who 'stood his own counsel'. He 'questioned all the evidences, and in a manner so arranged and pertinent, that the spectators waited with impatience for his turn to call on them, and listened with delight during the discussion'.[16] He was found guilty but received the King's pardon, along with six other men who were also acquitted. The remaining three men were hanged. 'At 11.00 o'clock the gun was fired and their souls took flight in a cloud, amid the observations of thousands.'[17] Morrison remained in the navy until he drowned when his ship the *Blenheim* went down with all hands off the coast of Madagascar on 1 February 1807.

A Return to God

Morrison's return home was surrounded by publicity and notoriety. Others managed a less traumatic reintroduction to their old lives. The lapsed missionary George Vason left Tonga on board the *Royal Admiral* in August 1801 after increasing turmoil and political instability convinced him that his life might be in danger. He worked his way back to England as a sailor and then returned to his pre-missionary life as a bricklayer. But it was not an easy transition for the Tongan landowner and favourite of the chief. As soon as he boarded the ship he began to dread his return. He preferred, he said, to find an island somewhere 'where I might end my days as a hermit, and in unbroken retirement repent of my past'. He feared the censorious gaze and the condemnation of others: 'I began to reflect on my past strange life and conduct and look forward with shame and anxiety to a return to my native country', he wrote. His four years in Tonga proved hard to forget. They had challenged his religious beliefs and shaken his moral certainties. He found he was in no hurry to resume his life as a European. 'I felt an insuperable reluctance', he admitted, 'to return to the confinement of a particular spot, and the labours of a weekly employment.'

His return to England was hailed as an act of grace by his friends and family. Vason found himself surrounded by many people anxious to ensure the repentance of his sins and the salvation of his soul. It was not long before the tattooed Tongan beachcomber became a respected member of the church and a pillar of the community. He married a fellow church member and was appointed keeper of a local workhouse. He was a changed man from the young missionary who entered so wholeheartedly into Tongan life and culture. He became taciturn and withdrawn, although his contemporaries admired what they described as his steadiness of character. His reputation as an honourable and worthy member of society culminated in his appointment as governor of Nottingham gaol. In 1810 Vason published an account of his life in Tonga. He did so with a specific agenda. His was a narrative of sin and redemption, of conversion and salvation. It was first published in 1810 and again in 1840, each edition carefully framed within an evangelical context. By this time he had sorely regretted his previous lapse from grace and wanted his story to serve as an example and a warning to others. He was sixty-six years of age, a fully redeemed Christian and a stalwart of the community when he died of a stroke in 1838.

For a brief moment in the history of the Pacific, men such as George Vason had been at the vanguard of European knowledge and expansion. They were the true pioneers of the nineteenth century, travelling culturally to places unvisited and unexplored by others. It was a terrifying experience but, as we have come to know, it was also an exhilarating one. D. H. Lawrence believed Melville's days on the islands were the happiest of his life. 'For once he is really reckless', he wrote. 'For once he takes life as it comes . . . For once he is careless of his actions, careless of his morals, careless of his ideals.'[18] It was a state of being that the sailors would never experience to the same degree. John Jackson would agree. He was one of those who never returned to Europe. He explained why:

> There was a fascination in this kind of life, not only in the youthful and green portion of it, but lasting into and through the yellow and sere; and even now that I am verging on the allotted period . . . of threescore and ten . . . I still have a yearning, even at this age, for the sweets of that exhilarating, wild natural life, so distinct from the artificial, craving, envious, selfish, and greedy life of civilization![19]

Those sailors who made it back home tell us how hard their journeys were. When they first set sail from Europe they were no different from others of their own class, race and status. They became special by virtue of the trials, dangers, successes and failures they shared on the islands. Those differences were not always visible. Not all of them wore evidence of their adventures on their bodies like O'Connell, Vason and Cabri. Others carried them deep in their minds. Returned beachcombers often write of nervousness, sleeplessness, anxiety and depression. Many disliked wearing European clothes, finding them constrictive and uncomfortable. They also did not enjoy the food they had anticipated for so long. Others found that their experiences had taken a physical toll that incapacitated them and increased their difficulties at assimilation. They were often ill, crippled, disfigured and unable to work. They were unfit for the physical demands of the sailor's life and had no prospects on shore. Despite the ordeals, dangers and uncertainties that were so large a feature of their island lives, they found it hard to adapt to life back in Europe. Archibald Campbell, who ended his days in Scotland in the meanest of circumstances, and Samuel Patterson, who peddled the story of his Pacific adventures throughout the American countryside, were always trying to raise funds to return to their island homes. 'From my soul', wrote one returned sailor, 'I had rather go back to those far-off islands, and dwell among the solitudes of those specks in the sea, than to be among civilized men.'[20]

The beachcombers' days of greatness, of cultural significance, ended with their departure from the Pacific. Although their native adventures came to an end, their lives continued and it is hard not to view their post-island lives as a deterioration in colour and intensity. As time passed, public interest faded and European concerns were directed elsewhere. The public was less and less intrigued with the stories and adventures of returned sailors. The men themselves were a long way from the exotic dangers of their island lives. They would never again experience such dramatic and life-changing events. Their lives were now limited and circumscribed by the constraints of their home culture. Island life may have been uncertain and unstable but it was also unforgettable and unrepeatable. Others would never see what they had seen; they would never know what they had known. It was a lonely state of affairs and it provoked a lingering sense of nostalgia for the excitement of that earlier existence.

Throughout the rest of his life, William Mariner, for instance, remained affected by his time as a beachcomber. Although George Vason had been gone for five years when Mariner arrived in the islands, their experiences were similar. Both were accepted by the Tongans, both had lived contented native lives and both returned to lead productive and successful lives in Europe. And their post-island

James O'Connell danced on stage, performing the story of his
native life for American audiences.

histories contain a similar sense of loss. Mariner was still a young man, only nineteen years old, when he returned to England after an absence of six and a half years, but his character had changed. He no longer dreamed of going to sea, his eyes sparkling at the thought of exotic adventures. He had become withdrawn and moody. He was taciturn and sedate with a marked disposition to rest and quiet. His adventuring days were over and he never saw his Tongan family again, despite promising that he would return. He became a stockbroker in London and like George Vason lived a life of respectability and propriety. His eventual death was a foolish accident. The boy who had survived shipwrecks, native massacres and tribal wars in Tonga drowned in the Surrey Canal in London. He was fifty-three years old.

We know that he never forgot his time on the islands. When he first returned to London, he met up with an old friend from Tonga, Jeremiah Higgins. Higgins was a fellow sailor who had been with him on the *Port au Prince*. Like Mariner, he too had survived the massacre on their arrival in Tonga and had lived with the islanders. Although he had not lived with the royal family and had returned home a year earlier, Higgins was a fellow beachcomber. He knew what it was like to live precariously within a foreign world. He had shared the same dangers, known the same culture and loved the same people. In Mariner's London sitting room the boys used to act out their adventures for the entertainment of family and friends. It was the closest they ever got to the 'exhilarating, wild, natural life' they had once known on the islands.

This is where we shall leave them. It is their last performance. They are dressed Tongan fashion with bare chests and lengths of cloth wrapped around their waists. They sway and dance and stamp their feet. Higgins sings while Mariner beats out a rhythm 'according to native method'. The lamplight shines on their young faces as they recreate the world they knew so well. They lose themselves in their memories. As they dance, their friends see strange, barbaric marks covering their hips and thighs. It is their first sight of the traditional tattoos worn by all Tongan males and in the cold London light, thousands of kilometres from the warmth of the Pacific, they marvel at the patterns which look like soft blue satin on the boys' white skin.

Notes

Preface

1 Trevor Bentley, Pakeha Maori: *The Extraordinary Story of the Europeans Who Lived as Maori in Early New Zealand*, Penguin Books, Auckland, 1999.

CHAPTER ONE
The White Heathen of the South Seas

1 Horace Holden, *A Narrative of the Shipwreck, Captivity & Sufferings of Horace Holden*, Ye Galleon Press, Fairfield, Washington, 1975 pp. 55–56; 1 edn 1836.

2 I. C. Campbell, 'European Transculturists in Polynesia, 1789–1840', PhD thesis, University of Adelaide, 1976. See Appendix, pp. 455–58 for a brief history of the term 'beachcomber'.

3 Quoted in Harrison Hayford, Hershel Parker and G. Thomas Tanselle (eds), *The Writings of Herman Melville: Omoo*, Northwestern University Press and the Newberry Library, Evanston and Chicago, ·1968 p. 81.

4 Quoted in Greg Dening, *Beach Crossings: Voyagings across Times,*

Cultures and Self, The Miegunyah Press, Melbourne, 2004, p. 270.

5 H. E. Maude, *Of Islands and Men: Studies in Pacific History,* Oxford University Press, Melbourne, 1968. See Chapter Four for an overview of beachcomber history, pp. 134–77.

6 H. E. Maude, *Of Islands and Men,* pp. 134–69.

7 Quoted in Neil Rennie, *Far-fetched Facts: The Literature of Travel and the Idea of the South Seas,* Clarendon Press, Oxford, 1995, p. 41.

8 Herman Melville, *Typee: A Peep at Polynesian Life,* Penguin, London, 1972, pp. 49, 50.

9 George Robertson, in H. Carrington (ed.), *Discovery of Tahiti, A Journal of the Second Voyage of the H.M.S. 'Dolphin' round the World,* The Hakluyt Society, London, 1948, p. 148.

10 Quoted in Anne Salmond, *The Trial of the Cannibal Dog: Captain Cook in the South Seas,* Penguin Books, Auckland, 2004, p. 49.

11 H. Stonehewer Cooper, *Coral Lands,* Southern Reprints, Papakura, New Zealand, 1987, vol. 1, p. 242; 1st edn 2 vols 1880.

12. Rod Edmond, *Representing the South Pacific: Colonial Discourse from Cook to Gauguin*, Cambridge University Press, Cambridge, 1997, p. 64. See also Bernard Smith, *European Vision and the South Pacific*, Clarendon Press, Oxford, 1960, pp. 248–50. Smith demonstrates the romantic ideal at work in the public perception of the *Bounty* mutineers.

13 See Edmond *Representing the South Pacific*, and Greg Dening, *Mr Bligh's Bad Language: Passion, Power and Theatre on the* Bounty, Cambridge University Press, Cambridge, 1992. Both texts discuss the political dimensions of the *Bounty* mutiny.

14 Julian Thomas, *Cannibals and Convicts: Notes of Personal Experience in the Western Pacific*, Cassell & Company Ltd, London, 1886, pp. 17, 373, 393.

15 Cooper, *Coral Lands*, vol. 2, pp. 99–100.

16 This observation belongs to Edmond, *Representing the South Pacific*, p. 63.

17 J. M. Walsh, *Overdue: A Romance of Unknown New Guinea*, States Publishing, Sydney, 1925, p. 59.

18 The Rev. Robert Thomson, *The Marquesas Islands: Their Description and Early History*, Institute for Polynesian Studies, Hawaii, 1980, pp. 57–58; 1st edn 1841.

19 Thomas, *Cannibals and Convicts*, p. 7.

20 Quoted in Maude, *Of Islands and Men*, pp. 160–61.

21 The Rev. James Orange (ed.), *Life of the Late George Vason of Nottingham*, Henry Mozley, Derby, 1840, p. 35.

22 Quoted in Jennifer Terrell, 'Joseph Cabri and his Notes on the Marquesas', *Journal of Pacific History*, XXVII: 2 April 1982, p. 102.

23 For an analysis of the psychological element in European response to
the beachcomber see I. C. Campbell, 'European Transculturists'.

CHAPTER TWO
Accidental Authors

1 From Melville's letter to Nathaniel Hawthorne, dated June 1851. See Lynn Horth (ed.), *The Writings of Herman Melville: Correspondence*, vol. 14, Northwestern University Press and the Newberry Library, Evanston and Chicago, 1993, p. 193.

2 Harrison Hayford, Hershel Parker and G. Thomas Tanselle, (eds), *The Writings of Herman Melville: Omoo*, Northwestern University Press and the Newberry Library, Evanston and Chicago, 1968, p. 27.

3 Quoted in Jonathan Lamb, V. Smith and N. Thomas (eds), *Exploration and Exchange: A South Seas Anthology 1680–1900*, The University of Chicago Press, Chicago and London, 2000, p. 158.

4 William Torrey, *Torrey's Narrative . . .*, A. J. Wright, Boston, 1848, p. v.

5 See discussion in Greg Dening, *Mr Bligh's Bad Language: Passion, Power and Theatre on the* Bounty, Cambridge University Press, Cambridge, 1994, p. 41.

6 Sir Everard Im Thurn and L. Wharton (eds), *The Journal of William Lockerby . . .*, Fiji Times and Herald Ltd, Fiji, 1982, pp. 20, 83; 1st edn 1825.

7 Greg Dening (ed.), *The Marquesan Journal of Edward Robarts 1797–1824*, Australian National University Press, Canberra, 1974, pp. 105–106.

8 Samuel Patterson, *Narrative of the Adventures and Sufferings of Samuel Patterson*, Ye Galleon Press, Fairfield, Washington, 1967, p. 141; 1st edn 1825.

9   William Diaper, *Cannibal Jack: The True Autobiography of a White Man in the South Seas*, London, Faber & Gwyer, 1928, introduction.

10 Dening, *Mr Bligh's Bad Language*, p. 73.

11 See Harrison Hayford et al. (eds), *Omoo*, p. 335 for detailed reviews.

CHAPTER THREE
The Myth of the Castaway

1   For all information on Alexander Selkirk and his island sojourn I am indebted to Diana Souhami, *Selkirk's Island: The True and Strange Adventures of the Real Robinson Crusoe*, Weidenfeld & Nicholson, London, 2001.

2   Woodes Rogers, *A Cruising Voyage round the World*, Dover Publications Inc, New York, 1970, p. 92; 1st edn 1712.

3   Rogers, *A Cruising Voyage round the World*, p. 94.

4   Greg Dening, *Mr Bligh's Bad Language: Passion, Power and Theatre on the* Bounty, Cambridge University Press, Cambridge, 1992, p. 308.

5   Rogers, *A Cruising Voyage round the World*, p. 96.

6   Quoted in Souhami, *Selkirk's Island*, p. 127.

7   For a discussion of Steele's treatment of Selkirk's story see Souhami, *Selkirk's Island*, pp. 170–71.

8   William Cowper, from *Verses Supposed to be Written by Alexander Selkirk, During his Solitary Abode in the Island of Juan Fernandez*, 1782, quoted in Souhami, p. 225.

9   Daniel Defoe, *Robinson Crusoe*, Wordsworth Classics, London, 1994, p. 16.

10 Christopher Lloyd, *The British Seaman*, Collins, London, 1968, p. 102.

11 James Oliver and William G. Dix, *Wreck of the* Glide, Wiley & Putnam, New York and London, 1848, p. 190.

12 John Twyning, *Shipwreck and Adventures of John P. Twyning*, 2nd edn, London, 1850, p. 20; printed for the benefit of the author.

13 Defoe, *Robinson Crusoe*, p. 112.

14 Peter Bays, *A Narrative of the Wreck of the* Minerva, B. Bridges, Market-Hill, Cambridge, 1831, p. 97.

15 James Morrison, *The Journal of James Morrison*, The Golden Cockerel Press, London, 1935, p. 85.

16 Morrison, *The Journal of James Morrison*, p. 85.

17 H. Stonehewer Cooper, *Coral Lands*, Southern Reprints, Papakura, New Zealand, 1987, vol. 2, p. 115; 1st edn, 2 vols, 1880.

18 John Coulter, *Adventures in the Pacific*, William Curry Jun. and Company, Dublin, 1845, p. 100.

19 Bill Pearson, *Rifled Sanctuaries: Some Views of the Pacific Islands in Western Literature*, Auckland University Press/Oxford University Press, Auckland, 1984, p. 25.

20 Lieve Spaas, 'Narcissus and Friday: From Classical to Anthropological Myth', in Lieve Spaas and Brian Stimpson (eds), *Robinson Crusoe: Myths and Metamorphoses*, Macmillan, London, 1996, p. 98–109.

21 Sir Everard Im Thurn and Leonard Wharton (eds), *The Journal of William Lockerby*, Fiji Times and Herald Ltd, 1982, p. 21; 1st edn 1925.

22 E. H. Lamont, *Wild Life among the Pacific Islanders*, University of the South Pacific, Rarotonga and Suva, 1994, pp. 353–54; 1st edn 1867.

23 Markman Ellis, 'Crusoe, Cannibalism and Empire', in *Robinson Crusoe:*

Myths and Metamorphoses, Macmillan, London, 1996, p. 49.

24 Defoe, *Robinson Crusoe*, p. 74.

25 For an in-depth discussion of the mutineers on Tubuai see Dening, *Mr Bligh's Bad Language*, pp. 88–96.

26 Point made by Dening, p. 92.

27 I. C. Campbell, *'Gone Native' in Polynesia: Captivity Narratives and Experiences from the South Pacific*, Greenwood Press, Westport, Connecticut, 1998, p. 30.

28 Vanessa Smith, 'Crusoe in the South Seas', Lieve Spaas et al. (eds), *Robinson Crusoe*, pp. 62–77, identifies beachcombers as 'mimic' Crusoes.

29 For a discussion of beachcombers as absconders from European society see Smith, 'Crusoe in the South Seas', p. 63.

30 Alfred Lord Tennyson, 'Locksley Hall', 1842.

CHAPTER FOUR
Going to Sea: Surviving the Journey

1 William Torrey, *Torrey's Narrative*, A. J. Wright, Boston, 1848, p. 29.

2 Daniel Defoe, *Robinson Crusoe*, Wordsworth Classics, London, 1994, p. 2.

3 Sigmund Freud, 'A Disturbance of Memory on the Acropolis', in James Strachey and Anna Freud (ed. and trans.), *The Standard Edition of the Complete Psychological Works of Sigmund Freud*, Hogarth Press and Institute of Psycho-Analysis, London, 1964, vol. 22 pp. 239–48.

4 James O'Connell, *A Residence of Eleven Years . . .*, Australian National University Press, Canberra, 1972, p. 53; 1st edn 1836.

5 John Martin (ed.), *An Account of the Natives of the Tonga Islands*, Constable and Co., Edinburgh, 3rd edn, 1827, p. xxiv.

6 Harrison Hayford, Hershel Parker and G. Thomas Tanselle (eds), *The Writings of Herman Melville: Redburn*, The Northwestern University Press and the Newberry Library, Evanston & Chicago, 1969, p. 5.

7 John Hawkesworth, *An Account of the Voyages and Discoveries in the Southern Hemisphere*, vol. 1, W. Strahan and T. Cadell, London, 2nd edn 1773, p. i.

8 Benjamin Morrell, *A Narrative of Four Voyages to the South Sea, North and South Pacific Ocean . . . from the Year 1822–1831*, J & J Harper, New York, 1832, p. xi.

9 Quoted in Nathaniel Philbrick, *In the Heart of the Sea*, Flamingo, London, 2000, p. 32.

10 Harrison Hayford, Hershel Parker and G. Thomas Tanselle (eds), *The Writings of Herman Melville: Omoo*, The Northwestern University Press and the Newberry Library, Evanston & Chicago, 1968, p. 38–39.

11 The following description of shipboard life is indebted to Stephen R. Bown, *Scurvy*, Penguin Books, Camberwell, Victoria, 2003, Chapter 1.

12 Greg Dening, *Mr Bligh's Bad Language: Passion, Power and Theatre on the* Bounty, Cambridge University Press, Cambridge, 1992, p. 68.

13 Quoted in Joan Druett, *Hen Frigates: Wives of Merchant Captains Under Sail*, Simon & Schuster, New York, 1998, p. 175.

14 Hayford, Parker and Tanselle (eds), *The Writings of Herman Melville: Omoo*, p. 40.

15 See Druett, *Hen Frigates*, p. 133.

16 Quoted in Bown, *Scurvy*, p. 28.

17 Druett, *Hen Frigates*, p. 142.

18 Bown, *Scurvy*, p. 29.
19 Jonathan Lamb, *Preserving the Self in the South Seas 1680–1840*, The University of Chicago Press, Chicago and London, 2001, p. 117.
20 Dening, *Mr Bligh's Bad Language*, p. 68.
21 Anne Salmond, *The Trial of the Cannibal Dog: Captain Cook in the South Seas*, Penguin Books, Auckland, 2004, p. 62.
22 Bown, *Scurvy*, p. 179.
23 The symptoms of scorbutic nostalgia and scurvy in general are discussed by Lamb in *Preserving the Self*, pp. 9, 114–31.
24 Jonathan Lamb, V. Smith and N. Thomas (eds), *Exploration and Exchange: A South Seas Anthology 1680–1900*, The University of Chicago Press, Chicago and London, 2000, p. xviii.
25 Quoted in Greg Dening, *Beach Crossings: Voyaging Across Times, Cultures and Self*, The Miegunyah Press, Melbourne, 2004, p. 288.
26 The divisions that demarcate a seaman's life are more fully examined by Greg Dening, *Mr Bligh's Bad Language*, pp. 81 ff.
27 Herman Melville, *White-Jacket or The World in a Man-of-War*, Oxford University Press, Oxford, 1990. All quotations appear in Chapter XXXIII.
28 My discussion of the theatricality of flogging is indebted to Greg Dening, *Mr Bligh's Bad Language*, pp. 113–56.
29 Richard Henry Dana, *Two Years before the Mast*, Wordsworth American Library, London, 1996, p. 82.
30 See Dening, *Mr Bligh's Bad Language*, p. 116.
31 See, for example, James Wilson, *A Missionary Voyage to the Southern Pacific Ocean . . .*, printed by S. Gosnell for T. Chapman, London, 1799, published for the benefit of the Society; William Ellis's *Polynesian Researches, During a Residence of Nearly Six Years in the South Sea Islands*, London: Dawsons of Pall Mall, London, 1967, 2 vols, 1st edn 1829; and Charles Wilkes, *Narrative of the United States Exploring Expedition*, Lea and Blanchard, Philadelphia, 1845, 5 vols.
32 Leonard Shaw, 'A Brief Sketch of the Sufferings of Leonard Shaw on Massacre Islands' in Benjamin Morrell, *A Narrative of Four Voyages . . . from the Year 1822 to 1831*, J. & J. Harper, New York, 1832, pp. 441–48.

CHAPTER FIVE
Stranded in a Strange Land

1 John Jackson, 'Jackson's Narrative', in J. Elphinstone Erskine, *Journal of a Cruise . . .*, Dawsons of Pall Mall, London, 1967, p. 415; 1st edn 1853.
2 Jackson, 'Jackson's Narrative', p. 429.
3 I. C. Campbell, *'Gone Native' in Polynesia: Captivity Narratives and Experiences from the South Pacific*, Greenwood Press, Westport, Connecticut, 1998, p. 102.
4 For discussion of the stages of liminality see Arnold Van Gennep, *The Rites of Passage* (trans. Vizedom and Caffee), Routledge & Kegan Paul, London, 1960.
5 Campbell, *'Gone Native'*, p. 101.
6 See Campbell, *'Gone Native'*, pp. 52–59 for discussion of Mariner's experiences in Tonga.
7 Jackson, 'Jackson's Narrative', p. 412.
8 E. H. Lamont, *Wild Life among the Pacific Islanders*, University of the South Pacific, Rarotonga and Suva, 1994, p. 131; 1st edn 1867.

9 William Cary, *Wrecked on the Feejees*, Ye Galleon Press, Fairfield, Washington, 1972, pp. 11–12; 1st edn 1887.

10 William Endicott, *Wrecked among Cannibals in the Fijis*, Marine Research Society, Salem, Massachusetts, 1923, p. 39.

11 Campbell, *'Gone Native'*, p. 106.

12 William Mariner in John Martin (ed.), *An Account of the Natives of the Tonga Islands*, Constable and Co., Edinburgh, 3rd edn, 1827, Chapter 10; 1st edn 1817.

13 Peter Bays, *A Narrative of the Wreck of the* Minerva . . . , B. Bridges, Market-Hill, Cambridge, 1831, p. 45.

14 James O'Connell, *A Residence of Eleven Years in New Holland and the Caroline Islands*, Australian National University Press, Canberra, 1972; 1st edn 1836. O'Connell's editor Saul H. Riesenberg disputes a number of personal details supplied by O'Connell.

15 James O'Connell, *A Residence of Eleven Years*, p. 106.

CHAPTER SIX
Strategies for Survival: The Mechanics of Going Native

1 Joseph Conrad, *Heart of Darkness and The Secret Sharer*, ed. Franklin Walker, Bantam Books, New York, 1971, pp. 3–132; all quotations refer to this edition; 1st edn 1902.

2 Quoted in I. C. Campbell, *'Gone Native' in Polynesia: Captivity Narratives and Experiences from the South Pacific*, Greenwood Press, Westport, Connecticut, 1998, p. 95.

3 I. C. Campbell, 'European Transculturists in Polynesia, 1789–1840', PhD thesis, University of Adelaide, 1976, p. xiii.

4 George Keate, *An Account of the Pelew Islands . . .*, printed for Captain Henry Wilson, London, 1803, p. 13; 1st edn 1788.

5 See discussion in I. C. Campbell, *'Gone Native'*, pp. 95–110.

6 Quoted in Campbell, *'Gone Native'*, p. 61.

7 Campbell, *'Gone Native'*, p. 99.

8 Stephen Greenblatt, *Marvelous Possessions: The Wonder of the New World*, The University of Chicago Press, Chicago, 1991, p. 104.

9 Greenblatt, *Marvelous Possessions*, p. 141.

10 Greg Dening, *Beach Crossings: Voyaging across Times, Cultures and Self*, The Miegunyah Press, Melbourne, 2004, p. 313.

11 Quoted in Greg Dening (ed.), *The Marquesan Journal of Edward Robarts 1797–1824*, Australian National University Press, Canberra, 1974, p. 8.

12 John Twyning, *Shipwreck and Adventures of John P. Twyning . . .*, printed for the benefit of the author, London, 1850, p. 117.

13 For an in-depth discussion of the role of women in beachcomber assimilation see Campbell *'Gone Native'*, pp. 106–107.

14 Point made by Campbell, *'Gone Native'*, p. 107.

15 Quoted in Campbell, *'Gone Native'*, p. 61.

16 See Greg Dening, *Mr Bligh's Bad Language: Passion, Power and Theatre on the* Bounty, Cambridge University Press, Cambridge, 1992, p. 258, who argues that by letting himself be tattooed, the beachcomber was repaying the generosity and hospitality of the natives by consenting to become like them.

17 Horace Holden, *A Narrative of the Shipwreck, Captivity & Sufferings of Horace Holden & Benj. H. Nute*, Ye Galleon Press, Fairfield, Washington, 1975, p. 51; 1st edn 1836.

18 Rod Edmond, *Representing the South Pacific: Colonial Discourse from Cook to Gauguin*, Cambridge University Press, Cambridge, 1997, p. 70.

19 Point made by Edmond, *Representing the South Pacific*, p. 93.

20 Harrison Hayford, Hershel Parker and G. Thomas Tanselle (eds), *The Writings of Herman Melville: Omoo*, Northwestern University Press and the Newberry Library, Evanston and Chicago, 1968, p. 27.

21 The following discussion is indebted to Campbell, *'Gone Native'*, pp. 111–24.

22 This incident is reported in Dening, *Beach Crossings*, p. 294.

23 Dening (ed.), *The Marquesan Journal of Edward Robarts*, p. 126.

24 Robarts in Greg Dening (ed.), *The Marquesan Journal of Edward RobartsI*, The Australian National University Press, Canberra, 1974, p. 79.

25 William Cary, *Wrecked on the Feejees*, Ye Galleon Press, Fairfield, Washington, 1972, p. 23; 1st edn 1887.

CHAPTER SEVEN
Drama and Role Play in the Life of the Beachcomber

1 James Morrison, *Journal of James Morrison*, The Golden Cockerel Press, London, 1935, p. 32.

2 James Oliver and William G. Dix, *Wreck of the* Glide, Wiley & Putnam, New York and London, 1848, p. 97.

3 George Keate, *An Account of the Pelew Islands*, printed for Captain Henry Wilson, London, 1803, p. 52; 1st edn 1788.

4 Greg Dening, *Performances*, The University of Chicago Press, Chicago, 1996, p. 20.

5 Victor Turner, *Anthropology of Performance*, PAJ Publications, New York, 1988, p. 24.

6 Erving Goffman, *The Presentation of Self in Everyday Life*, The Penguin Press, London, 1969, p. 63; 1st edn 1956.

7 Quoted in Richard Schechner, *Between Theater and Anthropology*, University of Pennsylvania Press, Philadelphia, 1985, p. 118.

8 E. H. Lamont, *Wild Life among the Pacific Islanders*, University of the South Pacific, Rarotonga and Suva, 1994, p. 132; 1st edn 1867.

9 Dening, *Performances*, p. 112.

10 Quoted in Goffman, *The Presentation of Self*, p. 66.

11 Robert Coffin, *The Last of the 'Logan'* ..., Harold Thompson (ed.), Cornell University Press, Ithaca, New York, 1928, p. 66.

12 John Twyning, *Shipwreck and Adventures of John P. Twyning* ..., printed for the benefit of the author, London, 1850, pp. 124–25.

13 Quoted in I. C. Campbell, *'Gone Native' in Polynesia: Captivity Narratives and Experiences from the South Pacific*, Greenwood Press, Westport, Connecticut, 1998, p. 45.

14 Quoted in I. C. Campbell, *'Gone Native'*, p. 46.

15 For further details of Whippy, Davis and Young see I. C. Campbell, *'Gone Native'*, pp. 62–68, 43–46.

16 Sir Everard Im Thurn and Leonard Wharton (eds), *The Journal of William Lockerby*, Fiji Times and Herald Ltd, Fiji, 1982, pp. 63–64.

CHAPTER EIGHT
On the Margins and in Despair

1 Everett V. Stonequist, *The Marginal Man: A Study in Personality and Culture Conflict*, Charles Scribner's Sons, New York, 1937. Stonequist's study concerns the sociological and psychological impact of marginality in societies where individuals leave one social group or culture without making a satisfactory adjustment to another.

2 Rod Edmond, *Representing the South Pacific: Colonial Discourse from Cook to Gauguin*, Cambridge University Press, Cambridge, 1997. Chapter Three discusses the political ramifications of the Marquesan beach.

3 Herman Melville, *Typee*, Penguin, London, 1972, p. 332.

4 D. H. Lawrence, *Studies in Classic American Literature*, Heinemann, London and Toronto, n.d., pp. 217–29.

5 Lawrence, *Studies*, p. 218.

6 John Jackson, 'Jackson's Narrative' in J. Elphinstone Erskine, *Journal of a Cruise*, Dawsons of Pall Mall, London, 1967, p. 422; 1st edn 1853.

7 Morris Frelich (ed.), *Marginal Natives at Work: Anthropologists in the Field*, Schenkman Publishing Company, Cambridge, Massachusetts, 1977, p. 22.

8 Peter Bays, *A Narrative of the Wreck of the* Minerva *Whaler of Port Jackson*, B. Bridges, Market-Hill, Cambridge, 1831, p. 88.

9 Bays, *A Narrative of the Wreck of* Minerva, p. 82.

10 E. H. Lamont, *Wild Life among the Pacific Islanders*, University of the South Pacific, Rarotonga and Suva, 1994, p. 306.

11 Samuel Patterson, *Narrative of the Adventures and Sufferings of Samuel Patterson* . . . Ye Galleon Press, Fairfield, Washington, 1967, p. 19; 1st edn 1825.

12 Patterson, *Narrative of the Adventures and Sufferings*, p. 95.

13 Patterson, *Narrative of the Adventures and Sufferings*, pp. 106–107.

14 Lamont, *Wild Life among the Pacific Islanders*, p. 312.

15 'The lure of the native' is a phrase used by Anthony Pagden in *European Encounters with the New World*, Yale University Press, New Haven and London, 1993, p. 37.

16 Point made by I. C. Campbell in 'European Transculturists in Polynesia, 1789–1840', PhD thesis, University of Adelaide, 1976, Chapter 4.

17 John Jackson, 'Jackson's Narrative', p. 450.

18 D. H. Lawrence, *Studies*, p. 137.

19 Samuel Patterson, *Narrative of the Adventures and Sufferings*, p. 101.

20 E. H. Lamont, *Wild Life among the Pacific Islanders*, p. 353.

21 Patterson, *Narrative of the Adventures and Sufferings*, p. 31.

CHAPTER NINE
Too Close to Cannibalism

1 I. C. Campbell, *'Gone Native' in Polynesia: Captivity Narratives and Experiences from the South Pacific*, Greenwood Press, Westport, Connecticut, 1998, p. 75.

2 Quoted in Vanessa Smith, *Literary Culture and the Pacific: Nineteenth-Century Textual Encounters*, Cambridge University Press, Cambridge, 1998, p. 44.

3 John Jackson, 'Jackson's Narrative', in J. Elphinstone Erskine *Journal of*

a Cruise . . ., Dawsons of Pall Mall, London, 1967, p. 427.

4 William Arens, *The Man-Eating Myth, Anthropology and Anthropophagy*, Oxford University Press, New York, 1979; and Peter Hulme, *Colonial Encounters: Europe and the Native Caribbean 1492–1797*, Methuen, London and New York, 1986. Arens and Hulme both outline the ideological impulses that traditionally underlie accusations of cannibalism.

5 Quoted in Neil Rennie, *Far-fetched Facts: The Literature of Travel and the Idea of the South Seas*, Clarendon Press, Oxford, 1995, p. 160.

6 Arens, *The Man-Eating Myth*, p. 19.

7 Michel de Montaigne, 'Of Cannibals', *Essays of Montaigne*, Charles Cotton (trans.), William Carew Hazlitt (ed.), vol. 1, Reeves & Turners, London, 1877, p. 259.

8 Montaigne, 'Of Cannibals', p. 249.

9 Herman Melville, *Typee: A Peep at Polynesian Life*, Penguin Classics, 1986, p. 62; 1st edn 1846.

10 Quoted in Rennie, *Far-fetched Facts*, p. 182.

11 Peter Bays, *A Narrative of the Wreck of the* Minerva . . . , B. Bridges, Market-Hill, Cambridge, 1831, pp. 47–48.

12 For example R. M. Ballantyne's *Coral Island* as argued by Gananath Obeyesekere in 'Cannibal Feasts in Nineteenth-century Fiji: Seamen's Yarns and the Ethnographic Imagination', in Frances Barker, Peter Hulme and Margaret Iverson (eds.), *Cannibalism and the Colonial World*, Cambridge University Press, Cambridge, 1992, pp. 63–86. Obeyesekere also regards the narratives of William Endicott and John Jackson as examples of seamen's yarns rather than reliable ethnographic sources.

13 Quoted in Rennie, *Far-fetched Facts*, p. 179.

14 John Jackson, 'Jackson's Narrative', p. 426.

15 See discussion in Introduction by Sir Everard Im Thurn and Leonard Wharton (eds.), *The Journal of William Lockerby* Fiji Times and Herald Ltd, Fiji, 1982; 1st edn 1925.

16 William Endicott, *Wrecked among Cannibals in the Fijis*, Marine Research Society, Salem, Massachusetts, 1923, pp. 62–63.

17 Quoted in Leonelle Wallace, 'Tryst Tropique: Pacific Texts, Modern Sexuality', PhD thesis, University of Auckland, 1996, p. 63; quote refers to a comment noted in Georg Langsdorff, *Voyages and Travels in Various Parts of the World, During the Years 1803, 1804, 1805, 1806 and 1807*.

18 See Introduction by Rev. J. Hadfield in *Cannibal Jack: The True Autobiography of a White Man in the South Seas*, Faber & Gwyer Ltd, London, 1928; and Julian Thomas (Vagabond) *Cannibals and Convicts*, Cassell & Company Ltd, London, 1886, p. 16.

19 See Preface to William Diaper, *Cannibal Jack*.

20 Introduction to *Cannibal Jack*, p. xvii.

21 Samuel Patterson, *Narrative of the Adventures and Sufferings of Samuel Patterson*, Ye Galleon Press, Fairfield, Washington, 1967, p. 100; 1st edn 1825.

22 Frances Barker et al. (eds.), *Cannibalism and the Colonial World*, Cambridge University Press, Cambridge, 1998, p. 2.

23 Mary Louise Pratt, 'Fieldwork in

Common Places', in James Clifford and George E. Marcus (eds), *Writing Culture: The Poetics and Politics of Ethnography*, University of California Press, Berkeley and Los Angeles, 1986, p. 33. Pratt is talking specifically about an anthropological experience but the distinctions apply equally well to beachcomber life.

24 James O'Connell, *A Residence of Eleven Years . . .*, Australian National University Press, Canberra, 1972, p. 194; 1st edn 1836.

25 The following story is taken from Owen Chase, *The Wreck of the Whaleship* Essex, London Review, London, 2000. All quotations that follow refer to that edition.

26 William Torrey, *Torrey's Narrative*, A. J. Wright, Boston, 1848, pp. 129–30.

27 Christopher Legge, 'William Diaper: A Biographical Sketch', in *Journal of Pacific History*, vol. 1, 1996, p. 86.

28 Thomas, *Cannibals and Convicts*, p. 8.

CHAPTER TEN
Voices from the Beach

1 John Martin (ed.), *An Account of the Natives of the Tonga Islands*, Constable and Co., Edinburgh, 3rd edn, 1827, vol. 1, p. 330.

2 Sir Everard Im Thurn and Leonard Wharton (eds), *The Journal of William Lockerby*, Fiji Times and Herald Ltd, Fiji, 1982, p. 69.

3 Robert Coffin, *The Last of the 'Logan'* . . ., Harold Thompson (ed.), Cornell University Press, Ithaca, New York, 1941, p. 77.

4 H. E. Maude, *Of Islands and Men: Studies in Pacific History*, Oxford University Press, Melbourne, 1968. Maude describes the beachcombers' 'genuine and mutual affection and

understanding' with regard to their native hosts, p. 168.

5 Martin, *An Account of the Natives of the Tongan Islands*, vol. 1, p. 76.

6 Herman Melville, *Typee: A Peep at Polynesian Life*, Penguin Classics, London, 1986, p. 37; 1st edn 1846.

7 Quoted in Neil Rennie, *Far-fetched Facts: The Literature of Travel and the Idea of the South Seas*, Clarendon Press, Oxford, 1995, p. 181.

8 Melville, *Typee*, p. 180.

9 Quoted in Rennie, *Far-fetched Facts*, p. 182.

10 See Greg Dening, *Beach Crossings: Voyaging across Times, Cultures and Self*, The Miegunyah Press, Melbourne, 2004, p. 97.

11 See Greg Dening, *Islands and Beaches, Discourse on a Silent Land: Marquesas 1774–1880*, The Dorsey Press, Chicago, 1980, p. 147. Dening argues that Melville's Pacific works continually challenge contemporary prejudices. See also Bill Pearson, *Riffed Sanctuaries: Some Views of the Pacific Islands in Western Literature*, Auckland University Press/Oxford University Press, Auckland, 1984, pp. 66 ff.

12 Niel Gunson, *Messengers of Grace: Evangelical Missionaries in the South Seas 1797–1860*, Oxford Univeristy Press, Melbourne, 1978, p. 36.

13 George Vason, *An Authentic Narrative of Four Years' Residence at Tongataboo . . . 1796*, Longman, Hurst, Rees, and Orme, London, 1810, appendix p. 227.

14 Martin, *An Account of the Natives of the Tonga Islands*, p. xxxi.

15 Harrison Hayford, Hershel Parker and G. Thomas Tanselle (eds), *The Writings of Herman Melville: Omoo*, Northwestern University Press and

the Newberry Library, Evanston and Chicago, 1968, pp. 334–40.

16 Edward Lucett, *Rovings in the Pacific from 1837–1849*, Longman, Brown, Green and Longmans, London, 1851, vol. 1, p. 293.

17 Hayford et al., *Omoo*, p. 336.

18 Lucett, *Rovings*, pp. 223–24.

19 Torrey is a problematic beachcomber. Bill Pearson in *Rifled Sanctuaries* doubts he was a beachcomber, while Greg Dening believes there is enough verifiable information in his account to accept he did spend some time with the Marquesans.

20 E. H. Lamont, *Wild Life among the Pacific Islanders*, University of the South Pacific, Rarotonga and Suva, 1994, p. 98; 1st edn 1867.

21 Coffin, *The Last of the 'Logan'*, p. 110.

22 James Oliver and William Dix, *Wreck of the* Glide . . ., Wiley & Putnam, New York and London, 1848, p. 125.

CHAPTER ELEVEN
The Return Home

1 John Slade, *Old Slade; or Fifteen Years Adventures of a Sailor . . .*, John Putnam, Boston, 1844, p. 84.

2 Cabri's story can be found in Jennifer Terrell, 'Joseph Kabris and his Notes on the Marquesas', *Journal of Pacific History*, XXVII: 2 April 1982, pp. 101–12; and in Greg Dening (ed.), *The Marquesan Journal of Edward Robarts 1797–1824*, Australian National University Press, Canberra, 1974; and *Beach Crossings: Voyaging across Times, Cultures and Self*, The Miegunyah Press, Melbourne, 2004.

3 Terrell, 'Joseph Kabris', p.105.

4 R. K. Porter, *Travelling Sketches in Russia and Sweden*, 2 vols, Richard Phillips, London, 1813, vol. 2, pp. 43–44.

5 Dening, *The Marquesan Journal*, p. 7.

6 See Dening, Introduction to *The Marquesan Journal*, pp. 1–29.

7 Melville's letter to Nathaniel Hawthorne, dated June 1851.

8 Hershel Parker, *Herman Melville: A Biography Volume 1, 1819–1851*, The Johns Hopkins University Press, Baltimore and London, 1996, pp. 773, 753. Parker provides an extremely detailed analysis of Melville's post-beachcomber years.

9 Gay Wilson Allen, *Melville and his World*, Thames and Hudson, London, 1971, p. 96.

10 Howard Horsforth and Lynn Horth (eds), *The Writings of Herman Melville: Journals*, Northwestern University Press and the Newberry Library, Evanston and Chicago, 1989, pp. 4–7.

11 Quoted in Allen, p. 130.

12 Melville's letter to Nathaniel Hawthorne, dated June 1851.

13 The length of O'Connell's stay is disputed by his editor, Saul H. Riesenberg, who believes it was closer to three years. See Saul H. Riesenberg, 'The Tattooed Irishman', *The Smithsonian Journal of History*, vol. 3, no. 1, Spring, 1968, pp. 1–18.

14 See Riesenberg, 'The Tattooed Irishman', p. 13.

15 James Morrison, *The Journal of James Morrison . . .* The Golden Cockerel Press, London, 1972, p. 123.

16 Greg Dening, *Mr Bligh's Bad Language: Passion, Power and Theatre on the* Bounty, Cambridge University Press, Cambridge, 1992, p. 45.

17 Dening, *Mr Bligh's Bad Language*, p. 48.

18 D. H. Lawrence, *Studies in Classic*

American Literature, Heinemann, London and Toronto, n.d., p. 141.

19 William Diaper, *Cannibal Jack: The*

True Autobiography of a White Man in the South Seas, Faber & Gwyer Ltd, London, 1928, p. 82.

20 Slade, *Old Slade*, p. 76.

Bibliography

Primary Texts

Bays, Peter, *A Narrative of the Wreck of the* Minerva *Whaler of Port Jackson, New South Wales, on Nicholson's Shoal, 24° S. 179°...*, B. Bridges, Market-Hill, Cambridge, 1831.

Campbell, Archibald, *A Voyage round the World from 1806 to 1812; in which Japan, Kamschatka, the Aleutian Islands, and the Sandwich Islands Were Visited; Including a Narrative of the Author's Shipwreck on the Island of Sannack, and His Subsequent Wreck in the Ship's Long-boat: With an Account of the Present State of the Sandwich Islands, and a Vocabulary of Their Language*, 3rd American edn, James Smith (ed.), University of Hawaii Press, Honolulu, 1967; 1st edn 1822.

Cary, William, *Wrecked on the Feejees*, Ye Galleon Press, Fairfield, Washington, 1972; 1st edn 1887.

Coffin, Robert, *The Last of the 'Logan'. The True Adventures of Robert Coffin, Mariner, in the Years 1854 to 1859 Wherein Are Set Forth His Pursuit of the Whale, His Shipwreck on Rapid Reef, His Life among the Cannibals of Fiji, and His Search for Gold in Australia, As Told by Himself and Now First Published*, Harold Thompson (ed.), Cornell University Press, Ithaca, New York, 1941.

Diapea, William [William Diaper], *Cannibal Jack: The True Autobiography of a White Man in the South Seas*, Faber & Gwyer Limited, London, 1928.

Endicott, William, *Wrecked among Cannibals in the Fijis: A Narrative*

of Shipwreck & Adventure in the South Seas, Marine Research
Society, Salem, Massachusetts, 1923.

Hayford, Harrison, Hershel Parker and G. Thomas Tanselle (eds),
The Writings of Herman Melville: Omoo, by Herman Melville,
Northwestern University Press and the Newberry Library,
Evanston and Chicago,1968, vol. 2.

Holden, Horace. *A Narrative of the Shipwreck, Captivity & Sufferings
of Horace Holden & Benj. H. Nute*, Keith Huntress (ed.), 4th edn,
Ye Galleon Press, Fairfield, Washington, 1975; 1st edn 1836.

Im Thurn, Sir Everard, and Leonard C. Wharton (eds), *The Journal
of William Lockerby, Sandalwood Trader in the Fijian Islands
During the Years 1808–1809*, Fiji Times and Herald Ltd, 1982;
1st edn 1925.

Jackson, John [William Diaper], 'Jackson's Narrative', in
J. Elphinstone Erskine, *Journal of a Cruise among the Islands of
the Western Pacific, Including the Feejees and Others Inhabited by the
Polynesian Negro Races, in Her Majesty's Ship* Havannah, Dawsons
of Pall Mall, London, 1967; 1st edn 1853.

Keate, George, *An Account of the Pelew Islands, Situated in the
Western Part of the Pacific Ocean; Composed from the Journals and
Communications of Captain Henry Wilson, and Some of His Officers,
Who in August, 1783, Were There Ship-wrecked, in the 'Antelope', a
Packet Belonging to the Honourable East India Company, by George
Keate, Esq., F.R.S. and S.A. The Fifth Edition, to Which Is Added
a Supplement, Compiled from the Journals of the* Panther *and*
Endeavour, *Two Vessels Sent by the Honourable East India Company
to Those Islands in 1790*, 5th edn printed for Captain Henry
Wilson, London, 1803; 1st edn 1788.

Lamont, E. H., *Wild Life among the Pacific Islanders*, University of
the South Pacific, Rarotonga and Suva, 1994; 1st edn 1867.

Martin, John, *An Account of the Natives of the Tonga Islands, in the
South Pacific Ocean. With an Original Grammar and Vocabulary
of Their Language. Compiled and Arranged from the Extensive
Communications of Mr William Mariner, Several Years Resident in
those Islands. By John Martin, M.D.*, 2 vols, printed for the
author, London, 1817; 2nd edition, 2 vols., John Murray,

London, 1818; 3rd edition, 2 vols, Constable and Co., Edinburgh, 1827.

Melville, Herman, *Typee: A Peep at Polynesian Life*, Penguin Classics, London, 1986; 1st edn 1846.

Morrison, James, *The Journal of James Morrison Boatswain's Mate of the* Bounty *Describing the Mutiny & Subsequent Misfortunes of the Mutineers Together with an Account of the Island of Tahiti*, Owen Rutter (ed.), The Golden Cockerel Press, London, 1935.

O'Connell, James, *A Residence of Eleven Years in New Holland and the Caroline Islands*, Saul H. Riesenberg (ed.), Australian National University Press, Canberra, 1972; 1st edn 1836.

Oliver, James, and William G. Dix, *Wreck of the* Glide, *with Recollections of the Fijis, and of Wallis Island*, Wiley & Putnam, New York and London, 1848.

Patterson, Samuel, *Narrative of the Adventures and Sufferings of Samuel Patterson, Who Made Three Voyages to the North West Coast of America, and Who Sailed to the Sandwich Islands and to Many Other Parts of This World before Being Shipwrecked on the Feegee Islands*, Ye Galleon Press, Fairfield, Washington, 1967; 1st edn 1825.

Robarts, Edward, *The Marquesan Journal of Edward Robarts 1797–1824*, Greg Dening (ed.), Australian National University Press, Canberra, 1974.

Shaw, Leonard, 'A Brief Sketch of the Sufferings of Leonard Shaw on Massacre Island', in Benjamin Morrell, *A Narrative of Four Voyages . . . from the Year 1822–1831*, J & J Harper, New York, 1832.

Terrell, Jennifer, 'Joseph Kabris and His Notes on the Marquesas', in *Journal of Pacific History*, vol. 27, no. 2, April 1982, pp. 101–12.

Torrey, William, *Torrey's Narrative: Or, the Life and Adventures of William Torrey*, A. J. Wright, Boston, 1848.

Twyning, John, *Shipwreck and Adventures of John P. Twyning, among the South Sea Islanders: Giving an Account of their Feasts, Massacres, &c. &c. with the Certificates of Wesleyan Missionaries Who Lived in the Islands.* 2nd edn printed for the benefit of the author, London, 1850.

Vason, George [George Veeson], *An Authentic Narrative of Four Years' Residence at Tongataboo, One of the Friendly Islands, in the South-Sea, by--------- Who Went thither in the* Duff, *under Captain Wilson, in 1796*, Longman, Hurst, Rees, and Orme, London, 1810.

Secondary Texts

Allen, Gay Wilson, *Melville and His World*, Thames & Hudson, London, 1971.

Anderson, Charles Robert, *Melville in the South Seas*, Dover Publications Inc., New York, 1966.

Arens, William, *The Man-Eating Myth, Anthropology and Anthropophagy*, Oxford University Press, New York, 1979.

Bargatzky, Thomas, 'Beachcombers and Castaways as Innovators', in *Journal of Pacific History*, vol. 15, no. 2, 1980, pp. 93–102.

Barker, Francis, Peter Hulme and Margaret Iverson (eds), *Cannibalism and the Colonial World*, Cambridge University Press, Cambridge, 1998.

Bentley, Trevor, *Pakeha Maori: The Extraordinary Story of the Europeans Who Lived as Maori in Early New Zealand*, Penguin Books, Auckland, 1999.

Bown, Stephen, *Scurvy*, Penguin Books, Camberwell, Victoria, 2003.

Calder, Alex, Jonathan Lamb and Bridget Orr (eds), *Voyages and Beaches: Pacific Encounters, 1769–1840*, University of Hawaii Press, Honolulu, 1999.

Campbell, I. C., 'European Transculturists in Polynesia, 1789–1840', PhD thesis, University of Adelaide, 1976.

—, *'Gone Native' in Polynesia: Captivity Narratives and Experiences from the South Pacific*, Greenwood Press, Westport, Connecticut, 1998.

Chard, Chloe, *Pleasure and Guilt on the Grand Tour: Travel Writing and Imaginative Geography 1600–1830*, Manchester University Press, Manchester and New York, 1999.

Chard, Chloe and Helen Langdon (eds), *Transports: Travel, Pleasure, and Imaginative Geography 1600–1830*, Yale University Press, New Haven and London, 1996.

Chase, Owen, *The Wreck of the Whaleship* Essex, *A First-hand Account of One of History's Most Extraordinary Maritime Disasters*, London Review, London, 2000.

Conrad, Joseph, *Heart of Darkness and The Secret Sharer*, Franklin Walker (ed.), Bantam Books, New York, 1971.

Cooper, H. Stonehewer, *Coral Lands*, 2 vols, Southern Reprints, Papakura, New Zealand, 1987; 1st edn 1880.

Coulter, John, *Adventures in the Pacific*, William Curry Jun. and Company, Dublin, 1845.

Dana, Richard Henry, *Two Years before the Mast*, Wordsworth American Library, London, 1996.

Defoe, Daniel, *Robinson Crusoe*, Wordsworth Classics, London, 1994.

—, *Robinson Crusoe and the Farther Adventures of Robinson Crusoe*, Collins, London and Glasgow, 1969.

Dening, Greg, *Beach Crossings: Voyaging across Times, Cultures and Self*, The Miegunyah Press, Melbourne, 2004.

—, *Islands and Beaches: Discourse on a Silent Land, Marquesas 1774–1880*, The Dorsey Press, Chicago, 1980.

—, *Mr Bligh's Bad Language: Passion, Power and Theatre on the Bounty*, Cambridge University Press, Cambridge, 1992.

—, *Performances*, The University of Chicago Press, Chicago, 1996.

— (ed.), *The Marquesan Journal of Edward Robarts 1797–1824*, Australian National University Press, Canberra, 1974.

Dodge, Ernest, S., 'A William Lockerby Manuscript in the Peabody Museum of Salem', in *Journal of Pacific History* 7, 1972, pp. 182–88.

Douglas, Mary, *Purity and Danger: An Analysis of the Concepts of Pollution and Taboo*, Routledge, London and New York, 1996.

Druett, Joan, *Hen Frigates: Wives of Merchant Captains Under Sail*, Simon & Schuster, New York, 1998.

Edmond, Rod, *Representing the South Pacific: Colonial Discourse from Cook to Gauguin*, Cambridge University Press, Cambridge, 1997.

Ellis, Markman, 'Crusoe, Cannibalism and Empire', in *Robinson Crusoe: Myths and Metamorphoses*, Lieve Spaas and Brian Stimpson (eds), Macmillan, London, 1996.

Ellis, William, *Polynesian Researches, During a Residence of Nearly Six Years in the South Sea Islands*, 2 vols, Dawsons of Pall Mall, London, 1967; 1st edn 1829.

Frelich, Morris (ed.), *Marginal Natives at Work: Anthropologists in the Field*, Schenkman Publishing Company Inc., Cambridge, Massachusetts, 1977.

Freud, Sigmund, *The Standard Edition of the Complete Psychological Works of Sigmund Freud*, James Strachey and Anna Freud (ed. and trans.), Hogarth Press and Institute of Psycho-Analysis, London, 1964, vol. 22.

Geertz, Clifford, 'Making Experiences, Authoring Selves', in *The Anthropology of Experience*, Victor Turner and E. Bruner (eds), University of Illinois Press, Chicago, 1986.

—, *Works and Lives: The Anthropologist as Author*, Stanford University Press, Stanford, 1988.

Goffman, Erving, *The Presentation of Self in Everyday Life*, The Penguin Press, London, 1969.

Greenblatt, Stephen, *Marvelous Possessions: The Wonder of the New World*, The University of Chicago Press, Chicago, 1991.

Gunson, Niel, *Messengers of Grace: Evangelical Missionaries in the South Seas 1797–1860*, Oxford University Press, Melbourne, 1978.

Hawkesworth, John, *An Account of the Voyages and Discoveries in the Southern Hemisphere*, 2nd edn, 3 vols, W. Strahan and T. Cadell, London, 1773.

Herbert, Walter, T., *Marquesan Encounters: Melville and the Meaning of Civilization*, Harvard University Press, Cambridge, 1980.

Horth, Lynn (ed.), *The Writings of Herman Melville: Correspondence*, Northwestern University Press and the Newberry Library, Evanston and Chicago, 1993, vol. 14.

Howe, K. R., *Nature, Culture, and History, the Knowing of Oceania*, University of Hawaii Press, Honolulu, 2000.

Hulme, Peter, *Colonial Encounters: Europe and the Native Caribbean 1492–1797*, Methuen, London and New York, 1986.

Lamb, Jonathan, Vanessa Smith and Nicholas Thomas (eds),

Exploration and Exchange: A South Seas Anthology 1680–1900, The University of Chicago Press, Chicago and London, 2000.

Lamb, Jonathan, *Preserving the Self in the South Seas 1680–1840*, The University of Chicago Press, Chicago and London, 2001.

Langsdorff, Georg H. von, *Voyages and Travels in Various Parts of the World, During the Years 1803, 1804, 1805, 1806, and 1807*, H. Colburn, London, 1813–14.

La Perouse, J. Francois Galaup, Comte de, *Voyage of La Perouse around the World*, 4 vols, M.L.A. Milet-Mureau (ed.), London, 1798.

Lawrence, D. H., *Studies in Classic American Literature*, Heinemann, London and Toronto, n.d.

Legge, Christopher, 'William Diaper: A Biographical Sketch', in *Journal of Pacific History*, vol. 1, 1996, pp. 79–90.

Lloyd, Christopher, *The British Seaman*, Collins, London, 1968.

Lucett, Edward, *Rovings in the Pacific from 1837–1849*, 2 vols, Longman, Brown, Green, and Longmans, London, 1851.

Maude, H. E., *Of Islands and Men: Studies in Pacific History*, Oxford University Press, Melbourne, 1968.

McArthur, Norma, 'Essays in Multiplication: European Seafarers in Polynesia', in *Journal of Pacific History*, vol. 1, 1996, pp. 91–105.

Melville, Herman, *Moby Dick*, Oxford University Press, Oxford, New York, 1988; 1st edn 1851.

—, *White-Jacket or the World in a Man-of-War*, Oxford University Press, Oxford and New York, 1988; 1st edn 1850.

Montaigne, Michel de, 'Of Cannibals', in *Essays of Montaigne, Vol. 1*, Charles Cotton (trans.), William Carew Hazlitt (ed.), Reeves & Turners, London, 1877.

Obeyesekere, Gananath, 'Cannibal Feasts in Nineteenth-century Fiji: Seamen's Yarns and the Ethnographic Imagination', in *Cannibalism and the Colonial World*, Barker, Hulme and Iverson (eds), Cambridge University Press, Cambridge, 1998.

—, *The Apotheosis of Captain Cook: European Myth-Making in the Pacific*, Princeton University Press, Princeton and Hawaii, 1992.

Orange, James, Rev. (ed.), *Life of the Late George Vason of Nottingham*, Henry Mozley, Derby, 1840.

Pagden, Anthony, *European Encounters with the New World*, Yale University Press, New Haven and London, 1993.

Parker, Hershel, *Herman Melville: A Biography Volume 1, 1819–1851*, The Johns Hopkins University Press, Baltimore and London, 1996.

Pearson, Bill, *Rifled Sanctuaries: Some Views of the Pacific Islands in Western Literature*, Auckland University Press/Oxford University Press, Auckland, 1984.

Philbrick, Nathaniel, *In the Heart of the Sea*, Flamingo, London, 2000.

Porter, R. K., *Travelling Sketches in Russia and Sweden*, 2 vols, Richard Phillips, London, 1813.

Pratt, Mary Louise, 'Fieldwork in Common Places', in *Writing Culture: The Poetics and Politics of Ethnography*, James Clifford and George E. Marcus (eds), University of California Press, Berkeley and Los Angeles, 1986.

—, *Imperial Eyes: Travel Writing and Transculturation*, Routledge, London and New York, 1992.

—, 'Scratches on the Face of the Country; or, What Mr Barrow Saw in the Land of the Bushmen', in *'Race', Writing and Difference*, Henry Louis Gates Jr. (ed.), University of Chicago Press, Chicago and London, 1986.

Ralston, Caroline, *Grass Huts and Warehouses: Pacific Beach Communities of the Nineteenth-Century*, Australian National University Press, Canberra, 1977.

Riesenberg, Saul, H., 'The Tattooed Irishman', in *The Smithsonian Journal of History*, vol. 3, no. 1, Spring, 1968, pp. 1–18.

Rennie, Neil, *Far-Fetched Facts: The Literature of Travel and the Idea of the South Seas*, Clarendon Press, Oxford, 1995.

Robertson, George, *Discovery of Tahiti: A Journal of the Second Voyage of the HMS 'Dolphin' Round the World*, H. Carrington (ed.), London, 1948.

Rogers, Woodes, Captain, *A Cruising Voyage Round the World*, Dover Publications Inc., New York, 1970; 1st edn 1712.

Sahlins, Marshall, *How 'Natives' Think: About Captain Cook, for Example*, University of Chicago Press, Chicago, 1995.

Salmond, Anne, *The Trial of the Cannibal Dog: Captain Cook in the South Seas*, Penguin Books, Auckland, 2004.

Schechner, Richard, *Between Theater and Anthropology*, University of Pennsylvania Press, Philadelphia, 1985.

—, *Essays on Performance Theory 1970–1987*, Drama Book Specialists, New York, 1977.

Schultz, Albert, J., 'A Note on William Lockerby's Fiji Manuscript', in *Journal of Pacific History*, vol. 13, 1978, pp. 115–16.

Sharrad, Paul, 'Imagining the Pacific', in *Meanjin* vol. 49, no. 4, 1990, pp. 597–606.

Slade, John, *Old Slade; Or Fifteen Years Adventures of a Sailor: Including a Residence among Cannibals on Wallace Island*, John Putnam, Boston, 1844.

Smith, Bernard, *European Vision and the South Pacific 1768–1850*, Clarendon Press, Oxford, 1960.

Smith, Vanessa, 'Crusoe in the South Seas: Beachcombers, Missionaries and the Myth of the Castaway', in *Robinson Crusoe: Myths and Metamorphoses*, Lieve Spaas and Brian Stimpson (eds) Macmillan, London, 1996.

—, *Literary Culture and the Pacific: Nineteenth-Century Textual Encounters*, Cambridge University Press, Cambridge, 1998.

Smythe, Mrs, *Ten Months in the Fiji Islands*, John Henry and James Parker, Oxford and London, 1864.

Solomon-Godeau, Abigail, 'Going Native', in *Art in America*, July, 1989, pp. 118–61.

Souhami, Diana, *Selkirk's Island*, Phoenix, London, 2001.

Spaas, Lieve, 'Narcissus and Friday: From Classical to Anthropological Myth', *Robinson Crusoe: Myths and Metamorphoses*, Lieve Spaas and Brian Stimpson (eds), Macmillan, London, 1996.

Spaas, Lieve, and Brian Stimpson (eds), *Robinson Crusoe: Myths and Metamorphoses*, Macmillan, London, 1996.

Stonequist, Everett V., *The Marginal Man: A Study in Personality and Culture Conflict*, Charles Scribner's Sons, New York, 1937.

Thomas, Julian [Vagabond], *Cannibals and Convicts: Notes of Personal Experience in the Western Pacific*, Cassell & Company Ltd, London, 1886.

Thomas, Nicholas, *Colonialism's Culture: Anthropology, Travel and Government*, Polity Press, Cambridge, 1994.

—, *Entangled Objects: Exchange, Material Culture, and Colonialism in the Pacific*, Harvard University Press, Cambridge, Massachusetts, 1991.

Thomson, Robert, Rev., *The Marquesas Islands: Their Description and Early History*, Institute for Polynesian Studies, Hawaii, 1980; 1st edn 1841.

Turner, Victor, *Dramas, Fields, and Metaphors: Symbolic Action in Human Society*, Cornell University Press, Ithaca and London, 1974.

Turner, Victor, *The Anthropology of Performance*, PAJ Publications, New York, 1988.

—, *The Ritual Process: Structure and Anti-Structure*, Penguin, London, 1969.

Van Gennep, Arnold, *The Rites of Passage*, Vizedom and Caffee (trans.), Routledge & Kegan Paul, London, 1960.

Wallace, Leonelle, 'Tryst Tropique: Pacific Texts, Modern Sexuality', PhD thesis, University of Auckland, 1996.

[Wallis, Mary]. *Life in Feejee, or, Five Years among the Cannibals. By A Lady*, The Gregg Press, Ridgewood, 1967, 1st edn 1851.

Walsh, J. M., *Overdue: A Romance of Unknown New Guinea*, States Publishing, Sydney, 1925.

Wilkes, Charles, *Narrative of the United States Exploring Expedition*, 5 vols, Lea and Blanchard, Philadelphia, 1845.

Wilson, James, *A Missionary Voyage to the Southern Pacific Ocean*, published for the benefit of the society, printed by S. Gosnell for T. Chapman, London, 1799.

Index